# THE MAKING OF A GINGER NUT
# NATURE OR NURTURE?

## By Malcolm Day

'Ginger' Nut fell in the cut and frightened all the fishes,
along came a big one and swallowed him up,
and that was the end of 'Ginger' Nut.

The Making of a Ginger Nut

Spiderwize
Remus House
Coltsfoot Drive
Woodston
Peterborough
PE2 9BF

www.spiderwize.com

ISBN: 978-1-908128-92-8

# CONTENTS

# PREFACE

This book shares the journey of my early life in a thought-provoking and humorous way. It contains tales of fun, relives moments of sadness and recalls many of the 'cheeky' things I got up to as a child. They are all stories and recollections of experiences that have shaped the man I have turned out to be; or have they? Was it 'nature' or was it 'nurture'? This is a common thread that runs throughout the book. Anyone who lived through the 1950s and 60s, will be able to relate to many of the tales. Memories will be evoked, smiles will appear and tears will be shed, as each recollection takes the reader through what was a relatively poor but happy childhood, living in Shirley on the edge of affluent Solihull.

Born in 1953, I was the scruffiest of five children, raised during the post war years. Being relatively poor, my Mom was forced to make our clothes and cut our hair, which has definitely had an impact on my appearance today. Indeed Mom and Dad often had to "make do and mend" on many occasions, generally leading to Dad embarking on one of his not always successful 'special' projects. At an early age, I soon developed a sense of humour as a defence mechanism against the teasing I received about my ginger hair, unusual clothes and improvised accessories.

However, despite these hard circumstances I was very fortunate to have three significant male role models in my life, all of whom feature extensively in the book: my grandfather

William, my father Ernie and my uncle Les. These three men were very influential in so many ways. They created the passion for the things I love, taught me how to respect and appreciate people whatever the circumstances and most importantly, how to make people laugh.

Although it has taken only twelve months to write the substance of my book, I had previously been jotting down memories and ideas for four years in a little notebook bought specifically for this task by my daughter Kerry. Each night as I climbed into bed I would record any recollections or memories that had come to me during the day.  By the time I started to write, there were many random scribblings, only some of which have been included. I could probably write a further book using those stories that are still to tell.

I hope the reader will experience the many emotions I have had in my early life. In particular: fun, love, pain and sadness, all coated with a generous helping of humour. Thanks have to go to Mom, Dad, Gran, Grampy and my Uncle Les, for the many memories that make up the biggest part of this book. Whilst I was growing up they all influenced my life enormously. Whether it was from nature or nurture I have my view, but ultimately you will need to decide. Finally, last but not least, I have to acknowledge Heather, my wife of 37 years, because she provided me with the inspiration, support and belief that I could fulfil a dream. This was a dream that my English teachers, if alive today, would find very hard to believe. Many of them seemed more intent on a handing out a beating with the 'slipper', instead of advice or encouragement about how to improve my writing skills. In fact, at times, they made me feel completely inadequate and beyond help. I hope 'The Making of a Ginger Nut' proves them all wrong, evokes memories and brings more than the odd smile to your face.

# INTRODUCTION

I don't have many regrets in my life and would change very little of what has happened to me, apart from perhaps one thing. In May 1983 my Dad was diagnosed with lung cancer, without doubt a result of his many years spent smoking. It was a terrible shock to us all, particularly as Mom had been diagnosed with ovarian cancer not much more than twelve months earlier. Mom had already made a fantastic recovery, the start of thirty years of remission, but Dad's prognosis was not so positive. Doctors told Mom that Dad had only a few months to live. Unlike today when patients are told the truth, Dad was informed it could be treated successfully with tablets and radiotherapy. Not only did the doctors keep the truth from him, but Mom did as well. She felt by 'pretending' everything would turn out for the best, she was protecting Dad. Mom also asked all of her five children to respect her wishes and to keep up the pretence, so Dad would not know he was dying. We all did as Mom asked. I don't know about everyone else, but for me it was difficult, and besides, how did he not know he was deteriorating fast? Dad was never fat, but within a matter of a few months he went from the strong, wiry character I always knew to a shadow of his former self. Cancer is a horrible disease that respects no one, taking away people's dignity and self-respect with remorseless force.

On August 25, the day before he died, Dad was not the same person I once knew. The cancer had done its worst, causing Dad indescribable pain and discomfort, although he wouldn't show it. That was typical of him, he never wanted to show any sign of weakness. Despite his poor physical condition he still kept an inner strength, right to the end. Although he had been confined to bed for weeks, even on the last day of his life he ate breakfast and struggled out of bed, with Mom's help, to visit the bathroom. However he managed I shall never know! The family doctor, Doctor Crean, said, "I have given him enough morphine to knock out a horse," yet still he would not give up the fight. That was my Dad.

The one big regret I have is that on that last evening as I sat beside him, I was not allowed to give the game away. I so wanted to hold his hand, thank him for everything he had done for me and to tell him I loved him. Those weren't the sort of actions and words you did or said to Dad, so he would have guessed something was wrong for sure; not what Mom wanted. Over the last thirty years I have agonised as to whether I should have spoken to him frankly, particularly as I feel he knew he was dying anyway. While we sat talking for the last time he said to me, "Fifty nine is no age is it? I am lucky though, because I always felt I should have died alongside my mates in the war." Even after he spoke I still kept up the pretence that Mom so desperately wanted. I never gave him false hope, but neither did I tell him the truth.

That night, for the very first time, Mom agreed for a Macmillan nurse to sit with Dad, while she got some well-deserved sleep. Early next morning I was awoken by the sound of the telephone. It was Mom bringing us the news that Dad had passed away in the night. It was almost as though he had waited, so that Mom was not on her own to cope with the inevitable.

Strong to the very end, Dad had finally given up the fight while the nurse was with him. I can still remember the very words I said to Mom when she called to tell me the news. "Oh, that's great!" Taken out of context it might seem as if I was pleased he had died; in a way I was. I was just pleased that Dad was no longer suffering, had no pain and could finally rest in peace. For the last few weeks, cancer had taken away his dignity, self-respect and the Dad we all once knew.

Whilst I can remember what Dad looked like in those final weeks, my strongest memories of him are when I was growing up. He will always be that strong, protective, witty Dad, I so respected and who was a major influence in 'the making of a ginger nut': both Nature and Nurture.

Have you ever wondered how strange it is that we frequently have memories (like the one I just recalled), facts, and in my case jokes or witty comments that suddenly appear at the fore of our brains almost out of nowhere? Their appearance can be stimulated by situations, sights, sounds and smells, or sometimes by nothing in particular. They are almost like comets that orbit the solar system, making an appearance from time to time, only to disappear again to the back of our brain as quickly as they appeared. The facts retrieved may be vitally important or at the other extreme, just trivia. The memories can be of critical points in our life, or of insignificant happenings that may seem quite unimportant. The memories are like a box of old photographs stored at the back of a cupboard or drawer, occasionally discovered by accident or, most likely, after many hours of painstaking search.

One of my earliest memories was on the morning of my second birthday. Mom had spent a considerable amount of her valuable time making and decorating a beautiful cake in readiness for the birthday party she had organised for the afternoon. The cake was on the dining table in the kitchen, while my Mom got on with tidying the house. She was a very hard working and house-proud lady and despite being a mother of three under-fives at this time, she cleaned the house from top to bottom every day. When I was growing up the kitchen was the main room in the house, as we spent most of our time there. It was reasonably large, with enough space for a dining table, armchairs and even a television in later years. It had a solid fuel boiler used for producing our hot water, so it was also the warmest room in the house. Although I didn't realise it at the time, this is likely to be the main reason we spent a lot of time there. When growing up, money was always tight, so Mom and Dad could not afford to heat the whole house. On this particular morning while Mom was out of the kitchen I decided the cake looked too good to resist. I took the end out of the barrel of my grey, soft, plastic water pistol, stuck it in the top of the cake and took it behind an armchair to eat. I repeated the same action numerous times so by the time my Mom returned it resembled a Chinese chequers board: very little cake but plenty of holes. You can imagine how cross she was, having to spend more time and effort making another cake before everyone arrived for the party. The most vivid part of my memory is the replacement cake, which was covered in Cadbury's milk chocolate and decorated with Smarties, my favourite sweets.

My Mom never let me forget what I had done. She would tell the story to everyone and constantly remind me throughout my childhood. So is this really a memory or is it a 'virtual recollection': a film, created in my head, about a time gone by? Was I reminded about the incident so many times by Mom that I imagined how it had all happened and built a picture of everything in my mind? I suppose I will never know. Maybe many of my other memories are also 'virtual recollections'. Only when I was alone and have never been reminded of the occasion can I really be sure it all actually happened as I remember it. Memories like the time my Mom would not let me have a drink of milk, until I had said the word 'milk'. I remember standing in the kitchen, pointing up at the bottle of milk on the window sill, saying defiantly "mup, mup", and Mom insisting, "You are not having any until you say milk." I don't remember whether or not she gave in to me, but I recall being determined not to say the word.

Or what about the time when I told my first joke; did it really happen as I remember? Again I was in the kitchen, with Mom; all of my earliest memories seem to involve the kitchen and my Mom. She was making a pink blancmange and kept stirring it vigorously. I asked why she needed to stir the blancmange so often and she replied, "Because if not, it will develop a skin when it sets. Everything that sets has a skin."

"The sun doesn't," I said as quickly as anything. Even at this early age (about five) had I already been influenced by my Dad's sharp wit? Surely not.

You may be wondering why I started my book in this strange way. It is because I have been prompted to put 'pen to paper' by a conversation much later in life, one that I often recall. It is something that was said to me in passing by Heather, my wife, soul mate, best friend and the most important person in my life. Almost forty years ago, during the time we were courting – an old fashioned word younger readers may need to look up – she told me about a psychology lecture she'd had at college, regarding 'nature' and 'nurture'. For some unknown reason I often remember our first discussion on the subject and will always try to ponder the answer.

'Nature or nurture' is an age old debate surrounding the relative importance of a person's inherited qualities (nature) versus personal experiences (nurture) in determining their individual differences in physical and behavioural traits. It has long been known that certain physical characteristics are biologically determined by genetic inheritance. Colour of eyes, straight or curly hair, pigmentation of the skin and certain diseases are all a function of the genes we inherit. Other physical characteristics, if not determined, appear to be at least strongly influenced by the genetic make-up of our biological parents. Height, weight, hair loss (something I can relate to), life expectancy and vulnerability to specific illnesses are positively correlated between genetically related individuals. These facts have led many to speculate as to whether psychological characteristics such as behavioural tendencies, personality attributes and mental abilities are also 'wired in' before we are even born.

The phrase 'nature versus nurture' is thought to have been first used by the English Victorian Francis Galton in his discussion of the influence of heredity and environment on a person's social development. To untangle the effects of genes and environment, scientists will perform 'adoption' and 'twin' studies. These are investigations which try to separate the variation in a population into genetic and environmental components. Although this appeals to the statistical and logical side of my nature, I believe for most people it would not make enjoyable reading. Neither do I think the average reader will be interested in Sigmund Freud's theory about personality development being formed through the interaction of id, ego, and super-ego. I have therefore decided to look at my life and the influences and experiences I have encountered, to try and form my own view on the answer to the question.

A classification of the 'Big 5' personal traits can be remembered by the acronym OCEAN:

**O**penness to experience

**C**onscientiousness

**E**xtraversion

**A**greeableness

**N**euroticism

*'Openness'* is a general appreciation for art, adventure, unusual ideas, imagination, inquisitiveness, and variety of different experiences. People who are open to new experiences are academically curious, appreciative of art, and sensitive to beautiful things. When compared to closed people they tend to be, more creative and more aware of their own feelings. Open

people will generally have a diverse vocabulary, outstanding ideas and a colourful imagination. They pick up new ideas quickly, may use complicated words and spend time reflecting on things.

'**Conscientiousness'** is a tendency to be self-disciplined, acting respectfully, and setting targets or expectations. This quality shows a preference for planned rather than spontaneous behaviour. It influences the way in which we control, regulate, and direct our impulses. Conscientious people are usually well prepared, pay attention to detail, get tasks completed right away, like order and generally follow schedules.

'**Extraversion'** is regarded as having positive emotions and a tendency to look for stimulation and the company of others. Extraverts enjoy being with people, and are often thought of as being full of energy. They tend to be enthusiastic, action-packed individuals who are likely to say "Yes!" or "Let's go!" to opportunities for excitement. When in a group they tend to talk a great deal, be assertive, and draw attention to themselves. Conversely when in company introverts often lack the enthusiasm and activity levels of extraverts. They are inclined to appear quiet, low-key, deliberate, and more reserved in social company.

'**Agreeableness'** is a tendency to be empathetic and cooperative rather than mistrustful and unfriendly towards others. This quality reflects individual differences in general concern for social harmony. Getting along with others is important to 'agreeable' individuals. They are mostly considerate, friendly, generous, obliging, and willing to compromise their interests for others. 'Agreeable' people also have an optimistic view of human nature. They believe people are fundamentally honest, decent, and trustworthy. 'Disagreeable' individuals place self-interest above getting along with others. They are normally unconcerned with others' well-being, and are less likely to go out of their way to help someone else. Sometimes their suspicion about a person's motives causes them to be dismissive and uncooperative.

Finally **'Neuroticism'** is the tendency to harbour negative emotions, such as anger, anxiety and depression. It is sometimes referred to as emotional instability. Those who score highly in neuroticism react emotionally and are susceptible to stress. They are more likely to view commonplace situations as threatening, and minor obstructions as hopelessly difficult. Their negative emotional reactions can persist for unusually long periods of time, which means they often appear to be in a bad mood. These problems with emotional regulation can reduce the ability of a person scoring highly on neuroticism to think clearly, make decisions, and cope with stress. At the other end of the scale, individuals who have low scores in neuroticism are less likely to get upset and are more emotionally stable. They tend to be calm and free from persistent negative feelings. Freedom from negative feelings does not mean that low scorers will necessarily experience a lot of positive feelings. Neurotic people are easily disturbed, get irritated, stressed out or upset very easily, have frequent mood swings and worry about things.

We will all have a perception of how as an individual we relate to the classification of personal traits; I am no exception. I have included the diagram below as I thought before I start it may be helpful to score myself on a scale of 1 to 5 against the 'Big 5'. Now there is another story for later!

| | 1 | 2 | 3 | 4 | 5 | |
|---|---|---|---|---|---|---|
| CLOSED | ███ | ███ | ███ | ███ | | OPEN |
| SPONTANEOUS | ███ | ███ | ███ | | | CONSCIENTIOUS |
| INTROVERT | ███ | | | | | EXTRAVERT |
| DISAGREEABLE | ███ | ███ | ███ | ███ | | AGREEABLE |
| STABLE | ███ | | | | | NEUROTIC |

The blacker the rows in the table, the more I feel I meet the personal trait on the right-hand side of the table and the whiter the rows the more I feel I have an affinity for the characteristic on the left.

In summary I feel I am "an open-minded, logical thinking, introvert, who cares for and considers others, while being able to cope with the stresses and problems thrown at me by life". These personal traits, together with other emotional, attitudinal, and behavioural response patterns give me my individual personality. This book is a rambling of my memories, using them to try and unravel the reasons why 'I am who I am'. Was I born to have these characteristics or are they due to the influences of my family, how I was brought up and my life experiences? I have not yet fully considered the detailed content of the remaining chapters and hence have not formed a conclusion to the answer. Nevertheless my statistical background and logical nature already suggest to me I may never be convinced one way or the other; that it is likely to be a combination of both 'nature' and 'nurture'. Let's wait and see.

# Chapter 1

## THE ORIGIN OF A SPECIES

I was born to Ernest Murray and Gwendoline Day on **Sunday** 6 December 1953, in Solihull hospital; only a few miles away from where I have lived for most of my life. The first thing to say is the popular nursery rhyme "Monday's child" is not always correct. For those of you who are not familiar with the words from A. E. Bray's Traditions of Devonshire (1838), they go like this:

> Monday's child is fair of face,
>
> Tuesday's child is full of grace,
>
> Wednesday's child is full of woe,
>
> Thursday's child has far to go,
>
> Friday's child is loving and giving,
>
> Saturday's child works hard for a living,
>
> But the child who is born on the Sabbath Day
>
> Is happy, bonny, blithe and gay.

I have to point out some of it is true, but not all. My personal view is supported by the fact there has been considerable variation and debate about the exact attributes of each day and even over the days. For example, James Orchard Halliwell had Christmas Day instead of the Sabbath and an early version of the rhyme appearing in 'Harper's Weekly' in 1887, had "Friday's child is full of woe". This perhaps reflected traditional superstition associated with bad luck on Friday; many Christians associate Friday with the Crucifixion. In addition to Wednesday's and

Friday's children's role reversal, the fates of Thursday's and Saturday's children were also exchanged.

Can you guess which one of the four words undeniably does not describe me: happy, bonny, blithe or gay? I am definitely handsome, easy-going and brightly-coloured or attractive, but I cannot be described as cheerful. I have to say for some reason I rarely smile or laugh and it is really difficult for me to put on an acceptable facial expression when having my photograph taken. I have lost count of the number of family photographs spoilt by a 'silly' expression on my face, but it does have its advantages. I have a great face for playing poker, or games where you need to hide your feelings and it has helped me many times to tell a joke or 'tall' story. I am not the only one to have noticed this trait. My two children Kerry and Matthew often made fun of me when they were growing up, usually when I laughed or smiled. Then they would say, "Oh! What's up? Dad's smiling!" It wasn't just close family either, even strangers noticed it.

One occasion in particular was when I was about 13 or 14 years old and I was cajoled into helping out Mrs Swan (a friend of my Aunty Barbara). She and my Aunty occasionally worked at the Shirley Golf Club in Monkspath, as 'Silver service' waitresses. The golf club members were mostly well-to-do Jews and liked things done properly. Myself and Carl, the son of another waitress, were more or less told we were 'helping out' at a club tournament, 'The Clancy', which was held annually in early May, attracting players from all over the UK. I know it was early May, because that year it coincided with the day of the FA Cup Final. I was not best pleased. We were going to be 'helping out', by caddying for club members. Not my cup of tea really; what's the saying, "to play golf is to spoil an otherwise enjoyable walk"? The only saving grace was that we were getting paid for it. However, we could not tell anyone, because the local scout group were also helping out, and they were doing it for nothing. I am not sure but I have a feeling the scout leaders were pocketing all of the money for the scout hut.

Anyway, I was one of the first lads chosen. It must have been for my looks, it certainly was not for my strength and physique, because I was tall and thin at that age. It was often said of me, that "there was more fat on a chip and I had muscles like sparrow's ankles". The player I was to caddy for started by knocking a few practice balls on the driving range and my first job was to collect them all up at the end. In just five minutes I had collected about 20 golf balls, whilst dodging many more furiously raining down on me like giant hailstones. I cannot imagine that would be allowed today, with all of the Health and Safety rules and regulations in place and the current culture of suing anyone for anything. I went back to my player to find out my next job with some trepidation, because I knew sooner or later I was going to have to carry his bag; there were no buggies or trollies in those days. I was not looking forward to this because the bag was probably as big and as heavy as I was. I would be on my knees well before the ninth hole. To my relief he said, "Do you always look that miserable? I don't think I can stand looking at your face all morning, so I have asked my mate to caddy for me. Take this for your trouble." He handed me a new, crisp, blue five pound note for the 15 minutes of work I had done; that was twenty quid an hour! At that time I had to work five Saturday evenings at the Plough restaurant in Monkspath to earn a fiver.

"Thanks mate," I said with a huge smile on my face, "it's a pleasure doing business with you." There was still time to go back to the reception tent and caddy for someone else, but I thought, "No, don't be greedy," so I took to my heels and excitedly ran home to watch the FA Cup final after all.

I need to give you a potted history of my Mom and Dad at this point, so you can begin to appreciate their characters, which will help you to understand later whether I am like them or not. Have I inherited their ways or been influenced by their values, principles and behaviours?

Sadly I never got to find out much about Dad's early life. He was always a very private man, rarely talking about himself or his family. In fact I have no memory of ever meeting any of his family; not even my gran or granddad, four aunts and uncles and countless cousins. He never completely cut himself off from them, but there was only rare contact. Letters were scarce and the only visit I am able to recall is when my Mom and Dad went down to London to see Doris (whom I assumed to be his stepmother), after his Dad had died. I am certain Dad never went to granddad's funeral; I don't even think the family told him he had passed away until it was too late. Clearly something had happened between them to create this situation. I will probably never know what, but I do feel sad that it came to this. My view is life is too short to hold grudges and I strongly believe in the saying "to err is human, but to forgive is divine". I wish they had made up at some point, because somehow I feel we have all missed out on a significant part of our family history.

The only patchy details I have about his childhood are that he was born at 5 Aldis Street, in Tooting, London, on 11 July 1924, to Bertie Enoch and Lillian Estelle (nee Duncombe). Dad was one of six boys: Wilf, Reg, Bert, my Dad (Ernest) and Alf, with his youngest brother Jimmy dying at a very early age from polio, or so I thought. I asked my sister Sue about this recently and she said she understood he died of diphtheria. Both diseases were prevalent at the time, but it appears diphtheria may have been the most likely to cause death in the 1930s. It sounded as though the boys were always getting into trouble; I know my Dad started smoking at the age of eight! By all accounts his father was really strict. The only thing Dad told me about granddad was, when they were naughty, he would take off his belt and chase the boys down the garden and over the fence. The last one over was the one to 'get the buckle'.

I don't believe he ever told me anything about his mom; it is all a bit of a mystery really. One story was she started drinking and so they split up and granddad then moved in with a lady called Doris. I have no idea how old Dad was when this all was supposed to have taken place. Apparently Doris and granddad lived together for the rest of his life but never actually got married. We always referred to her as Doris Day! A few months before my Mom died she told me something really interesting, which puts this version in doubt. Mom revealed there was always uncertainty about the real reason for the splitting up and a different possibility was my granddad had been having an affair with Doris while still married to Dad's mom! This theory was supported by an incident when Mom and Dad went to visit Doris after granddad died; the same, one and only time I remember them visiting any member of his family. When asked about a photograph which bore a great resemblance to my granddad when he was younger, Doris explained that it was her son from a previous relationship. However, Mom and Dad were left with a strong feeling that it was really granddad's son! Since deciding to write my book I have considered trying to find out more about Dad's side of the family, but decided I would prefer not to know.

The detail of my Dad's life from 1938, until he met Mom, is also rather patchy. I know he ran away from home to work on a farm in Cornwall at the age of 14, and later I think he moved up to Birmingham and worked at Beckett's farm near Wythall, which is still there today. In 1943, when he was just 19, he joined the army for roughly five years and while recovering from an injury sustained in combat, met Mom.

With Mom it is exactly the opposite; I know plenty about her childhood. She and Dad were 'poles apart' in this respect. Mom was very open about her life, or was it my Gran and Grampy who told me all about it? I spent a lot of my time in their company when I was younger. These were wonderful times which provided me with many happy memories.

Mom was born on 26 May 1928, at 1130 Stratford Road, Monkspath, or Home Farm as it was known then. She had a brother called Les, of whom I also have great memories. When I was young, it was almost as though I became the son he never had. In 1928 with only about a dozen houses in Monkspath and surrounded by fields, Home Farm could be described as very rural; not like it is today. When Mom was little there were no other girls of her age locally, so she mainly played with dolls, did a lot of reading, needlework, listened to the radio, or played board games. There were two or three boys about Les' age, so she often tagged along with them. They would all spend many happy hours catching butterflies, picking wild flowers and playing games like paper chase. Often they would go fishing in the nearby River Blythe for minnows, sticklebacks and bullheads, or go for long, leisurely bike rides along the local country lanes in Earlswood. The outdoor life and making up your own games was essential in the 1930s; there were no computers or televisions then. The most they had at that time was a wireless (an early type of radio) or wind-up gramophone. The environment in which Mom grew up must have been wonderful; it is my idea of heaven. Do I feel like this because of nature or nurture? I don't know for certain but I am sure nurture had a big part to play, with experiences encountered during the many happy days I spent with my grandparents at Home Farm.

You can imagine Home Farm was an ideal place for Mom and Les to have pets. They always had a dog around; over the years there was Gyp, Lassie, Judy and Dawn, to name just a few. Mom once had a large black and white rabbit named Wilfred. She would dress him up in her dolls' clothes and wheel him about in a pram; that is until he got fed up and scratched her! They also had chickens, ferrets, fish and pigs. One story I remember in particular was that Mom and Les had a little chicken, whose mother had rejected it. He would follow them around and often sat on my Grampy's shoulder. One Sunday, after a large, filling lunch, my Grampy fell asleep in his armchair. Mom and Les put the chicken on his shoulder along with a handful of crumbs on his head. They took great delight in seeing the chicken scratching for crumbs in his hair, but she wasn't sure her Dad was impressed! I think my Grampy had the last laugh, because as far as my Mom could remember it grew into a large black cockerel, eventually ending up on the dinner table.

Mom went to school in Shirley, about three miles from Home Farm. There was no transport so she and Les would walk to school every day. When World War II started, Mom and Les were at Sharmans Cross School in Solihull Road, Shirley. Strangely enough just a few yards away from where I lived, up until a few months ago. (The school though has long since gone, replaced with a small, modern housing estate). Sharmans Cross School was a two storey building for both boys and girls, but at the start of the war they apparently only attended for half days. It was boys in the morning and girls in the afternoon for one week and then the reverse the following week. This was because the school had no air raid shelters; children were taught in classrooms on the ground floor only. If the alarm was sounded during school time they had to sit under the desks until the all clear was given. If the air raid sirens sounded on the way to or from school, Mom and Les had to go to, or return to, whichever place was the nearest. They always had to carry their gas masks with them wherever they went; I cannot begin to imagine how scary it must have been.

School wasn't like it is now. They had all of the same lessons, English, maths, history, geography, needlework and cookery, but Mom also had to learn how to 'wash and iron in the correct manner'. Daily country dancing and PE were also on the curriculum. It was also a time of food rationing, so there was no obesity in those days. Apparently Mom's best subjects were maths and needlework, something she continued in later life.

My Grampy built his own air raid shelter at Home Farm so it soon became a regular safe haven for many people, not just for the family. Mom remembers how Cousin Winnie, her husband, Winnie's Dad and dog Peggy would arrive at tea time each evening, stay the night and return home the next morning. Mr and Mrs Vinden would also do the same. Mom recalled how Mrs Vinden was an actress known as Maud Gill. I have checked this out and it's true; she was an english character actress, chiefly in comic roles. Born in London, she made her name playing Thirza Tapper, the title character in Eden Philpotts' comedy play 'The Farmer's Wife', which ran for several years in London. She later repeated the role in Alfred Hitchcock's silent film version of the play. What Mom didn't recall, or didn't know, was Mr E. Stuart Vinden, her husband, was also an actor. Records show he was a regular in more serious plays such as Shakespeare at the Birmingham Repertory Theatre in the early 1920s.

Other people who stayed over regularly were Mr Hunt and Mr Knight, two mysterious characters, who I know nothing about. Therefore, every evening during the war, there was a large gathering at Home Farm. Despite food being rationed, my Gran always shared anything she had. Gran was used to providing hospitality, her parents having run a guest house called Earlsmere House, in Earlswood during WW1. I still have the original visitor's book; Mom must have kept it all those years. It makes very interesting reading today because most visitors came from Birmingham just a few miles away. They usually took two or three weeks' holiday there, nearly always promising to return in the future. Can you imagine nowadays, spending your annual holiday seven or eight miles down the road? I imagine it was because Earlswood Lakes station was on the popular Tysley to Stratford-upon-Avon line. Every comment in the book is complimentary e.g. "We are very grateful to all members of the family for the kind and sociable spirit they have shown us", or as one soldier from Princess Patricia's Canadian Light Infantry put it, "This is to state we have stayed two days and found everything to be very clean, comfortable and moderate terms". The guests from farthest afield were Mr and Mrs Charles Rowley of Tasmania Australia, who were looking forward to coming back for a longer stay "providing Mr and Mrs Manley and family order the weather to make our visit even more enjoyable". Some things never change! There is even a record of Gran's parents having an afternoon tea party at the guest house for a school outing. The letter reads:

*My Dear Mrs Manley*

*As promised, a line to let you know our party on Saturday will number 90 children and 50 adults. Do not worry about it, just arrange for the children to sit down first. Teachers and friends will wait on them and when they have finished they can play football ... etc..., while we take our teas. We are hoping for fine weather and a very happy time with you.*

*Yours very sincerely*

*Frank Townley*

*PS Hope to arrive about 4-30*

My Grampy also 'did his bit' when people stayed during the war. He would catch local rabbits to supplement the meat rations, which were always very scarce. Everyone must have eaten really well at Home Farm. One evening Mom recalls a ring of incendiary bombs being dropped around the house. She said, "For a while it was as though the house was on fire, until they were put out by the Home Guard." The next morning she and Les excitedly collected all of the fins from the burned out bombs in the surrounding fields, ending up with two buckets full!

Mom left school at 14 and started work in a garage called Archers, which was on the corner of Stratford Road and Marshall Lake Road, in Shirley. What she really wanted to do when she grew up was to become a nurse, but her headmistress and my Gran both insisted she would "be best suited to office work". So that was what she had to do, hating every moment of it. This surprises me somewhat because Mom did a similar thing to me when I first left school. I would have thought she might have had empathy for me and reacted differently. (Chapter 10)

Not to be put off, when Mom was 16 she applied to do voluntary work at Solihull hospital, along with two friends. Initially she worked on a geriatric ward, but soon moved to maternity where, at 17, for the first time she saw a baby born. I think a nurse would have been an ideal vocation for her; she loved children and many years later when Dad died of cancer she nursed him at home and on her own. There was no support in 1983 like there is today, with carers in abundance and Marie Curie nurses to take the strain and give support. Having very recently helped care for Mom under similar circumstances, along with my brothers and sister, I sometimes feel guilty she cared for Dad on her own. I don't think any of us realised at the time, the stress and the pressure she must have been under. I suppose I shouldn't feel guilty, because that's the way she wanted it to be. We were there to support her psychologically, but the actual nursing she wanted to do for herself. I imagine it was to protect Dad's dignity. He would not have wanted his children tending to his personal needs, especially towards the end when he was so frail (a sad shadow of his former self). Only a few months ago after Mom's death I discovered some notes she had made about her life. An extract about this time reads: *"When Kerry was about a year old Ernie became ill. They discovered he had cancer of the lung and there was nothing they could do. Sadly he died four months later, at home on 26 August 1983, aged 59 years. Once again my children were a tower of strength during Ernie's illness and after his death. If it hadn't been for all of them I could not have cared for him as I did at home."* Perhaps we all did more than we realised and really did give Mom the support she needed to fulfil her wish of having Dad die in his own bed.

It was around the time of the voluntary work at the local hospital that Mom first met Dad. Piecing together details about Dad's war years has involved some research on the internet and examining his old army papers. With World War II on-going, Dad had enlisted into the army, in Shrewsbury, on 3 December 1942. He joined the Kings Shropshire Light Infantry (KSLI) and was given the army number 14376712. When he left the army he was in Company 'A' of the Depot Battalion of the Royal Army Service Corp (RASC). What happened in between is unclear. I have been unable to trace Dad's army records; he is probably one of the 70 per cent of personnel who don't have any. Therefore, most of what I have uncovered has come from his Service Book, Transfer Certificate and Release Note.

Dad was just 18 years of age, 5 feet 7$^1/_2$ inches tall; not yet fully grown and weighing just 9 stone and 11 pounds. He was described as having brown hair, grey eyes and a fresh complexion. From this description he was obviously still a young lad, like many other young men of his age, signing up to fight for their country, not knowing what the future would hold. Within five weeks he had passed his rifle training before going on to train as a carrier driver on the Wrekin in Shropshire. This was additional to warfare training, which must have been pretty gruelling and tough. Dad's life in the army was a time he always said he wanted to forget. However, when we were young he would tell us a few 'snippets' of information about army life during World War II. Even before his war had started he recalled one occasion whilst training in a thunderstorm. He and his new mates were all wearing standard issue rubber mackintosh capes to protect themselves from the wet conditions. They were following each other by holding on to each other's capes, like a giant caterpillar. The rain was lashing down, it was dark and the visibility was poor when suddenly lightning struck! It hit the back of one of his colleagues, knocking him to the floor and killing the soldier holding on to his cape immediately behind him. He had no chance of survival. I can only begin to imagine what it must have been like, seeing a mate killed in front of you, even before you went to war.

Following his preliminary training, Dad was sent to France to fight against the Germans on the front line. He said he had lived on rations of cigarettes and chocolates for several weeks at a time, something I am certain contributed to his poor health in later years. It is hard for us to imagine the conditions soldiers faced at this time. If the personnel responsible for supplying the front lines were living on cigarettes and chocolate, how did others fare? He told me about the times he had to run across fields, zigzagging his way from one end to the other, just to avoid the gunfire; like a rabbit running in a car's headlights. When reaching the far side he had to dive head first into the hedge with his rifle and backpack on, covering his head to protect himself from the thorns and brambles. I will never forget the sense of urgency that he portrayed in this story and the fear he must have gone through.

It was on one of these occasions that Dad got injured, less than 12 months into his army career and just before his 20th birthday. He was crossing a field when a shout went out to drop to the floor as mortar fire was being aimed in their direction. It was a ploughed field with deep furrows, ideal for taking cover. Unfortunately, as Dad dived to the ground he had his rifle caught under his right foot, instead of to the side of it. Mortars whistled above their heads, sending shrapnel in all directions as they exploded. A piece of shrapnel hit Dad's foot, which lay above the furrow. He said he never felt anything at the time; it was only later that he noticed his boot was damaged and saw his heel had been blown off. I am certain it could have been worse. He never said, but I got the feeling *not all* of his mates made it that day.

Dad was brought back to England, had surgery and more specifically a silver plate put in his heel. Secretly, I felt he was quite proud of this fact and it never seemed to physically affect his life anyway. While in hospital, he was visited by a friend of his Dad's, from London, called Charles Bunce. He became a great friend to Dad, who always affectionately referred to him as 'Bunny'. As fate would have it Uncle Bunny was lodging at Home Farm (my Mom's home) at the time and my Gran made him some of her special cakes to take to Dad. When Dad was discharged from hospital and sent on leave to recuperate, Gran agreed he could stay at Home Farm. Mom said when she first met him she thought he was 'gorgeous'. It is often said that I am very much like Dad in looks, so I can understand why she thought this! During the time he was staying at Home Farm Mom went to a dance at Earlswood village hall with her cousin Betty. By the time the dance finished it was late and dark. Mom's journey home involved quiet country lanes so Dad, being ever the gentleman, offered to go and fetch her. Mom said, "Things went on from there!"

Money was short and food was still being rationed, so there were no 'slap up' meals or fancy restaurants. They went to the pictures and had a snack meal in a local café. This was a regular occurrence, as they went to the cinema two or three times per week. Back in the early 1940s one film was shown Monday to Wednesday, a different one from Thursday to Saturday and a third one on Sunday.

Dad got on well with most people and soon became one of a much larger circle of Mom and Les' friends. Every Saturday night they went to the Bull's Head in Earlswood where about 25 friends met up for a drink and a sing-along. One night the landlady short-changed Dad, saying he only gave her a ten shilling note and not £1. Dad was as honest as the day is long and knew he had given her a £1 note. In the 1940s a pound was a lot of money and not that common. When he challenged her she said, "I never make mistakes, I have served more times than I can remember." Dad being Dad quickly replied, "Where love, Winson Green Prison?" He, like me, was quick witted and rather cheeky. That didn't go down well and she threw him out. I am sure the landlady regretted doing it, because the following Saturday the pub was empty. Every one of the group of friends supported Dad and went to the nearby Red Lion instead!

When Dad's sick leave ended he was stationed in Egypt and India until his transfer to the army reserve in July 1947. I only got to hear a little about life in Egypt, and just about times when he was off duty! There were two stories in particular Dad told more than once.

The first story was about leaning out of a train window, which was pulling out of the station. Everyone was doing the same, saying their goodbyes to friends and colleagues. Just as his carriage reached the end of the platform a small Egyptian lad ran up to the window and pulled the glasses off the nose of the soldier standing next to him. It was perfect timing; nothing could be done to stop the thief as he disappeared into the crowd. Seemingly this was a regular occurrence, with many a soldier losing his spectacles in this way.

The second story was when Dad was on leave and doing a bit of sight-seeing in Cairo. It was the height of summer and extremely hot, so not the best time to be doing the touristy bits. Dad, feeling very tired, hot and dusty, towards the end of the day was approached by a local street seller. "Glass of orange juice, Johnny?" he said. (All soldiers were referred to as Johnny by the locals; it was the only name they knew) This was a daft question. Dad was desperate for some refreshment, so quickly replied, "Yes please." Unfortunately, or perhaps fortunately for Dad the guy had run out of water. "Won't be long Johnny, just going to fetch some water," the vendor said as he rushed down to the banks of the Nile to collect a container of 'fresh' water. My Dad's face must have been a picture. The Nile was filthy dirty, with the majority of locals washing themselves and their clothes in the river on a regular basis. Needless to say, Dad made a sharp exit before the drinks vendor returned. It must have been a long wait for a refreshing drink.

In 1947 Dad left the army for a position with the reserves. He won three medals during his time; none of them for distinguished service, but his release papers did say some very complementary things about him:

**Military Conduct** *"Exemplary"*

**Testimonial** *"Private Day has given excellent service both at home and overseas and has carried out all duties assigned to him with zeal and ability. He is recommended as honest, sober, trustworthy and hardworking".*

I am not sure whether or not these were standard comments or personalised specifically for Dad, but I do know before I found his release papers just a few months ago, this is a description I could have written myself.

When Dad came home from the army he and Mom got engaged and a few years later, on 25 June 1949 (a month after mom's 21st birthday), they got married at St James' Church Shirley. Not surprisingly Uncle 'Bunny', the person who was responsible for bringing Mom and Dad together, was Dad's best man. Mom recalled that most things were still on ration, so there was no 'big do'. She said, "Clothing coupons were in short supply, so I borrowed my friend's wedding dress and your Dad wore his demob suit. The reception was held at Home Farm and friends contributed food for a wedding breakfast buffet. I had a bouquet of pink roses and lilies of the valley and my bridesmaids had bouquets of sweet peas. Just like my own dress, the two bridesmaids' dresses were also borrowed. Despite rationing it was still a lovely day and I did manage to get a new pink and grey silk dress, together with a blue hat and coat for the honeymoon in Ilfracombe."

Houses were in short supply straight after the war, so Mom and Dad initially lived at Home Farm along with Gran, Grampy, her brother Les and his wife, my Aunty Barb. It wasn't long before Mom got pregnant, with my sister Susan arriving on 24 June 1950 almost 12 months after they were married. On 2 June 1952 when Sue was nearly two Mom and Dad moved into their first family home. This was 84 Arbury Hall Road, a three bedroomed council house in Shirley, just a couple of miles away from Home Farm. This proved to be their *only* family home, as it was the place where they both spent the rest of their lives, including their final days. The weekly rent and rates were £1-8s-0d, equivalent to £1.40 today, which was a large proportion of Dad's £5 per week wages. Mom said food was much cheaper then though. She recalled how the weekend joint of meat cost just 5 shillings; that is 25p in today's money.

By the time I arrived in 1953, Dad was working for Uncle Bunny as a milkman. Now, according to Mom, their family was complete; one boy and one girl. But clearly, I was such a lovely baby, Mom and Dad decided to have another, so along came Graham 18 months later! This was definitely the last. That is, until Mom and Dad decided to foster Jonathan. Brother Jon was born on 18 October 1959 to an unmarried mother from Coventry. Apparently his Dad was a doctor and his mother a nurse who was in no position to be able to offer him the home he needed.

Jon went into foster care and had already lived with five different families before he came to us. Immediately prior to Mom and Dad fostering Jon, he was being looked after by a family who lived in the same road as Uncle Les and Aunty Barb. The family fostered many children and from what I can gather it was more of a job, rather than offering a loving and caring environment for the children. I remember Mom saying, one day when Jon was about six months old he was put outside in his pram and left to cry while his foster mother got on with her housework. She never went to him when he cried, which is probably why, when he came to us to live at nine months old, he never cried. It was almost as though he knew crying was a waste of time, because it didn't get you anywhere. When the foster mother eventually went to Jon, he had fallen out of his pram and was crawling about on the floor.

When the family ended Jon's period of foster care, Mom persuaded Dad to foster Jon. As a friend of the foster family, Mom had already seen Jon and had fallen in love with him. I have to admit he was a lovely looking baby. With his big, bush baby, blue eyes you could not fail to adore him. Mom knew she could offer Jon a better home, perhaps not in a material way, but certainly in a loving one. At 18 months old, Jon's biological mom decided to have him adopted. At the time it looked as though it wasn't going to be possible for us to adopt him. The social worker said some pretty horrible and hurtful things to Mom and Dad, who thought they were going to lose Jon. I believe she wanted someone else to adopt him. However, Jon's mom felt otherwise and was instrumental in influencing the final decision about who he should live with. She had visited Jon on many occasions when he was little and had kept in contact with Mom and Dad by letter. These letters were kept hidden away and only found after Mom died. They clearly showed Jon's mom was very happy with his new family and the brothers and sisters he had gained. I can still clearly remember the day we all went to Solihull's Magistrates' Court, for the final adoption. We were all dressed up in our 'Sunday best' and held hands as we proudly and excitedly walked up the steps to the court in Poplar Road. Sue was asked to make a sketch of the court room by Margaret McGuire (who lived next door). Margaret wanted to become a police woman when she was older and obviously thought it would help. The day Jon became an official member of our family was a very special day for us all.

Mom and Dad never regretted adopting Jon, even though times were hard and money was in short supply. You might have thought our family was finally complete, but five years later there was another surprise when Lawrence, affectionately known as Lol, was born. After that Mom and Dad always joked about there being seven days in a week, so Lol was definitely the last; completing our seven member family!

# Chapter 2

## EARLY HOME LIFE

To help ease the pressure on finances Mom took a number of part-time jobs. She worked for Bryant Homes, the local home builder, where she cleaned the new homes before the buyers moved in. I also remember her working for Bryant and Tucker in Shirley, making embroidered badges for sewing onto blazers and jackets. All of the money she earned went towards helping to run the home. I am not sure what we would have done without it, because we still struggled to make ends meet. We never had summer holidays and out of necessity Mom made many of our clothes. She was very accomplished at this; a dab hand with the sewing machine and an expert with a pair of knitting needles. I remember she spent many Sunday evenings cutting out material from paper patterns and making up clothes on her old Singer sewing machine, ready for school on Monday. The two most memorable items I can recall were a pair of black and white, small checked shorts and a royal blue jumper. The former were certainly different and as Mom pointed out they were special. "No one else will have a pair like them." That was true, everyone else at school wore plain grey pairs. My favourite jumper was ruined while sitting on the beach during a day trip to Rhyl, when a seagull with diarrhoea emptied the contents of its stomach all over me! Not only did we have many of our clothes made, but we also wore hand-me-downs: Graham received mine, Jon had Graham's and so on right down to Lawrence. You might be forgiven for thinking Lol was the one with the rawest deal, but I can tell you he wasn't, I was. Lol may have had to wear clothes we had all worn at some time or other, but at least he didn't have to wear Dad's old clothes like I did!

I don't remember feeling upset about having to wear them, or school mates making fun of me. Perhaps I have blotted it out of my memory, or maybe the other kids were jealous of them. I will never know, but I do feel having experienced this it influenced my choice of clothes later in life. Since my late teens I have always been keen to buy clothes that are different; not necessarily radically different in style, but certainly different in colour and pattern. I also think Graham and Sue were similar in this respect, whereas Jon and Lol were not. Perhaps as we got older Mom and Dad had more money and they never had clothes made for them.

In my mid-teens I remember Gra and I going shopping into Birmingham and buying a whole new outfit each, for the first time. We were both working part-time in restaurants and had some money to spend for the first time. We both liked the same trends and ended up buying very similar outfits. We bought black, three quarter length 'Crombie' overcoats, (complete with handkerchief and tie-pin), two-tone trousers, Ben Sherman checked shirts and appropriate shoes. I bought a pair of Loafers and Gra a pair of Brogues. We both thought we were the bees' knees. After wearing so many homemade clothes, it felt great to be able to choose some readymade items for my wardrobe. Although this first outfit was special, my most memorable outfit has to be the one I bought in 1972.

Straight after I picked up my first pay packet from a full-time job I bought a pale yellow, round collared shirt, with pale brown and yellow checked piping around the edge of the collar and sleeves. This was to be worn under a black, round necked jumper that had four large squares on the front, two white and two black; a bit like an extract from a chess board. The trousers were woollen, light grey Oxford bags, with extremely wide legs, turn-ups and red and white lines creating a tartan effect. The piece de resistance were the shoes. They were a pair of white leather and brown suede brogues, which I bought from Dolcis for £10. It was an awful lot of money back then, about half a week's wages, but worth every penny, because they were the one thing that attracted Heather to me. She had only ever seen one other pair like them and they were owned by a boy she really fancied. More about this later as it was a very important event in my life.

On the fashion front, even today I am attracted towards styles and colours that stand me out from the rest. My pet hate is denim jeans, particularly old men in baggy, denim jeans; I won't go anywhere near them. I suppose I may change as I get older, but I don't think so!

Despite not being well off, I can honestly say I never remember going hungry or wanting for anything. In fact I never really thought of us as being particularly poor. When we were all young and growing up Mom was once asked how she coped with such a large family, on such a moderate income. Her reply was, "There is always enough money to care for those you love and there will always be a little left over." When Mom and Dad had more than they needed they immediately shared it with the family and others less fortunate than themselves. I remember many Christmases when Mom and Dad would make up a parcel for a family poorer than we were. We all got involved with putting the parcel together, often wrapping up one of our own toys for children who would otherwise have nothing. These all went in a large cardboard box, together with cans and packets of food, to make some other family's Christmas special. For some reason I remember being told without our parcel the children would have no presents and just have a saucepan of boiled cabbage for their Christmas dinner. I can believe the former, but find the latter 'very hard to swallow'! On Christmas Eve a local charity would drive Mom and Dad to a designated family, somewhere in Birmingham, so they could deliver our parcel.

I had a very happy childhood really. I was always content with what we had and never resented Mom and Dad for not being able to provide us with too many special extras. I suppose 'special' is all relative. Graham and I had a very large, second hand Meccano set for Christmas one year and a second hand train set another. We thought they were fantastic and certainly got a lot of enjoyment out of them. However, I am not so sure we were as pleased with our football boots. Unlike most of our friends, we had to make do with a pair of second-hand rugby boots that Grampy was given by Mrs Clarke. Grampy was her gardener and Mrs Clarke's son went to a private boarding school.

A game of football with the other local lads on the big green at Swallows' Meadow was a regular occurrence. Come rain or shine, during the holidays, at weekends and in the evenings after tea, if the light allowed, we played football. Matches consisted of two sets of goals made from jumpers, with the size of the pitch depending on how many were playing (it could be anything from six to twenty two). Games started when there were enough of us gathered, and others could only join the game when there were an equal number of lads waiting to join in. So on a Sunday morning if I was late due to having to peel a 'ton' of spuds for dinner, I sometimes had to wait an age before I got a game. These were the unwritten rules, over which I had no control and which were generally applied to everyone except the oldest and best players. Despite this I was often blamed for Gra not getting a game. Mom went to her grave still believing that when Gra arrived late, through having to peel the potatoes for lunch, I used to tell the other lads not to let him have a game. I do not remember this being true. If it is true, I have completely blotted the memory from my mind and apologise unreservedly to my brother for a despicable act. Deep down though I don't believe I was ever capable of such a thing and regret that despite my protestations Mom never believed me.

There was a time in our football 'careers' when Gra and I wore the second-hand rugby boots or 'granny' boots, while others had the latest Puma or Adidas footwear. 'Granny' boots was the name given to them by 'Doppo' and 'Clarkie', because like most rugby boots in the 1960s they came right up over the ankles. They may have been the best rugby boots money could buy, but the other lads weren't very impressed. I am not sure about Gra, but I don't think it bothered me too much; I just let my feet do the talking. I suppose I was an average player, so when the captains chose their teams I usually got picked somewhere near the middle. Getting left until last wasn't good, because if there were an unequal number of players you might not get a game. There was only one thing worse than not getting picked at all and that was if you got put as an 'extra' player on one side. You then knew everyone else thought you were no good and unlikely to make much of a difference!

Football boots were not the only time I had to have below par footwear while growing up. When I was at Technical Grammar school I went on a week-long trip with the class to the school's 'Mountain Centre' in Wales. It was sort of an outward bound, come geography field trip centre, where we did walking, orienteering and activities to enhance our geography skills. All pupils were expected to take certain pieces of clothing, appropriate for the planned activities. One of the mandatory items was a pair of walking boots for hiking and rock climbing. You can probably guess, I didn't have a pair of boots and ended up taking a pair of black, canvas hockey trainers, which Dad 'water-proofed', by coating them in polyurethane. Dad was very good at improvising, something I picked up from him over the years. It wasn't that Mom and Dad could not afford a pair of boots for me, but rather me having strange feet. They told me I had an unusually large, raised instep, which meant shoes and boots didn't fit me very well. You will be pleased to hear I have managed to grow out of this and my high instep no longer causes me a problem.

Mr Townsend, the teacher in charge was not too sure about the reason, or whether the trainers were going to be suitable. It did not matter too much, because he never found out until we were on our first walk. He need not have worried though, because the trainers were a huge success. They gave me adequate support, I never had an accident in them and they kept my feet lovely and dry, for the first day anyway! After that the polyurethane coating started to crack and the trainers absorbed water like a sponge.

Clothes and footwear may have been something we had to 'make do and mend', but food was something we always seemed to have in plentiful supply. It was not gourmet cooking, but good old fashioned home cooking that was tasty and above all, filling. We always ate together as a family: Mom, Dad and the five children. Good table manners were something they both insisted on: elbows off the table, no talking with your mouth full, using your knife and fork properly and not leaving the table until everyone had finished. This is a tradition Heather and I carried on whilst bringing up our own children, a tradition which sadly seems to be slowly disappearing from general family life. I feel it is a practice we should all be striving to keep. Today, it seems people are 'too busy' to spend time together as a family. Mealtimes are when you can spend quality time together, talking about the day's events, discussing problems and making plans. It is a time for communication; the essential ingredient of any successful family. If children don't experience mealtimes with adults, when will they learn good table manners and the social skills necessary for later in life? We may not have been well off but this is a lesson we all got taught, after all "Good manners cost nothing!"

My clearest food memories are of Sunday mealtimes. Lunches were typically a minced beef pie or steak and kidney suet pudding, with vegetables and potatoes. Vegetables were always well salted, particularly when Dad thought Mom had not salted them and added a second lot, just to make sure. The main course was usually followed by a blackberry and apple pie or perhaps a steamed syrup or jam sponge, always with plenty of custard!

It was all served with lashings of the *'The Clitheroe Kid'*, a long-running BBC radio comedy show featuring Jimmy Clitheroe. Jimmy was a diminutive comedian playing the role of a cheeky schoolboy, who lived with his family at 33 Lilac Avenue. The show's other stars included his granddad, mother, long-suffering sister Susan and Alfie Hall, Susan's daft, tongue-tied boyfriend. Alfie was often drawn into Jimmy's reckless schemes. Susan was usually referred to as 'Scraggy-neck', 'Sparrow-legs' or occasionally 'the Octopus' in reference to her clinches with boyfriend Alfie. I always found this amusing and often used it as a weapon against my own sister Susan when she annoyed or upset me. Would you believe it, she has actually admitted to hitting me when I was little, just so she could cuddle me better! Despite this, more often than not she was good to me, often sneaking a hot water bottle and a plate of jam sandwiches upstairs when I had been sent to bed without any tea. At the time I thought Mom and Dad didn't know about it, but of course they did as Mom confirmed when I was much older. To get back to the radio series, it was made with a studio audience so there were frequent bouts of 'canned laughter' at Jimmy's schoolboy humour. I used to laugh at Alfie's bumblings as he tried to explain something, but always seeming to make things worse. Jimmy frequently listened at keyholes, where he usually got the wrong end of the stick, and even when he tried to do good, he usually messed things up. After the end credits, a short piece by Jimmy was usually inserted when he wound-up the show, tying up any loose ends in the plot and often reporting that Granddad had spanked him for what he had done.

Teatime was almost more predictable than lunch with tinned fruit and evaporated milk on the menu, together with bread and butter. If the timing was right we were able to buy a block of ice-cream from a van that drove around the streets. You always knew when the van was close by because you could hear its chimes, usually 'Greensleeves'. However, you were never exactly sure when it would arrive, or in fact if it ever would. I remember many Sundays when the chimes got tantalizingly close, but the ice-cream van never made an appearance in our road. Even when it did, the timing had to be just right, or the ice-cream would melt because we didn't have a fridge, let alone a freezer. Dad's favourite fruit was peaches, so he usually got his way, but there was the odd occasion when we had pears or even fruit salad as a special treat. Mom would often spend all Sunday afternoon baking cakes, jam tarts or scones so by teatime there was an enormous meat plate full, stacked five or six deep. The smell of the baking was wonderful and the taste even better, particularly when they were still warm. I don't remember there ever being any left for later, because with so many of us they were soon devoured.

We always ate well on Sundays but this did have its disadvantages; with so many of us for lunch there were always plenty of potatoes to peel and peas to pod. Mom and Dad always made us earn our pocket money by doing jobs around the house and rightly so! However the weekly 'spud bashing' always seemed to fall to me and then Gra, as he grew older. I got to be quite a dab hand at peeling potatoes and have never met anyone as quick or as good as I am. If potato peeling was an Olympic sport, I would get the gold medal every time! It is not surprising that I am so good, because I had plenty of practice and always had the added incentive of wanting to finish the task quickly so I could fit in a game of football before lunch.

When I was very young Sunday afternoons, as far as I can remember, were always spent in front of the TV together with the whole family. We did have a second-hand TV, although it was only black and white and had just two channels: BBC and ITV (Independent Television). The choice was not great so we usually watched a film. The only ones I remember were comedies starring either George Formby or Old Mother Riley.

George Formby was a British comedy actor, singer-songwriter and comedian. He sang light, comical songs, accompanying himself on the banjo ukulele, probably the most well-known being 'Leaning on a Lamppost'. He was a major star of stage and screen in the 1930s and 1940s, so on reflection his films must have been old even then when we were watching them.

Old Mother Riley was originally a music hall act, which ran from about 1934 to 1954 played by Arthur Lucan. Old Mother Riley was an Irish washerwoman character, devised by Lucan and whose daughter Kitty was played by Lucan's wife Kitty McShane. It was essentially a drag act, which became hugely successful; eventually performed in theatres, on radio and in films. We loved the films and would stay glued to the TV, spending most of our time laughing at the antics Old Mother Riley got up to. Coincidently it was this show that gave Jimmy Clitheroe his first big break in 1939 in an Old Mother Riley pantomime called 'The Old Woman who Lives in a Shoe.'

The first children's TV programmes I ever watched were 'Watch with Mother'. This was a cycle of children's programmes created by Freda Lingstrom and broadcast by the BBC from 1952 until 1973. To accommodate its target audience of pre-school children viewing with their mothers, Watch With Mother was broadcast at 1:30 pm each day. This was post lunch and before older children came home from school. The classic cycle comprised:

Picture Book on Mondays,

Andy Pandy on Tuesdays,

The Flower Pot Men on Wednesdays,

Rag, Tag and Bobtail on Thursdays and

The Woodentops on Fridays.

My favourite was without doubt Picture Book; I looked forward to it all week. The programme, which encouraged children to make things, was presented by Patricia Driscoll. I remember quite clearly the little string puppet sausage dog that got excited and jumped up and down on the desk beside her. I suppose, besides Mom, Patricia was the first true love in my life. She was a lovely looking Irish girl, with a soft, beautiful voice. I remember she had a catchphrase: "Do you think you could do this? – I am sure you could if you tried." When she whispered those words, my heart melted. I am certain I only watched it because she was on and not because of the programme itself.

Watching programmes on TV in the 1960s was not as reliable as it is today. Electronics were far from being advanced, which meant televisions could be quite temperamental. There were two frequent problems that occurred with not only ours, but most televisions. They were problems that usually prevented us from watching programmes uninterrupted. The first problem was a weak signal; even with a good signal the picture quality was quite poor. I remember many times when Dad would climb in to the loft to adjust the aerial. For the Day family it was quite an easy thing to do, because there were so many of us. We formed a human intercom system from the loft to the TV, so that Dad instantly knew what effect his adjustments were making. Dad was in the loft, Sue at the top of the stairs, me at the bottom, Graham by the sitting room door and Mom in front of the television. When Dad moved the aerial we relayed back to him when to stop. It was never a straightforward task, often involving many iterations of positioning the aerial in different places. Frequently we would have a 'great' picture only for it to disappear again as Dad climbed down from the loft. I soon learnt many new electrical terms, like 'bollocks' and 'bugger'; words which were precisely conveyed from Dad to Mom via our unique communication chain.

The second difficulty we had with the TV was the picture would 'roll' upwards, off the screen, only to appear again at the bottom. There was always a complete picture on the screen, it just wasn't all in the right place and it never stopped moving. We all knew what the problem was, it was the 'horizontal hold'. I did recently 'Google it', "*... a horizontal-hold control, which adjusts the horizontal deflection generator so that it conforms exactly to the control of the horizontal synchronizing impulses...*", but it didn't make much sense. I only know that Dad was the one who spent hours each week with his arm behind the TV adjusting the horizontal hold. There was also a 'vertical hold', which rarely caused us any problem. I can only assume this was a much more reliable and robust component.

One expenditure Mom was also able to cut back on was haircuts. She managed this by cutting our hair herself. Not only was it expensive for my Dad and four boys to visit the barber but it was also time-consuming. Sunday evening was generally the time we all queued up to have our hair cut. Dad was always first, followed by Lol, Jon, Gra and finally me. This was to ensure my two youngest brothers were able to go to bed at a reasonable time. We took it in turn to put on a black plastic cape and sit on a square, green stool while Mom cut our hair. The stool was an old dining room chair without the back attached and the plastic cape was far too small for me. It was so small that it cut into my neck. However the pain of being garrotted by the cape was nothing compared to actually having your hair cut. Mom had bought a pair of hairdressing scissors and a special comb for thinning out our hair. It was a two sided comb, with edges very similar to the electric clippers you can buy today. The cutting was carried out by inserting an old style, double edged Gillette razor blade. When Dad had his hair cut the blade was brand new, razor sharp and would cut through anything. Dad had a really dense head of hair; hair that was very thick and wiry. Consequently, you can imagine that by the time the razor had been used to cut his and three other lots of hair, it wasn't sharp anymore. Predictably by the time it got to me it was always as blunt as the back of a knife and would not 'cut butter hot', so much so that it pulled my hair out rather than cut it! Therefore, once a month the Sunday 'hair' night was something I didn't look forward to, or relish. Despite my endless protestations about the discomfort, Mom would not use a new blade and just told me to stop moaning. It was not all bad though because it never hurt when Mom used the scissors to cut my fringe. Fringes were all the rage in the 60s, something to do with 'The Beatles'.

Again it didn't bother me that Mom cut our hair because she did rather a good job of it. None of my mates ever commented upon it or made disparaging remarks, so I could not have looked very different from the rest of them. However my hair did get me into trouble with teachers at my Technical Grammar school. My hair was often referred to as 'a furry helmet' and it once got me a detention. One morning I arrived at school wearing light grey trousers, instead of the regulation charcoal grey ones and was accosted at the school entrance by Mr Collins, the

Headmaster. His nickname was 'The Acorn', I am not entirely sure why, but I think it was to do with his short rotund figure. He had a fearsome reputation for making and implementing draconian rules within the school. Mr Collins once made the national press with his enforcement of petty rules about sideburns. A handful of lads at the school arrived to take their A level maths examination, with sideburns they had grown over the previous two weeks. Just like I was accosted at the entrance to the school, so were these lads. Mr Collins told them to go home and get their sideburns removed, or else they would not be allowed to sit the exam. The rebellious boys didn't and consequently never got to take the examination.

Anyway this particular morning, it was my trousers and not my hair that got me into trouble, or so I thought. I had to line up outside the Head's office, ready to be chastised along with about six other lads buttonholed for breaking one of Collins' ridiculous rules. When Sir dealt with me he said, "What's wrong with your hair boy? You look like a girl with that fringe. Why haven't you got a parting?"

I replied with my stock answer, "I have got a 'cowlick' Sir and my hair won't stay down."

"Of course it won't boy, unless you get a proper haircut and stick it down with Brylcreem," he yelled.

Brylcreem was a brand of hair styling products for men. The first Brylcreem product was pomade, created locally in 1928 by County Chemicals at the Chemico Works in Bradford Street, Birmingham. Pomade was a greasy and waxy substance that was used to style hair: making hair look slick, neat and shiny. Unlike modern hair spray and hair gel, pomade did not dry and often took several washes to remove. It could easily be removed by using a high-detergent shampoo or other de-greaser such as washing-up liquid. Well, when I went home and told Mom what Mr Collins had told me to do, she was furious. Mom told me "Go and tell Mr Collins you can have a parting, *plastered down* with Brylcreem, if he is willing to wash your pillow case each week." I was never a straight 'A' student, but I wasn't daft either, so I spent a week making myself as inconspicuous as possible, trying to avoid Mr Collins and a confrontation that would mean me having to tell him what Mom had said.

When I was young, holidays abroad in places like Spain never really existed. Holidays for most families were usually spent in the UK, at old Victorian holiday towns like Weston-Super-Mare or Rhyl. However, for us a family holiday was something we didn't have until I was about fourteen. This wasn't to say we never had treats. Summer holidays were days out to places like Stratford-upon-Avon, Earlswood Woods, Malvern and Brueton park in Solihull, or if we were really lucky a day trip on Smith's coaches to Weston or Rhyl. Again I didn't feel as though I was missing out, because I didn't know any different and we still had memorable and enjoyable times. The most memorable times were our trips to the woods at Earlswood. These were only three miles from where we lived, but you could have been miles from anywhere. The woods had everything a child could want: trees of every size and shape, large expanses of bracken to hide in and a railway line that split the woods in two. The two halves of the wood were joined by a large foot bridge. The main structure was constructed of cast iron held together with the biggest rivets I have ever seen and the steps and crossing were made of enormous railway sleepers. Every time a train approached we all ran on to the bridge to wave to the driver. All of the trains back then were steam locomotives. They were large, dirty, thundering great trains, which you could hear coming down the track, five minutes before they came into view. This always gave us plenty of time to run to the bridge and gain a great vantage point to get the best view. They would sound their ear-splitting whistles and let off billowing steam as they fought their way up the gradient towards Earlswood station. The engines had a large tender full of black, dusty coal that the engineers would inevitably be shovelling into the furnace. The drivers were always covered in soot and sweat as they passed by, but they never failed to look up and wave at us on the bridge. We must have been and felt like Jenny Agutter and the cast of 'The Railway Children'. During the summer months we often found the vegetation on the railway embankments in the woods scorched and black, where sparks from the trains had set them alight. Sometimes the grass was warm and smoke would still be evident from a recent incident.

We would go as a whole family group together with my Uncle Les and Aunty Barb and female cousins Jo and Jack. There were also times when others were invited along, such as our neighbourhood friends and the Gardners – Aunty Barb's brother's family. Our group could number as large as eighteen or more. The adults prepared picnics, which we would eat under a large oak tree to be followed by games based on hide-and-seek.

We took it in turns for all of the children to hide and to be 'hunted' by my Dad and Uncle Les, followed by the roles being reversed. Dad and Les always had an unfair advantage. I have vivid memories of Dad in particular climbing huge trees, climbing so high he was often completely hidden from sight. There were so many trees in the woods it was like looking for a needle in a haystack.

We always seemed to be playing when I was small, generally games we could play out in the street without expensive equipment. Games we played can be partitioned into a number of categories: ball, skipping, chasing, singing and instructional games. There are countless games that I can remember and I am sure I have forgotten just as many. Ball games included Queenie-o-cocoa and Donkey. In the latter we threw a tennis sized ball against a wall and let it bounce, whilst jumping over it. Each time you jumped over the ball successfully without it touching your legs, you received a letter. The first person to collect all of the letters to spell out the word 'donkey' was the winner.

We didn't just play normal skipping games, but also French skipping, which was played with a large loop of elastic. Our elastic was always every colour of the rainbow, made from dozens of coloured elastic bands joined together, by looping them through one another. Two people were the 'enders' who stood inside the loop of elastic, stretching it into a rectangle shape, by standing with their feet slightly apart. To start the game the elastic was set at ankle height. The jumper had to perform different hops and jumps: jumps in, around and on the elastic. Sometimes the jumps were done to the chant of skipping rhymes or songs. If the jumper was successful in completing the rhyme (and the jumps) the height of the elastic was raised to the knees, then the thighs and finally the waist!

Chasing games were always popular and numerous: hide and seek, tig, den to den and paper chase. For some reason the person who did the chasing was always referred to as 'IT': I haven't a clue where this came from. The person who was 'IT' ran after the other players and tried to touch, or 'tig' them. When you were touched by the chaser they would say "Tig, you're IT". You then became 'IT' or the chaser.  There were just two main rules:

'IT' could not run after the same person all the time.

If you were caught by the chaser, you could not try to catch the person who caught you straight away.

We would sometimes play a variation called 'tig off-ground'. This meant if you were being chased you could have a short respite, by standing on something off the ground, like a wall or fire hydrant.

Singing games included "In and out the Scottish Bluebells", "The big ship sails through the alley alley oh", "The Farmers in his Den" and "London Bridge is falling down." However, the games which caused most controversy were the 'instructional' type games like "May I". One of us played the role of "mother" or "father" and the rest of us were the "children". To begin the game, the "mother" or "father" stood about ten yards in front of everyone else, facing away from the "children" who stood on the starting line. The mother or father gave instructions to each of the children in turn. For example, "Graham, take three giant steps forward". Graham then had to say "May I" before he carried out the instructions or else he would forfeit his go. Other instructions included actions like.

Take six baby steps forward.

Take two umbrella steps forward.

Hop forward like a frog, four times.

Walk like a crabwalk forward for the count of five.

The first of the children to reach the location of the mother or father won the game. Other variations of this game were "Simon says" or "What's the time Mr Wolf?"

There were a few games we played with accessories, such as marbles, go-karting and roller skating, but these were all done using second hand, or 'nicked' equipment. Dad built a kart for me, from an old pram and a few planks of wood; it was easily the best in the street. The main body of the kart was very substantial (probably a bit over the top) and steering was by a rope tied to the front axle. Dad could put his hand to anything, but usually went for bigger and better than everyone else. You will probably notice plenty of examples of this throughout the book. I am not sure how securely the go-kart was put together, but I never had any doubts about it. I had every faith in my Dad; why wouldn't I?

Our roller skates, bought from a jumble sale, were not your usual 'run of the mill' skates. Instead of rubber wheels that all of my mates had, ours had wheels made out of stone. This made them exceptionally heavy, as noisy as hell and challenging to stop in. On the three by two concrete slabs that made up the pavements outside of our house, I sounded like a runaway train. The skates also had the big advantage that it was easy to keep upright in them. They were so heavy it was impossible to fall over, a bit like "weebles wobble but they don't fall down". The most contentious items I played with were marbles, because some of them were obtained by 'ill gotten' means. This was a period in my life I am not particularly proud of, but you will have to wait a while to find out why.

From a very early age, probably about 18 months, I became really interested in jigsaws and soon grew into a bit of an expert. Starting with small six piece wooden jigsaws, I soon progressed onto larger, more difficult puzzles. By five or six I was having competitions with Dad to see who could do a certain jigsaw the quickest. Mom would time us and be the judge. I remember one in particular, which was a 120 piece puzzle of Davy Crocket, complete with beaver skin hat, fighting at the battle of the Alamo. I won convincingly, but did have a distinct advantage, by having put the puzzle together on numerous occasions. From an early age I religiously had to piece together the outside edges, before I could begin the middle pieces. One weekend Mom came home from a jumble sale with six new jigsaws for me. What a treat it was. Unfortunately they had no boxes or pictures and were all together in the same plastic bag. I think Mom thought it would keep me quiet for a few days, but they were all completed well before I went to bed.

It wasn't long before I was being bought much larger jigsaws for birthdays and Christmas; jigsaws up to 1,000 pieces. I had my own jigsaw board, large enough to do even the biggest puzzle I owned, that is until Mom and Dad bought me a 2,000 piece puzzle. This was some jigsaw, double the size of any other one I owned and entitled "The Village Green". There were plenty of 'green' and 'sky' pieces, all looking very similar and making it more difficult than any other puzzle I had ever completed. It was a challenge I was looking forward to. It was even too large to put together on my board, so Mom agreed I could put it on the kitchen table. After each session I carefully covered the jigsaw with a thick woollen tablecloth so that we could all eat our meals as normal. I spent all of my spare time on the puzzle; my Mom having to prise me away from it to get me to go to bed. Against my better nature this one evening I allowed Mom and Dad to help me with the jigsaw; they said it was so we could finish it quicker. About 9 o'clock, on Mom and Dad's instruction, I reluctantly went to bed, knowing that tomorrow I would complete the challenge.

I dreamt about which would be the last piece I put into the puzzle; would it be sky or would it be grass? Much to my chagrin I awoke the next morning to find out Mom and Dad had actually finished it for me. There it was, complete, no pieces missing and looking splendid. I think my Mom expected me to be excited and thrilled it was finished, but I wasn't. The whole point and excitement of doing a jigsaw reaches a climax when putting in the final piece and they had denied me that pleasure. A pleasure I should have had, because after all it was my jigsaw. To this day I have never understood how they could have done this to me and never forgave them. Perhaps that's petty but they did scar me for life and changed the way I do jigsaws forever. The first action I now take when I begin any jigsaw is to put a piece on one side. This is brought out towards the end, thus ensuring I am the one that puts in the last piece and gets the thrill and excitement of completing the puzzle; how sad is that?

We may not have had much money for clothes, toys and haircuts, but we nearly always had a pet in the house. The first was when Dad came home with a pure white Alsatian puppy called Sally. She grew in to a wonderful pet: intelligent, very faithful and extremely protective towards the children. Sally was definitely a one off, the only white Alsatian in the locality and extremely large for a bitch. She would have been perfect, an ideal show dog, if it were not for her one ear, which flopped down to one side like a rabbit's. Although Sally was a smart dog, she was extremely clumsy. Every four weeks, she would cut her paw without fail. I do not remember ever seeing the actual cuts, but Mom assured us she had. It would certainly explain why Sally left a trail of blood, on the lino in the hall, for a few days every month!

White must have been my Dad's favourite colour, because he also bought a pair of white mice to keep. They were lovely little pets, with pink eyes and long pink tails. There was no problem with a cage because you've guessed it, Dad made one. We also got the bedding for free. Sue, Gra and I took it in turns to ask Dewhurst's the butchers in Cranmore Boulevard for a bag of sawdust. They always had a never ending supply of the stuff, because they used it to put on the floor to soak up blood from the meat. Now I don't know whether you know anything about the life cycle of white mice, but a female becomes sexually mature at three months, has a gestation period of less than three weeks and can have anything up to 11 young at a time. It was just Dad's luck that he was sold a male and female, therefore within six months his cage was overcrowded and he had to make one of his specialities. It was made out of an old radio, it had several floors, joined by stairs and multiple boxes for bedding. He even made a sign for it saying 'The Mouse Hotel'. However after 12 months our two mice had turned into 63 and even the hotel was too small. Dad and I took them down the road onto a piece of waste land and set them free. I am not entirely sure why we had to get rid of them. I often wonder if Dad had got fed up with making cages, Mom had put her foot down, or we couldn't carry bags of sawdust big enough back from the butchers.

# Chapter 3

## FIRST SCHOOL DAYS

I first attended school at the age of five and my first school was Cranmore Infants, in Shirley, right next to where Uncle Les and Aunty Barb lived. It was that close, I could literally stand behind the bike shed and peer into their back garden. In 1958 there were no 'rising fives', so I started mid-term in class five, exactly when I was five years old. I am not sure exactly how the system worked, but those children with summer-term birthdays went into class six and were treated differently from the rest of us. In particular they had beds in their classroom and were made to have a sleep each afternoon. I can remember my first teacher quite clearly. Her name was Miss Murphy, a lady I admired and loved. I have kept the Christmas card she gave me a few weeks after I started.

Memories of lunch times for the first week are still very clear in my mind; because I was new I was put on the 'Fussers' table. This was a large wooden table placed at the front of the hall for about eight children, who as the name suggests were a bit picky with their food. The dinner ladies obviously didn't know me at that time because I usually ate everything that was put in front of me. I also ate very rapidly; too quickly for my Mom and Dad's liking. They were always telling me to slow down and to chew my food, and often said they could see potatoes going down my throat as I swallowed them whole. They claimed my Adams apple became distorted and my eyes nearly popped out of my head. It never made any difference; to this day I still eat far too quickly. When you came from a large family like mine, if you didn't eat quickly then your food got taken off your plate before you could finish it. I don't think the dinner ladies had seen anyone quite like me and they were not best pleased. They had quite a fearsome reputation, taking great delight in putting children in their place and making them feel humiliated. There was one occasion I can recall, which I am sure stuck in every child's mind. When you had finished your food and the dinner ladies gave their permission, you took your plate, knife and fork up to the serving hatch to be cleared away. Any scraps left on your plate were scraped in to the 'pig bin', which went off to be used as pigswill by the local farmer. This was a large black plastic dustbin, which by the end of lunch contained everything from vegetables, meat, gravy, pastry and custard, all mixed up and looking pretty disgusting. One day a young lad scraped his plate without permission, so one of the dinner ladies took potatoes out of the 'pig bin' and made him stay in the dining room until he had eaten them.

Those on the 'Fussers' table in particular were berated and made fun of; it was not a place you wanted to be. I lasted there exactly one week, which would have been less but I am certain the dinner ladies did their best to keep me there. I remember one lunch time when I was served pork, mashed potatoes and cauliflower. It doesn't sound too bad; it wasn't. I soon devoured the meat and potatoes, but left the veg. The reason being, it was a whole cauliflower. When I say a whole cauliflower I mean the whole stalk, but no florets. I had to sit at the 'Fusser' table until school restarted, having to miss my play time.

I must have impressed the dinner ladies because I eventually went on to be a server; one of a select band of children chosen to collect dinners and hand them out to everyone else. It was a very responsible job that came complete with apron. There were half a dozen of us who, each day, left class early to meet in the equipment cupboard off the dining hall, prior to the hordes arriving. There was always a teacher with us who asked mental arithmetic questions while we were waiting; I was usually the first one to put my hand up with the answer. I also became a biscuit trolley monitor, pushing the trolley up and down the corridor at break-time and selling biscuits to every class. The selection wasn't great, but the biscuits were very popular; every child bought something. There were Burton's 'Jammie Dodgers', chocolate marshmallows and orange or mint 'Bingos'. They were to be eaten with our free daily bottle of milk, a feature of 1960's school life due to Ellen Wilkinson the first woman Minister of Education. She had long been a campaigner against poverty and in 1946 managed to persuade Parliament to pass the School Milk Act, which ordered the issue of one-third of a pint of milk, free to all pupils under eighteen. At one time I loved my milk, gulping it down alongside a Jammie Dodger. That was until the winter of 1962-63.

The winter of 1962–1963, also known as 'The Big Freeze of 1963' was one of the coldest winters on record. Temperatures plummeted and the local Earlswood lakes and rivers began to freeze over. At the time, in the Central England temperature records extending back to 1659, only the winter of 1683–84 had been significantly colder. In December 1962 a cold easterly wind set in and a blizzard swept across the country creating snow drifts in places as high as 20 feet. They blocked roads and railways, left villagers stranded and brought down power lines. In January the country started to freeze solid with temperatures as low as −16 °C (3.2 °F). Even the sea froze for 1 mile out from the shore at Herne Bay in Kent. Icicles hung from every roof, some of them were more than a metre long. The thaw didn't set in until early March; the 6th March was the first morning of the year without any frost anywhere in Britain. Temperatures may have risen to normal quite quickly, but I remember drifts of snow in the hedgerows of Earlswood well in to April. We had a fish pond at the time, which Dad had built out of old bricks and concrete. The fish were perch from the local canal and not surprisingly they never survived, with the water freezing solid to a depth of three feet.

At the time Gra, Jon and I shared one of the larger bedrooms. With no double glazing or central heating, every morning our bedroom windows were frozen from top to bottom, with patterns that looked like flowers and ferns created by some exceptionally talented artist. Each day I scratched the patterns off the glass with my finger nails to reveal whether or not it had snowed overnight. On the coldest nights moisture from our breath condensed on the cold internal walls and froze, forming a sparkly frost. It was on mornings like this that Dad would get up early to fetch the milk in immediately after the milkman delivered it. If not the milk froze, expanded above the neck of the glass bottle and pushed the foil top upwards. Dad never got up late, so we could depend upon our milk for breakfast; frozen milk was not good for pouring over cereals! In 1963 the milk was delivered by Mr Rowney in his car; a huge great black vehicle with a massive boot. It had to be to hold crates of milk. I don't know what happened to him, but a few years later we were receiving milk from the Co-op. I have clear memories of paying the milkman for Mom on a Saturday. She would be busy in the kitchen when he arrived, so would give me the money to take to the door. I had to give him our 'Divi' number and obtain a receipt, which was not much bigger than a postage stamp. Jack, our milkman, had a huge leather pouch for carrying his money, which he shook to sort out the coins for our change. The jangling of the coins and the smell of the leather are senses that will stick long in my memory. Incidentally, our 'Divi' number was '292823'. I repeated it so many times over the years I shall never forget it.

Anyway, unlike Dad, the school caretaker was not an early riser and this particular morning dozens of crates of school milk had more milk out of the bottles than in them. This was still the case at 10 o'clock, our break time for biscuits and milk. I recall our teacher telling us to hold the bottles on the radiator to thaw the milk out. This allowed it to melt and then we could drink it. It took all break time to even begin to thaw. The full fat cream separated out from the rest of the milk and curdled in a thick, congealed lump on top. We were all made to drink our milk before returning to lessons. I was not physically sick, but it was revolting and put me off milk for life. I have not drunk a glass of milk since that fateful day.

Despite a number of these poor experiences I can honestly say I never once 'wagged' off school. Mom didn't have to tell me twice, or try to blackmail me into going to school. However she did have to spend more time getting me ready for school than she did with Sue or Gra. This is mainly because I always looked scruffy, or so my Mom always said. She may have made me some lovely trousers and knitted me attractive jumpers, but I never looked smart. The main problem was my hair, because I had what is often referred to as a 'cowlick', and a 'burnished chestnut' one at that. Many colourblind people often referred to my hair colour as ginger, but I called it burnished chestnut. A cowlick is a section of hair that stands straight up, or lies at an obscure angle to the rest of the hair, often forming a spiral pattern. The term "cowlick" originates from a cow's habit of licking its young, which results in a swirling pattern in the calf's hair. The most common site for a human cowlick is in the crown, but they can show up anywhere. Mine was on my forehead, to the right hand side. Mom would spend an age trying to get my hair to look half decent before school, usually while I was having breakfast. She would slap on loads of thick, slimy, green, opaque setting lotion, which, unlike Brylcreem, dried quickly and set hard. However, on several occasions, not before it slipped off the comb and into my cornflakes!

When I look back at old photographs I can see why Mom complained about my smartness – I did look a little unkempt at the side of brother Gra. His appearance was always pristine, tidy as could be and not a fair hair out of place, a little angel really. Anyway after my hair had set in place, we would go off to school hand in hand, Gra like a little cherub and me only barely acceptable. When Mom collected us each afternoon, she would despair. Gra and I would run out of school together; Gra still looking as he had done first thing, but me looking like a 'rag bag'. Mom said she always wanted to disown me, because I looked like I had been 'dragged through a hedge backwards'. My hair was all over the place, as though it had not seen a comb all day, my shirt was out and my tie usually around the back of my neck. As if that wasn't bad enough, my shoes were muddy and scuffed, my laces undone and my socks were down around my ankles! Every day I was given the same message about how messy I looked. I don't know when, but I think Mom's persistence must have paid off, somewhere along the line. When I became a teenager I started to take great pride in my appearance and now I go nowhere without a comb, for what bit of hair I still have. In recent years I can recall several occasions when I arrived at work without my comb, so the first task of the day was a special visit to the chemist to buy one. I probably have around half a dozen in the house at any given time. It is sad to say Heather often refers to me as 'Malcomb'.

Irrespective of my appearance and despite not looking like a true scholar, I loved school and seemed to do reasonably well in most subjects apart from English. I suspect this has something to do with the fact I rarely read books, unless it was for gaining information. Growing up I could count the number of real books I read on both hands and all but one of these were paperbacks written by Edgar Rice Burroughs. He was an American author, best known for his creation of the jungle hero Tarzan, and Dad had a pile of his books in his bedroom cupboard. I went through a phase of reading most of them, including 'Tarzan of the Apes',

'Tarzan and the Forbidden City' and 'Tarzan and the Leopard Men'. The title of the other solitary book I read sticks vividly in my mind – it was 'Hudson Bay', a biography of the French Canadian fur trader and explorer Pierre Raddison. The part of the story I recollect most clearly is the first chapter when he was captured by Mohawk Indians, while out duck hunting. He was adopted by them, learnt their language and way of life and joined them in their wars. Raddison eventually went on to form the Hudson Bay Trading Company.

Even at school while my class mates were reading 'Biggles' from the library, I would steer well clear of any type of fiction and choose 'Animals of Asia' or 'Amazing Fish of the Natural World'. I have always had different tastes to the majority of people, being able to boast that I have never read any James Bond books or even seen one of the Bond films either. For some reason I am not the remotest bit interested.

I believe that genetically I am not inclined towards reading 'stories', but feel I could have been encouraged more as a child. I can honestly put my hand on my heart and say I do not ever remember Mom or Dad reading me a book or telling me a story. It was not just me either, Sue and Gra would tell you exactly the same thing. For this reason I always found it difficult to read to Matt and Kerry when they were young, but at least I tried. Perhaps I only tried because Heather was always keen we should read to them, as she loves reading. I do feel though that even if Mom and Dad had read to me, things would not have been very different. I say this because despite Heather and I reading to our children, Matt still doesn't read a great deal, whereas my sister

Sue and brother Jon, who were in a similar situation to me, are always reading books. Perhaps they are genetically different, they are that way inclined and it is nature and not nurture, which is the major influence.

English is not just about reading, but it certainly helps when it comes to writing. I always wanted to write interesting and exciting essays, but I do not remember any of my English teachers giving me advice, help or encouragement to improve my writing skills. Not once can I recall any constructive comment on my English work, pointing out what was wrong and how I could address things. I have probably learnt more during my time at work and from Heather, Mrs. Literacy herself! I certainly was not taught any of the grammar she currently teaches six and seven year olds; even when I was at Technical Grammar school. Until I met Heather I could never spell onomatopoeia, let alone know what it meant. The term means the imitation of a sound and the commonest occurrences of them include animal noises, such as "oink" or "meow". Other popular ones are "splash" and "tick tock". This is only one example of how today's children are learning at a standard far higher than I ever did, so I cannot accept consecutive Government's claims that standards of education are getting worse. I believe it is just that 'today' there is so much to learn. Long gone is the *Renaissance man:* people such as Leonardo da Vinci, Michelangelo, Galileo Galilei, and Nicolaus Copernicus. Da Vinci was a painter, sculptor, architect, musician, scientist, mathematician, engineer, inventor, anatomist, geologist, cartographer, botanist, and writer. He was without doubt a genius, but in the 21$^{st}$ century it takes a genius to know everything about just one of these subjects. I feel that today it is impossible to know the entirety of any subject, because human knowledge changes by the minute. What da Vinci knew in the early 16<sup>th</sup> Century is a mere fraction of what he could learn today. I always remember my 6<sup>th</sup> form Chemistry teacher telling the class he was teaching topics he only learnt at University. Standards move on, there is so much children have to learn today that some topics will have to suffer.

Heather has made me quite a pernickety person with regards to the spoken and written word. Many of her pet hates have rubbed off on me, something which she regrets when I pick her up on the very occasional slip she makes. There are two main ones: the first being when presenters and sports stars do not use adverbs. An adverb usually modifies a verb or a verb phrase. Many adverbs end in 'ly'. It is this ending which many people do not use. When interviewed after a match the Premier League manager will often say "The team played brilliant". You can say "The team played brilliantly" or "The team played brilliant football", but you cannot say "The team played brilliant". Next time you watch Match of the Day, listen out for it. The other dislike is the spelling of plurals and the use of apostrophe 'S'. I don't think there is a day goes by, without either Heather or I spotting a sign or notice like "Homemade sausage's for sale", or "Kates Café". I never used to be like this, but now I am always looking out for it, thanks Heather for that little bit of nurture.

I wrote earlier that I was not given any encouragement – I told a lie. My favourite teacher Miss Betteridge was always putting red kisses on my comprehension work and spellings.

Additionally an English teacher in my final GCE year stood up in front of the whole class, handed me back my essay and said "Day, this essay is crap!"

My favourite lesson and the one I excelled in the most was always Mathematics. It was this subject that got me into the top 'stream' at junior school. When I left Cranmore Infants I was initially put in to class 1A2 at Shirley Heath. This was for the group of children who did not quite have the ability to be in the top class. This was probably thanks to my final year teacher Mrs. Lloyd, a plumpish, grey haired and matronly lady who thought the sun shone out of my sister's backside. Mrs Lloyd had taught Sue four years before I was in her class and whenever I got anything wrong she would take great delight in telling me, "Susan could always do this," or, "Susan never did that." I should be grateful really, because Gra got "Susan and Malcolm never…" and poor old Jon got compared to all three of us!

After two weeks in class 1A2, the whole class had to take spelling and arithmetic tests, to see whether we needed to be put up or down a class. I recall quite clearly getting stuck about halfway through the spellings as they got harder and harder. The one word in particular I remember not having a clue how to spell was 'talk'. When the results were announced, it was decided myself along with a lad called Derek, would be put into 1A1 on a trial basis. I was told my spelling results had been below average, but my arithmetic was so good they were going to try me in the top class, to see how I would cope. From then on I never looked back, staying in the top stream throughout my time at Shirley Heath.

One of the other subjects I preferred at infant and junior schools was art and crafts; I loved making things. Perhaps I had listened to Patricia Driscoll's "Do you think you could do this? – I am sure you could if you tried" when I watched 'Picture Book'. Or perhaps it was the lovely Miss Betteridge I had in class 3 at Cranmore that encouraged me. The first and only object we made that year was a brightly coloured raffia mat. It was made from a thick circular piece of card, with a saw-tooth circumference and a half inch hole in the centre. Raffia was wound around the card; through the hole in the centre and into each consecutive 'V' of the saw-tooth, to make what looked like a wheel with raffia spokes. This was the starting point, after which we then wove different coloured raffia in between the 'spokes', starting at the centre and working our way outwards. Admittedly we only had art once a week, for about an hour, but it should not have taken all year for us to complete them. The reason why it took so long, was because I just loved standing next to 'Miss'. She was young, attractive and I suppose reminded me of my first love, Patricia Driscoll. In order to get close to 'Miss', once a week I would cut one of the raffia 'spokes' and take my mat up to her and say it had broken. She would then spend the next five minutes mending the broken 'spoke' with me standing at the table next to her, breathing in her heady perfume. This experience could only be topped when she replied, "Yes" to my question, "Please Miss, can I tell you who's talking?" After several weeks she caught on to what I was doing and had words with me; what a snitch I must have been! Despite the numerous running repairs on my mat, it turned out quite well. I managed to expertly hide all of the loose ends on the repaired 'spokes' underneath the raffia weaving. Mom was pleased with it anyway. She said it was wonderful and put it away in a cupboard for safe keeping!

The next item I remember making was a Toby jug at Shirley Heath Junior School. A Toby Jug, sometimes known as a Fillpot (or Philpot) is a pottery jug in the form of a seated person, or the head of a recognisable individual. Typically the seated figure is a heavily-set, jovial man wearing 18th century attire – a long coat and a tricorn hat. The tricorn hat forms a pouring spout and a handle is attached at the rear. My effort at making a Toby Jug, along with most of them made by the class, ended up looking nothing like this description. We made them by using jam jars and making the tricorn hat from card. The jug was then built up by covering them in numerous layers of newspaper soaked in glue. After many weeks of applying newspaper layers we used papier mâché to add the handle and features such as a nose and eyebrows. They were finally hand painted and varnished to complete the finished article. Art lessons involved us sitting at tables in groups of four with each table having its own paint pallets and pot of glue. Many older readers will remember the type of glue we were provided with. It came in the form of a powder and was prepared by adding water and stirring vigorously; a bit like wallpaper paste, but without the fungicide. My group was located towards the back of the room and managed to get through five times the amount of paste than any other table. The teacher regularly got frustrated with the rapidity with which we got through the glue and would ask, "What are you doing, eating it?" We never said anything, but little did he know that is exactly what Patricia was doing. As fast as we were provided with a pot of glue, Pat would stick her brush in the pot and suck the glue off. The rest of us on the table would look on in amazement, but were helpless in trying to stop her. The more we said anything the more she did it. Pat wasn't the most popular girl in the class and she was the only girl I steered well clear of when playing 'kiss chase' at playtime, just in case our lips ever got stuck together.

Kiss chase was not the only game we played at play time, in fact the boys didn't really want to play it. We only played when the girls made us! I would usually play 'Den to Den', 'British Bulldog', marbles or hopscotch. I went through a stage when I played hopscotch all the time with Roger and Andrew. At the time Roger was probably my best mate; I was always going to his house, after school, to play and have tea. Roger's Mom and my Mom sort of knew each other. Roger was born three days before me and our moms were in beds next to each other in hospital when we were born. We played hopscotch at every opportunity. There were only four hopscotch grids painted on the school playground so in order to get one of them, as soon as the bell sounded, we rushed outside to play. Designs of courses can vary. Those at Shirley Heath were painted like a sheet of lined paper from an exercise book, but with only seven lines. Just like the paper, the top line, or 'home' square, was much bigger than the rest. This square is where the player turns before completing the reverse trip. I won't explain the rules apart from saying the game starts by the players tossing a marker into the first square. The marker is typically a stone, coin or bean bag. Roger, Andrew and

I didn't use any of the usual items for markers, we used large paper clips, carefully engineered into unique, aerodynamic shapes that 'stopped on a sixpence' when landing on a square. We each had our own lucky, cautiously guarded markers, so as to steal an advantage on each other.

In the previous chapter I mentioned marbles obtained by 'ill gotten' means. At the time I was at Shirley Heath Junior School, probably about eight or nine, and playing marbles was very popular. I did have a few marbles of my own, but not that many. This soon changed when Mom bought me a pair of chocolate brown 'jelly bean' sandals. Strangely enough I have just Googled 'jelly beans' and have discovered this year they are making a come-back. I find that very hard to believe because 'jelly beans' are a hard-wearing, open sandal made of soft PVC. Functional, but not really trendy. Mine had a fantastic tread on the sole. There may have been no cushioning or support for my ankles, but the tread on them was perfect for holding a standard sized marble. When others were playing and concentrating on the match in hand, I would walk past, straight across the playing ring and on top of any wayward marbles. I think the record was five in one go. No one ever saw them disappear, knew where they had gone or suspected me of this foul deed! That is until my cousin Jo went home crying to her mom saying, "Malcolm's nicking other children's marbles, with his sandals." Mom and Dad soon put a stop to my antics, threatening to take me into school and reporting me to the Headmaster.

I would like to say this was the only time I cheated at anything, but there was one other occasion, which was not entirely my fault, it was more my Dad's. Every autumn when leaves fall from the trees it is also the time for conker tournaments. Children may not be allowed to play conkers at school today because of Health and Safety issues, but when I was growing up there were a few weeks in the year when boys played nothing else. Conkers is played by two players, using the seeds of the horse-chestnut tree threaded onto a piece of string, or shoe-lace. Each player takes it in turn to strike the other's conker until one of them breaks; it is usually the hardest conker that wins. New conkers from the current year's crop are always quite soft and are no match for conkers from previous years or ones that have been hardened. Hardening conkers can be done by keeping them for a year or more, baking them briefly, soaking or boiling in vinegar, or painting with clear nail varnish. It is quite easy to recognise a conker that has been hardened and they were often banned from games in the playground, as it was generally regarded as cheating. So to have a conker that looked like a new one, but was indestructible, was a great advantage. There was only one person I knew who could achieve this: my Dad. Dad spent half a day meticulously hollowing out the centre of a huge new conker, which he then filled with 'plastic wood'. This was a proprietary DIY material, purchased from the local hardware shop that set within two hours and became as hard as concrete. By the time Dad had finished, it was perfect. No one could tell the difference between my unbreakable, future champion conker and the real thing. Within a few hours it was already the envy of the neighbourhood, defeating everything in its way and becoming a 100-er plus. It didn't last very long though, because when I went home for lunch Mom said it was wrong and made Dad smash it with a hammer. I don't think Dad was best pleased, seeing his efforts smashed into a hundred pieces with one swift blow!

I may have given you the mistaken impression that all teachers at school were lovely – how wrong could you be! I was lucky enough never to have been in Mrs Sharp's class, a believer in the phrase "spare the rod and spoil the child". This is the notion that children will only flourish if chastised, physically or otherwise, for any wrongdoing. I may have been lucky but Gra wasn't, although he was such an angel and 'goodie two shoes' he never felt the full force of her wrath. One lad who did though was Johnny (not his real name, in an effort to protect his identity). On this particular day Johnny, who I have to admit was quite a naughty boy, did something wrong, was smacked by Mrs Sharp and locked in a stationery cupboard for the rest of the afternoon. Later that day Johnny got into even more trouble, but this time with his mother for not going straight home after school. After several hours there was still no sign of him, so his mom went down to the school to see if they knew where Johnny might be. Eventually someone realised and asked the caretaker to open up the school, only to find Johnny still locked in the cupboard. Nothing ever came of it; Mrs Sharp continued to teach and bully children in her class and poor Johnny was never quite the same again.

Teachers were not the only ones I learnt from at Cranmore School; some of my classmates were very bright as well. One in particular was Peta Jackson, a girl who lived a stone's throw from the school. One day in December 1960, we were all in class seated at our designated tables. Mine was towards the back of the classroom and Peta was sitting opposite me. I didn't believe her at first – how would she know that Father Christmas was really my Dad? My first thoughts were this couldn't be right because every Christmas morning had been the same, for as long as I could remember. Dad would get up first, light a fire and make everyone a cup of tea. All of the children would put on their dressing gowns and creep slowly downstairs to the kitchen. When the fire was blazing and teas had been drunk, we had to line up outside the living room, in increasing order of age. Gra first, Sue last and me in the middle. Dad would enter the room first, only to pop his head back around the door to say, "He's been." We would then rush excitedly in to the room to discover Santa had left us each a sack of presents under the tree. Mom and Dad told us they had to help Father Christmas pay for some of the presents so we never had quite as much as everyone else in the street. There was always one 'large' present and half a dozen smaller stocking fillers, including a Cadbury's selection box. The sacks were sitting under the Christmas tree, which Mom had dressed with dozens of ornaments and decorations about a week before. Mom always went to town on the tree; there were so many bits and pieces on it, it was always difficult to see any green at all. A few years previously Dad had bought a special set of fairy lights, which would be adorning the centre of a large display cabinet we owned. The cabinet was something else Dad just happened to come home with one day. I don't think Mom ever liked it and would regularly moan about it gathering dust. The lights were really special, a regular talking point and like no other lights I have ever seen before or since. Each one was about six inches tall and shaped like a candle and holder, with the candle part being a tube made of clear glass. Each light contained coloured oil, which when warm started to 'boil', making bubbles circulate inside the candle. By the time we had entered the room the lights were usually warm and the oil had started to react, some of them anyway. Those that were not 'bubbling' were easily started by carefully flicking the base of the light; this was always a treat for us at Christmas.

We had to take it in turns to open our presents, always the youngest first. This tradition carried on throughout the day, when Les and Barb's family and Gran and Grampy came to dinner. After a traditional lunch we would share presents and once again take it in turns to open them. In 1960 Cousin Jackie was the youngest, so she opened hers first, followed by Gra and finally ending up with Grampy, several hours later. By the time it came around to him opening his presents, Grampy was usually having 'forty winks'! We all knew what was wrapped up for him anyway: a packet of Park Drive cigarettes, some panatelas, a pair of socks and a box of his favourite new berry fruits or Liquorice Allsorts. We all enthused over what was bought for us, everyone saying, "Ooh, just what I always wanted." In Grampy's case it probably was.

Knowing Santa was my Dad meant from that year onwards Christmases were not the same. They never quite had the magic of my first seven. Never again did I ever get butterflies in my stomach, which made me sick, anticipating whether or not Father Christmas would arrive and leave me presents. Thanks Peta.

# Chapter 4

## FATHER CHRISTMAS AND ME

At first I found it very hard to believe Father Christmas was actually my Dad, because they were so different. After all, Father Christmas was a large, old man, who didn't seem very energetic, plodding around with a sack on his back. In fact I cannot think of two people who were more different. My Dad was as thin as a rake and always full of energy. Besides, I had only ever seen Santa with a beard and I don't ever remember Dad having one of those.

Dad had obviously changed from when he joined the army, not an awful lot though. I think it was more that he had grown up; now a family man and not a young lad just going off to war. I always remember him as being five feet ten and a half inches; the last half inch seemed to be important to him! He was still slim, probably weighing in at about ten stone. I would not describe him as thin, but perhaps wiry would be more appropriate. Yes, wiry looking. He resembled a prize welterweight boxer, with little or no fat and plenty of muscle. I suppose what made him look more daunting was a tattoo on his left forearm. The tattoo was of a dagger with a snake coiled around it. The colours were relatively dull, not like other tattoos I have seen. I am not sure whether the tattoo had always been like it, or if it was the heavy smoking that had faded it. It was certainly the smoking which gave him his dry skin and sallow complexion. Dad started smoking at the age of eight, and by the age of 30 he was smoking 40 cigarettes a day. They weren't just any old cigarettes either, they were Woodbines which were noted for being strong unfiltered cigarettes, popular in the early 20th century especially with soldiers during the two World Wars.

The smoking affected all of his skin, but particularly the fingers on his left hand, which were permanently stained a yellowy brown by the nicotine. I think Dad was conscious of the staining, because I can remember him trying to clean his fingers with lemon juice and a scrubbing brush on numerous occasions. Obviously we all lived with passive smoking until Dad gave up around 1982, but I can honestly say I never really noticed the smoke. I can only assume we must have been accustomed to it. With Dad constantly having a cigarette in his mouth, it soon became a source of fascination to me. I would stand and stare as he exhaled with his mouth pointing upwards, making smoke rings above his head – one of his party tricks. On one of these occasions I was standing next to his chair in the living room, watching closely as he lit yet another cigarette. I was five at the time and clearly remember that I was only just able to see above the arm of the chair. Dad could see the interest I was showing so he turned to me and said, "Would you like one?" I didn't need asking twice so gave a very hesitant but positive reply. "If I let you have one you will have to smoke it all," he said, "I am not going to waste it." I was nervous but still determined to find out what smoking was like, so promised I would. Dad lit a cigarette and handed it to me tentatively, making sure I didn't burn myself. I took one very small 'puff' on it and immediately started to cough as the smoke seemed to fill my head and burn the back of my throat. I pushed the cigarette back in Dad's direction, indicating I had had enough and wanted no more of it. "You promised me you would finish it," he said, "you need to smoke it all." I did have a further two cautious 'puffs' but things didn't get any better. By the end I was coughing profusely and I am sure my face had turned an awful shade of green. It was an unpleasant and memorable event in my life, but clearly a very valuable lesson. In today's environment Dad may have been prosecuted for giving a minor a cigarette, but I am convinced it had the desired effect on me, because since then I have never been tempted to take up smoking. There have been times when I have had a 'drag' on a mate's Park Drive or menthol cigarette to be seen as one of the lads, but that's as far as I have ever gone.

Dad was always clean shaven – invariably a shave was his first task of the day. If you got up early enough you could catch Dad standing at the kitchen sink with a towel around his neck and his face lathered up. He would look in a mirror, balanced precariously on the window sill and carefully shave his neck with his chin pointing outwards and upwards to stretch his skin. Sometimes I would be downstairs too late, but I always knew when Dad had already shaved. He would have little pieces of tissue paper stuck to his face to stop the bleeding from little nicks he had inflicted on himself. I don't think it was that often, it just made an impression on me when I saw it. It is something I do now anyway. After his shave Dad would dab his face dry, put Old Spice aftershave in the palms of his hands and apply it to his cheeks and neck. There wasn't the choice of aftershaves then as there are now. The only other brands I remember around at the time were Albany and Yardley. Dad thought Old Spice was the best having a rich woody oriental smell that was suitable for everyday use. I seem to remember it came in a red bottle with a silver screw top.

Once he had finished shaving he would concentrate on his hair. He had a good head of hair right up to the day he died. It was short, very thick, wavy and bushy, almost black when I was young but turning greyer as he got older. Mom said when she first met Dad it was burnished chestnut just like mine. He always had the same style: a side parting on his left hand side and brushed right and towards the back. Sadly very similar to what I have now, although Dad never had my bald spot. Again he would stand in front of the mirror and style his hair with a comb and brush. Like mine his hair tended to have a mind of its own, so it was held in place with plenty of Brylcreem. Obviously Mom didn't mind washing his pillow cases, or perhaps she was too respectful to say!

One day we noticed Dad had a certain sparkle about him. He always had a sparkle in his blue-grey eyes, but this was different and no one could put their finger on it. It lasted about a week, until one morning when I noticed the silver paint on his Old Spice bottle top was coming off. It was flaking into tiny little pieces, which stuck to his hands and then to his face as it mixed with the aftershave. I am sure it was the forerunner of the 'Glitterbug' cosmetics company, which specialises in sparkly glitter products for the face and body. Glitterbug produces make-up designed for "anyone in search of that extra sparkle", a great option for cheerleaders, dancers, and anyone else looking to add a little bling to their performance. Sorry but I think my Dad had been there, done that and worn the T-shirt fifty years ago.

I tell a lie really, because I didn't ever see Dad in a T-shirt. My memory suggests he always dressed the same unless he was going to work, in which case he usually wore his works' overalls. Dad generally dressed in grey or blue nylon trousers, an open necked nylon shirt and 'V-necked' jumper purchased from Marks and Spencers or through one of Mom's mail order catalogues. He would wear black or brown shoes, whichever were appropriate and they would always be beautifully polished, with a shine you could almost see your face in. Polishing his shoes was another of Dad's daily tasks before he went to work. He would spend far more time than I ever do dubbing and buffing them up; an outcome of his military service, I am sure.

I said Dad reminded me of a prize fighter. It wasn't just his looks, but it was his strength as well. Despite smoking 40 a day, Dad was very fit and had many a party trick to show-off his strength and great sense of balance. I for one would look on in awe and amazement as he did headstands or numerous press-ups on his knuckles or fingers. My favourite antic, which he often rehearsed, was when he balanced on two hands with his body out straight, parallel to the floor. When poised in this position he would then take one hand away and stay positioned like it for what seemed like forever. I have tried it many times, but have never succeeded once.

Dad also had extraordinarily quick reactions. I consider mine to be fast, but Dad's were lightning fast. Again he always had party tricks 'up his sleeve' to exhibit his speed and accuracy.

During the summer months we didn't need fly spray or fly paper to get rid of unwanted flies. Dad used his bare hands, a bit like something out of 'The Karate Kid'. He was highly effective with a success rate of about nine times out of ten. With his strength, speed and competitiveness Dad was a formidable opponent for anybody. He hated losing at anything, even when playing games with his children, no matter what age we were. I don't ever remember Dad letting me come first at anything, so on the few occasions I did win, I knew it was on my own merit and not a hollow victory. It's probably where I get my competitive nature from; I always like to win or have the last word, just like Dad. I have the feeling my quick reactions and good sense of balance are a result of nature, but the desire to win has resulted from nurture.

Dad also loved a challenge, especially when it came to the local fair at Tudor Grange Park. There was a fair every year at the time of Solihull Carnival. When we arrived Dad was not interested in the rides like everyone else, he typically made straight for the coconut shy or the air rifle side stalls. When Dad was throwing at the coconut shy you had to give him plenty of room. The crowds walking past would separate like 'the parting of the Red Sea' as he grabbed the wooden balls in his left hand, wound his arm up like a coiled spring and let fly. Dad nearly always hit a coconut, at least once in three balls. Frequently, he threw the balls so hard that if they hit anything they would ricochet back in to the crowd, causing the onlookers to dive for cover. He didn't win a coconut very often, because they rarely came off their post holder, no matter how hard he hit them.

Once he actually split the coconut in two and it still didn't fall to the ground. Dad reckoned they glued them on as soon as they saw him coming. The only time I recall him winning a coconut, we got it home only to find it was rotten inside.

On the air rifles stall he was just as competitive, but rarely scored enough to win at the first attempt. Again it wasn't Dad, it was just that the stall holders had 'fixed' the sights to reduce the number of winners. That didn't stop him for long, because by the second go Dad had worked out where to aim to allow for the bias in the sights setting. Soon he was well on his way to having enough tokens for a couple of goldfish or a large teddy bear.

Dad was a very proud man and one who didn't like to display any signs of weakness. Probably the best example of this is when I was about sixteen, making Dad approximately forty six. He was working at the Reeds Corrugated Cardboard factory at the time and the company started up a karate club, which Dad and I joined. Every Wednesday evening we met in the staff canteen and received instruction from a local black belt, who bought a handful of his protégés along with him. They were younger men with several years of experience and a few coloured belts to their names. We soon picked up all of the basic moves and blocks and after a month were excited to have a demonstration at our weekly class. This was held by our instructor and involved his protégés showing off their advanced knowledge, ending with a demonstration of breaking tiles and wooden planks. The latter was pretty impressive, with them smashing an inch thick piece of wood with their bare hands. The evening ended with the instructor asking if any of the new recruits wanted to have a go.

Clearly with such little experience, nobody in their right mind would be daft enough to try. Except of course my Dad! He didn't even have a karate suit, we were wearing joggers and a shirt. He lined up in front of the piece of wood with the protégés standing behind him, smiling and expecting him to fail miserably. Similar to the coconut shy, he positioned his left hand directly in front of the plank, wound his arm up like a coiled spring and let fly, splitting the wood cleanly in two. On the way home he told me he knew they were smirking behind his back and expecting him not to be successful. This made him all the more determined to prove them wrong – there was no way he was ever going to fail. I found this out very early on in life.

I can honestly say Dad didn't go looking for trouble, but equally he would not consider walking away from it either. When he was living at Home Farm, shortly after he and Mom were married, he was walking along the Stratford Road about half a mile from home when he got jumped on by three men. I am not sure why, but according to Dad's recollections I think they wished they hadn't, because Dad fought back and gave better than he got. I believe one or two of them came off worse than Dad did. His philosophy was, go for the biggest bloke in the gang and hit him hard, where it hurts. He always said if you go for the largest and hurt him, then the others will think twice before they join in. This is the attitude I constantly carry with me. Luckily I haven't been put in that situation because I am not sure I could carry it off. I am certain I would be more 'flight' than 'fight'. Incidentally the only fight I have ever been involved in was at the age of about ten when I had a disagreement with Graham, a lad in my class at Shirley Heath Junior School. I cannot remember what the argument was about, but I know we agreed to meet after school, on a piece of grass outside the shops at Tanworth Lane about 200 yards from the school gates. Quite a crowd of class mates gathered at the agreed spot with anticipation of a great spectacle. Suffice to say, I think they were slightly disappointed. In spite of a lot of huffing and puffing, very few blows were landed before it was stopped by some elderly man passing by.  Despite this I went home in tears on the back of my mate Pete's bike. Not because I was hurt or because of the scratches on my back, but because the pocket on my shirt had been ripped off. I knew Mom would be upset because she would have to repair it before I went to school the following day. Dad wasn't worried about the shirt, just that I was alright and I had given a good account of myself, particularly as Graham was the son of someone he worked with.

That confrontation near Home Farm is the only one Dad ever mentioned and I certainly don't ever remember him getting involved in any trouble. He put all of his strength into being protective of others, particularly his family. Our family came first and no one put one over on us, Dad made sure of that! A good example of this was one winter's evening close to Bonfire night, around about 6 o'clock. It was too dark to be playing football, but a group of mine and Gra's 'mates' were out and about keeping themselves entertained. There were seven or eight 13 to 16 year olds walking past our house, one of whom decided it would be a hoot if he threw two lumps of mud at our living room window. Our house was perfect for this prank. It had a large bay window and was on the corner, near a small green and very close to the gulley; an ideal route for a quick getaway. It just so happened Dad was watching TV in the living room at the time and quick as a flash he gave chase, still in his slippers and complete with fag in mouth. The group of lads took to their heels, up the gulley and along Cranmore Road with Dad close behind, catching them up with every stride he took. After 600 yards and with Dad about to overhaul them, they dived for cover in Clinton Road, down one of the drives leading to garages at the back of the houses. Later Dad admitted it was so dark he couldn't see a thing and because he didn't intend to physically apprehend them, knew he might never know who it was. That is, until a frightened little voice from out of the darkness said, "It wasn't me Mr Day". Dad recognised the voice straight away as being Doppo's – a red headed lad who lived down our road about six doors away. After giving them a 'ticking off', Dad returned home, satisfied he had caught the culprits, but with two large holes in the bottom of his slippers.

Dad didn't like anyone having a go, or mouthing off at him. He always stood his ground and verbally gave as 'good as he got'. One Saturday afternoon he caught a Midland Red bus home from Shirley. Just like buses today, he had to wait for ages to catch one and then two came along together, both going his way! The first was a number 150 that passed where Dad was going, but went on much further to Stratford-upon-Avon and the second was a number 181, which terminated one stop further on from Dad's destination. Forever thinking about others he waved the 150 past and hailed the 181. His thinking was the buses were fairly full and he didn't want to take a seat of someone who further along the route might want to go to Stratford. He paid his fare to the conductor and took a seat to travel home. In the sixties, buses required two people to operate them: a conductor and a driver. Five minutes later Dad alighted from the bus at St George's Road to take the short walk home. The bus was just pulling away when the driver wound down his window and shouted at Dad with a sarcastic voice, "What's the matter mate, was the other bus not good enough for you?" By now you can guess that was like 'a red rag to a bull'. Dad did no more than chase after the bus into Cranmore Boulevard where the bus was turning around in readiness for its return journey. The buses usually waited at least five minutes before they set off back towards Birmingham, but this one didn't. When the driver saw Dad coming, red faced and angry, he took off like a rally driver, with the wheels spinning and the conductor holding on for grim death. Thankfully we have better customer service from our buses today.

He may have been very protective, but he also demanded discipline within the home. There were certainly plenty of rules. I wasn't scared of my Dad, but I was definitely frightened to cross him. You never swore or smirked at him, answered him back or disobeyed him. With me being far from perfect, he was always threatening to hit me, but I only ever remember him doing it once and that wasn't very hard. I usually got punished in other ways, such as 'grounded', lost my pocket money, or got sent to bed without any tea. Dad also had very strong values and principles, which he passed on to his children, instilling in us the need for good manners. Please and thank you were a must, as was respect for your elders and politeness to strangers. One bizarre habit Dad passed on to me was the way in which he addressed people in the street when asking for directions or requesting information. He would always say, "Excuse me Squire, do you know where...?" Even then squire was not a word you heard every day, so today when I use the same expression, the recipient must wonder what planet I am from! Opening or holding the door for others and giving up your seat on the bus were other important lessons Dad taught us, but the one that will remain with me forever is, "A man never hits a woman, no matter what." I may have been able to get away with the odd lapse in any other of Dad's ideals, but not this one; he was always most insistent you never hit a woman. Therefore I wasn't allowed to hit my sister Susan, even when she was horrible to me or hit me first. She could do what she liked and I could not retaliate.

Dad was fairly strict and demanded respect, but he also had a good sense of humour. It wasn't always great, but he regularly made us laugh. His sense of humour was often dry, constantly making witty comments about life's goings on and what people said. Some people might say they were corny, because they were usually obvious and not very original. This wasn't Dad's only humorous side though, he would regularly come home with a whole load of new jokes. Certain ones were appropriate for someone of my age and some were not. That is why his jokes repeatedly got me into trouble at school. The lads in my class loved them. They didn't always understand them and occasionally needed me to explain the punch line, but they could never get enough of them.  At times this made me very popular; I was the class joker. However on the occasions I made them public in class, during lessons, I can definitely say the teachers were not as appreciative and I was not very popular.

Dad may have left home at 14 and not benefitted from a fantastic education, but he had many talents, including mental arithmetic and poetry. He could also put his hand to repairing anything or carry out any DIY job. Poetry wasn't going to be a vocation for Dad, only a pastime, but it did bring its own rewards. Growing up Mom always bought Brooke Bond PG tips tea in quarter pound bags, which came complete with picture cards to collect. Sets included African wildlife, Asian wildlife, British birds and British butterflies and usually comprised 50 cards, which could be stuck into books or on wall charts. We got through plenty of tea as a family, but it still took months to collect a full set. We usually ended up needing just one or two cards, which seemed to be as rare as 'hen's teeth'. This really frustrated Dad, so he would eventually put pen to paper and compose a poem to send off to Brooke Bond. It was typically about how we had been waiting for weeks to find a Jumping Hare or Bushy Tailed Galago, while collecting a dozen cards of the Black Rhinoceros. A week or two later we would receive a complete set of African wildlife along with a previous set such as British wildlife. The ultimate was when Brooke Bond changed the recipe to improve their PG Tips tea. Mom and Dad did not see it as an enhancement and were not best pleased, so once again Dad put pen to paper. It went like this:

*For donkey's years, Ma and me,*
*have drunk our daily brew,*
*We also raised a family*
*and made them like it too.*
*GP Tips our family crest,*
*the cards within to save,*
*All the animal and wild birds,*
*to our kids we gave.*
*Year after year, Ma and me,*
*on holiday we would go.*
*Taking kids and GP Tips,*
*to places we didn't know.*
*Wherever we went, Ma and me,*
*be it home or abroad.*
*We always had our GP Tips,*
*in one of our cases stored.*
*The kids have now all grown up,*
*and flown the family nest.*
*Now Ma and me have changed our brand,*
*of tea we all loved best.*
*The reason why, we told ourselves,*
*was not the price you see.*
*But the so called improved flavour,*
*was not for Ma and me.*

This is just as Dad wrote it: "GP Tips". What was that about? I do not remember Dad being dyslexic – perhaps the new brew was alcoholic.

If it had been, it would have affected Dad badly, because he was not a big drinker. That's not to say he didn't have a drink, but I don't ever remember him going off to the pub with his mates. There are just two occasions when I know Dad got drunk, mainly because he just wasn't used to it. The first was an occasion my Gran told me about. It was a wedding they were invited to and Dad had drunk so much he ended up sliding down the side of a piano, while he was singing some raunchy songs. The only other time was in Pesaro, Italy on holiday with me, Mom, Heather and Lol. We were only out there together by coincidence. Heather and I booked our holiday separately from Mom, Dad and Lol and it just so happened they booked exactly the same hotel as us, with their first week overlapping with our last one. We all decided to go out on this evening trip which included a meal, as much cheap wine as you could drink and a dance. Everybody had a fair bit to drink that night and we were all singing songs on the coach going back to the resort, sometime after midnight. Everyone that is except Dad, who was fast asleep on the back seat. When we arrived at the hotel, we had to wake him up to get him up to his room. Well that was a mistake, because as soon as we were inside reception Dad decided it was time for a sing song. The rest of us were creeping in, trying not to wake anyone else as instructed, while Dad was in full choral mood. Mom, Dad and Lol were all on the floor above us, so Heather and I left them in the lift. We could still hear him singing at the top of his voice and Mom saying, "Shhhh…" as we unlocked our door and made our way to bed.

Alcohol was definitely not Dad's thing, predominantly because of his stomach ulcer. He was more of a tea man, drinking mugs and mugs of it each day with plenty of sugar. He was very much a creature of habit, having his first tea of the day while he was shaving and at least one more before he left for work. We would often start our meals without Dad too, while he finished off his drink of tea. Tea after a meal was a definite 'no no', because it would give him severe indigestion, another side effect of his ulcer. More often than not Dad had a mug of tea in his hand. A vivid recollection I have is Dad sitting in his chair in the kitchen, with a mug of tea in one hand and a handful of rich tea biscuits in the other, perfect for dunking.

I am not sure whether Dad had always been good at mental arithmetic or whether it was having had plenty of practice on the darts board and spending hours reviewing form and working out odds on the races. He did love his horse racing, but he spent a lot of his time studying the form of dogs at Hall Green, Perry Barr and White City. I can see him now, sitting for hours in his chair in the kitchen, going through the back pages of the Birmingham Mail or Sporting Argus, picking his 'winners'. It may seem strange, but Dad had his own chairs, one in the kitchen and one in the living room, and you never sat in them even when he was not there. I think Dad got more fun out of selecting his 'winners' than he did placing bets on them. Bets were not large, because he couldn't afford a great deal. He was canny though, often putting on accumulator bets for small stakes, but potentially large winnings. An accumulator is a single bet which is linked to a number of other bets, the outcome being dependent on all of the bets winning. Odds for an accumulator are higher than those in a single bet, so present punters with a way of striking it rich with a relatively low stake.

Dad's favourite accumulator was when he picked two trap numbers to come first and second, in any order, in all races throughout the card at a given dog race meeting. His bet would be about one pound, but I remember him winning two to three hundred pounds on four or five occasions. It wasn't necessary for all races to come up trumps; it just needed his numbers to come first and second in three or four of the eight races. However, the more races that he predicted correctly, the more he won. When he had a big win it didn't last long; it was almost as though it was burning a hole in his pocket. However, Dad rarely spent it on himself. Most times I remember him treating Mom with a surprise present. Dad often went down to the Hall Green race track in York Road, mostly on a Friday night. We were usually in bed by the time he got home; hardly able to sleep with the anticipation of whether Dad would have a win and treat us. Most weeks we awoke on Saturday morning to find a small box of Payne's Poppets (chewy fruit sweets) waiting for us.

Dad really was a 'Bob the Builder' (can he fix it?). To my knowledge he didn't have any training, but he could fix anything be it a vacuum, washing machine, television, radio, toy or broken ornament. If the radio stopped working Dad would take it all apart, put it back together again and somehow it would be working. It wasn't always repaired quickly, but rarely did anything ever get the better of him. It wasn't just for us either, I can remember him mending a vacuum for Mrs Mcguire who lived next door and a fishing rod for Uncle Les. It was Les' favourite, an old, expensive Greenheart fishing rod. Greenheart (*Chlorocardium rodiei*) is an evergreen tree, native to northern South America, mainly in former British Guiana. The wood is extremely hard and strong, so hard that it cannot be worked with standard tools. Being extremely durable, even in marine conditions, Greenheart was used extensively in the building of docks and was an early choice for fishing rods. I am not sure how it got broken, but according to the local angling shops the top section became splintered beyond repair. I think my Uncle had a sentimental attachment to the rod, so understandably was distressed and desperate to get it fixed. My Dad offered to return it to its original condition, so Les agreed to let him try. Who else was more qualified? My Dad spent a week repairing and testing the rod and was delighted with the end product. That weekend Les took it fishing with him, but came back disappointed saying it broke whilst catching the smallest of fish. Dad didn't believe him and was adamant that my Aunty Barb must have been sitting on the end of it at the time!

He was far better at decorating than mending rods, and like everything else nothing ever stopped him from completing the job. Dad always decorated the house, did an excellent job and could even do it with just one hand. That may sound unbelievable but I remember him papering the hall stairs and landing with one arm in a sling! I still don't know how, but he hung the pieces of paper above and down the side of the stairs, with just one hand, up a ladder while supporting himself by resting his head against the wall. You might expect the final job to have been substandard, but it was just as professional as usual.

Without doubt Dad was a very strong person, but he also had his softer side. He was, in a way, what I often refer to as 'metrosexual'. I have always understood the definition to be a man who is not frightened to show his feminine qualities, but this may not be strictly correct. An alternative definition suggests the term originated as play on the term homosexual, in order to contrast heterosexuals who adopt fashions and lifestyles stereotypically associated with homosexuals. Probably the best known metrosexual is David Beckham, who uses skin care products, scented candles, costly colourful dress shirts, pricey designer jeans and even got derided when he wore a sarong. Dad did not go that far, or at least not to my knowledge, but apparently he was not afraid to show off his embroidery skills. Mom was always telling us how he produced some wonderful runners for their sideboard and that he was more precise at it than she ever was. One of Dad's other secrets was he was an avid collector, collecting many different things, many of which were often obscure and strange. When he was younger he was interested in Tyrosemiophilia, which is the hobby of collecting cheese labels. I believe it was a fad in the 1950s, which didn't last long, although long enough for Dad to collect hundreds of colourful, circular and triangular labels from all over the world.

Dad loved nothing better than spending his Saturdays by catching a bus into Birmingham and then walking home via every antique and old curiosity shop on the Stratford Road. He would always come home with some bargain he had found. They were mostly useful, but occasionally they weren't. Like the time he came home with a canvas bag full of old keys – hundreds of them, all different shapes and sizes. It is a good job he wasn't stopped by the police on the way home, because I am sure he would have been arrested on suspicion of being a burglar. I haven't managed to find a name for someone who collects keys, in fact I am sure there isn't a word for it. Dad is probably the only person ever to own so many keys. I am not quite sure why he bought them, it was probably a good idea at the time. They did prove to be really useful on a few occasions when we lost or broke a key. Dad would say "I have got one to fit that" and would then spend hours trying every key in the bag until he found one that was suitable. Invariably he always found one, which must have been very satisfying, but I cannot imagine anyone doing it today.

I hope I have portrayed Dad as a really strong person, both physically and mentally, because that's the way he was, but he was definitely not without his illnesses. The one complaint he suffered with throughout much of his life was a duodenal ulcer. This is a peptic ulcer in the duodenum, the first part of the small intestine. Symptoms are a burning or gnawing feeling in the stomach area lasting between 30 minutes and three hours, with the pain often misinterpreted as hunger, indigestion or heartburn. This type of ulcer is relieved by food, which is why Dad always ate regular but small meals. Duodenal ulcers tend to heal and recur, meaning the pain may last for a few days or weeks and then wane or disappear for a time. Studies have found correlations between diet, smoking and ulcer formation, which is why I am certain it was his poor diet during the war and smoking from an early age that contributed greatly to his illness. When I was about nine, Dad's ulcer perforated. A perforation is a hole in the gastro-intestinal wall, which can lead to catastrophic consequences, due to bleeding from the gastro duodenal artery. Mom didn't tell us at the time, but when Dad was admitted to hospital as an emergency case, two other patients with the same complaint died on his ward.

Dad had an emergency operation to try and stop the internal bleeding and spent the next three to four weeks in hospital. Mom visited every day and took one of us with her each time. A few days after the operation we knew Dad was starting to feel much better when he asked Mom to bring a mirror in for him; he was starting to take an interest in his appearance again. On the evening I went with Mom to visit Dad I noticed the mirror was on his over bed table, at the bottom of his bed alongside a glass, a jug of water and a handful of get-well cards. While reading who Dad's cards were from, much to Dad's annoyance Mom accidentally moved the mirror. Mom said it didn't matter because he wasn't going to have a shave that night. "The mirror is not for shaving," Dad said, "it is for when the matron does her rounds; I can see when she is coming." I was a little confused as to why Dad would want to know when she was coming, until he added, "If she sees me smoking I will be in big trouble." Unless she had no sense of smell at all, I cannot believe the matron did not know what was going on. That was my Dad though – he was addicted to smoking and would do anything to get his next fix of nicotine.

When Dad eventually came home, after spending a further few weeks in a convalescence home at Eastcote, money was very, very tight. There was definitely no money for his usual quota of cigarettes, so Mom bought a reduced allowance for Dad and rationed them out. Keeping the cigarettes 'out of his reach' was an ongoing battle for her; a battle she never won. When Mom left the house to go shopping she would hide the remainder of Dad's allowance somewhere in the house, perhaps just two single cigarettes. It would be a different hiding place every time and always in the most obscure places, but Dad always discovered them. No matter where they were it was just as though he could smell them, sniffing them out like a bloodhound. His recurring illness was a perfect opportunity for Dad to give up the habit, but he was adamant he enjoyed smoking and didn't want to stop. Sadly it eventually became his downfall, robbing the whole family of many more years of his company, wit and wisdom.

Before I started thinking about what I might write in this book, I thought that Dad and I did very little male bonding when I was growing up. However the more I think about it, the more I realise we spent lots of quality time together. I suppose I was correct in that we rarely went on organised trips or to places where we had to pay; those types of occasion I can count on one hand. There was a night at Hall Green dogs, a bingo session and a trip to the cinema to see "Battle of the Bulge". The latter was a birthday treat for me in 1965. Dad more than made up for this by spending many hours of quality time with me, doing things that cost nothing or very little. There were numerous times when we went for long walks in Monkspath, usually looking for golf balls, flowers, or cigarette packets. We searched for golf balls in the long grass verge and hedgerow running adjacent to Shirley Golf course. We used sticks to forage amongst leaves and under hawthorn bushes, coming away with two dozen or more used golf balls every couple of weeks. It makes you realise how good golf professionals are, or perhaps how bad the average club player is. If we weren't on the lookout for golf balls, we were having competitions to see who could spot the largest number of different wild flowers or brands of discarded cigarette packets. Things don't change, even then people threw away their rubbish at the side of the road. Mom and Dad always taught us to put it in our pockets and then in the bin when we got home. My favourite times were when we spotted wildflowers, or went blackberry picking in the hedgerows during late summer or early autumn. We got stung and scratched all over, but it was worth it. There is nothing quite as satisfying as arriving home with a bowl full of large, plump and tasty blackberries ready for a blackberry and apple pie. I honestly don't think there is anything better than a dish of warm blackberry and apple pie covered with piping hot custard. This is why in later years we always picked extra berries to ensure there were enough to freeze for times when they were not in season.

I suppose the oddest reason for going for a walk with Dad is one not many people can claim to have done. When I was still at junior school we went for a walk down Dog Kennel Lane, complete with a pram. The pram had a blanket strategically placed over it to prevent prying eyes from knowing our business. It was needed to carry coal we found in the 'Donkey Drive'. We collected coal that had been left by local gypsies after they had moved on to their next site. Some of it had been partly burned, but it could still provide much needed heat for our fire. Without it we would probably have gone cold. Coal was expensive, we had very little money and there were no extra benefits or fuel allowance to be had.

Dad's competitive streak meant he loved playing games, not always the usual ones, but often games he made up himself. The golf balls we found in Monkspath became very useful. Two flowerpots buried either end of the lawn in our back garden and we had a golf course to compare with Shirley Golf Club. We spent hours putting the balls into the holes from a distance of 20 feet or more. There were competitions to see who took the least number of shots to sink 16 balls. Most of them were holes in one with all of them taking no more than two putts. Dad was a natural left hander, which made it particularly awkward for me because I wanted to copy him. Although I am naturally right handed, when holding a cricket bat or golf club I am now classed as a left hander. I grew up copying Dad, putting my club in my left hand, which means this is one example of where nurture has triumphed over nature.

We couldn't always play outdoors, so Dad invented games for us to play indoors. The most memorable one was what we referred to as shove halfpenny football. Always looking to make the most of what we had, Dad utilised my 'jigsaw' board, turning it in to our very own White Hart Lane, the home of Spurs. This was Dad's favourite team. Dad drew a perfectly scaled pitch, complete with penalty spots and corner posts, on the three foot by four foot board. Teams comprised four or five old halfpence pieces, which were roughly the size of a current two penny piece and the ball was a farthing (now obsolete). The goal posts were clothes pegs, clipped to the edge of the board and teams were differentiated by one side being heads and the other tails. The game was played by players taking it in turns to flick one of their coins or 'men', either to kick the ball, or position it defensively to protect the goal. I suppose in a way it was dad's own form of Subbuteo. It was a simple game, but one which gave us many hours of fun and entertainment.

When I grew older Dad introduced me to playing darts. Dad would play at work during every break he had. He was better than an average player, but there were some even better players at Reeds Corrugated Paper, where he worked.  He was also probably past his best, because at this time he had already started to wear glasses and they don't make throwing 'arrows' any easier. Ever the competitor Dad would practise at home in the kitchen, where he had installed a dart board above where the coke fire used to be. This meant the oche (the line behind which the throwing player stands), was just in front of the sink and therefore no one could move in the kitchen while games were in progress. This annoyed Mom intensely, particularly when meals had to be prepared. She would usually lock herself away in the front room, watching TV with the sound turned up high. If she didn't have the volume turned up, she could hear the sound of the constant 'thud', 'thud', 'thud', as tungsten hit the board, on the other side of the wall. Dad would frequently try new combinations of barrels, stems and flights to try and gain maximum advantage and would even sometimes blame his sight. We would play 301 with a double to start and finish. Games were always competitive and the standard generally quite high, Dad made sure of that. We rarely got stuck on a double and scoring was usually reasonably high. I suppose I have to concede Dad had the upper hand on most days, but I was never far behind and it wasn't unknown for me to occasionally beat him. He did not like it and would always try and keep playing until he had the advantage. One thing you did not do was say anything to him about how poorly he was playing, or try and barrack him, to put him off his game. I mentioned previously Dad did not let me win at anything. Whether it was golf, shove halfpenny football, cards, dominoes or darts, he always tried his hardest. Just when I thought I was improving he would move up a gear and stay that one step ahead. When barracked or put under pressure most people get nervous, falter and get put off their game but not my Dad, it just seemed to spur him on and make him even more determined to win. He must have been the most competitive Father Christmas ever.

# Chapter 5

## IT ISN'T ONLY CATS THAT HAVE 9 LIVES!

According to myth, cats have multiple lives. In many countries, including Britain, they are believed to have nine lives, hence the title. The myth is attributed to the natural suppleness and speed cats exhibit to escape life-threatening situations. The myth also gains credence by the fact that falling cats usually land on their feet, using an instinctive righting reflex to twist their bodies around. However, if this book was being published in Germany or Spain the title of the chapter would have to be "It isn't only cats that have seven lives" or in Turkey and the Middle East it would be just six. When this book eventually goes global, I will probably have to change the heading, because in my case six or seven lives wouldn't be enough to make it appropriate. My Mom and Dad used to despair at the number of times I got into scrapes and unsafe situations, putting myself in danger but still emerging out from the other side. I didn't always make it unscathed; in fact I usually required first aid or occasionally hospital treatment.

Even as a toddler I was already losing the odd life. I don't remember many of the occasions when they occurred, but Mom and Dad were continually reminding me of how things always seemed to happen to me and never anyone else. Apparently there were two occasions, that they knew of, when I stuck my fingers in an electric socket. I suppose I was lucky really because the sockets in the kitchen were at the height of a normal light switch, which meant I needed to climb on a stool just to reach them. Dad always said it was standing on the stool that saved me. It prevented me from being earthed and ultimately, fried to a cinder. Out and about I was always falling over and cutting my knee or banging my head against a cupboard or paving slab. I once fell over the back of a park bench, hit my head and developed a lump as big as an egg, right above my right eye. Mom always recalled how she thought I was badly hurt, because I was crying hysterically. That is until they bought me an ice-cream. There was the time I tripped in the garden and landed on a bamboo cane, narrowly missing my eye by a few millimetres; I still have the scar to prove it.

A few years later Diane, a neighbour from across the road, crushed the index finger on my right hand in the cogs of a washing mangle. (A mangle or wringer, as it is sometimes referred to, was a mechanical laundry aid. It consisted of two large wooden rollers in a sturdy frame, connected by huge cogs and powered by a crank handle.) Mom kept ours on the coalhouse step, using it for wringing water from wet laundry on wash day. It was definitely quicker than today's spin dryers; removing almost every last drop of water from the clothes. The closer the rollers were adjusted the harder it was to turn the handle, and the dryer the clothes came out the other side. We all loved helping Mom with the mangle on wash day. On this particular occasion Sue, Diane and I were on the coalhouse step admiring the mangle. I don't think Diane had ever seen one like it. Her parents were relatively "well to do" compared to us and had an electric 'wringer', integrated into their top-loader. Anyway, I was standing with my hand near the large iron cogs when Diane decided to turn the handle, trapping my finger between a couple of them!

Growing up I had so many accidents. If I had been an only child I would have probably thought I wasn't being looked after properly. However Gra and Sue didn't suffer injuries like I did, so perhaps it was just me. It wasn't just accidents either. When I was a child I suffered from a number of persistent afflictions, which unfortunately didn't go away without medical treatment. From a very early age I suffered constantly from severe ear infections, which regularly gave me unbearable earache. I can remember many times when I had to cuddle Mom with a hot water bottle on the side of my face to try and ease the pain. The doctor gave me drops, which Mom applied using a glass pipette with a squeezy rubber handle. To prevent the drops from running out again Mom inserted two pieces of cotton wool, one in each ear. The ear infections affected my social life, when it stopped me from joining in with everyone else. I can remember one occasion at my Uncle and Aunt's house, watching the fireworks one bonfire night from a bedroom window. Everyone else was outside taking in the atmosphere of the smells and sounds. I can recall being distraught because it isn't quite the same watching fireworks and eating hotdogs behind glass. The earaches eventually stopped when I had my tonsils and adenoids removed at the age of about six.

I was always having antibiotics from the doctors to get rid of the infections. This was bad news for Mom and Dad, because I wasn't the best child for swallowing tablets. To make matters worse the tablets weren't particularly small either; generally the size of an adult's thumbnail. Dad usually broke them in half, and even then he struggled to get me to swallow one. Dad, bless him, never gave up though. He tried all sorts of tricks to get me to take my medicine. I would have them buried in a spoonful of jam, or there was the one and only time he tried blackcurrant vinegar. We always had a bottle of it in the house. Mrs. McGuire, from next door, regularly made huge quantities of the stuff and swore by its preventative powers. I remember quite vividly standing in the kitchen with my back to the sink and Dad's hand coming towards me with a large dessert spoon of blackcurrant vinegar. I just knew there was a dose of penicillin in there somewhere; Dad was trying to trick me. Immediately I felt the tablet on my tongue so I blew everything back down the spoon, covering Dad's clean white shirt in the process. I could tell he was not best pleased, but on this occasion he kept very calm. He told me it was really important I took the medicine, or else I wouldn't get better. Dad was determined not to be beaten. He decided to give me three pieces of bread, rolled up into round balls. One of them he said "contains a crushed penicillin tablet". He advised me to chew each one in turn, not knowing which piece of bread the tablet was in, and then to quickly swallow a spoonful of jam to take the taste away. It didn't sound very pleasant but I agreed to give it a try. One after the other, I chewed the bread pieces quickly, waiting to taste the bitterness of the tablet inside. Almost immediately after I put the third piece in my mouth, even before I had started chewing, Dad let me have the spoonful of strawberry jam. I gratefully swallowed it without any touching the sides of my throat. It was only after I showed him an empty mouth Dad revealed the penicillin had been in the jam; what a sneaky trick to play!

Just as if permanent earache wasn't bad enough, I also suffered from regular and prolonged nose bleeds. Everyone has had a nose bleed at some time or other, but mine seemed to happen at least once every week and usually lasted for several hours. They would just start for no apparent reason and Mom and Dad could do nothing to stop them. The doctor told them it was a relief valve for my body and that the bleeds would stop when it was ready. Mom and Dad tried everything: leaning my head backwards, pinching the bridge of my nose and even sticking cotton wool up my nostrils. You can imagine what I looked like when I had both a nose bleed and earache; there was cotton wool coming out of everywhere!

The nose bleeds got really bad one night. My nose had been bleeding for about two hours and would just not stop, so Mom and Dad called out the doctor. Doctor Essex arrived sometime after midnight, with his large black bag and a stethoscope around his neck. He said the bleeds were most likely caused by an exposed blood vessel in my nose and I had been suffering long enough. He decided to cauterise my nose that evening, which involved burning the affected area with acid. Mom had to hold my head still while he applied the solution and stuffed my nose with several yards of sterilised ribbon, which acted as a dressing. I am not even sure how he got that much tape up my nose. The doctor turned into some sort of magician, endlessly packing it up my nose. When he eventually stopped, the end of the tape was stuck to the side of my nose with a plaster. The whole thing made it very difficult for me to breath. I was under doctor's orders to refrain from eating solids for a week and told to take all fluids through a straw. It certainly did the trick – my nose stopped bleeding immediately and much to Mom and Dad's relief I soon fell asleep. However, the next morning a little of the tape had become dislodged from my nose, so Dad cut it off and reaffixed the new end to the side of my face again. This occurred several times more before Doctor Essex returned a week later to remove the dressing. When he took the plaster off and removed the tape, all that remained was a piece less than an inch long.

On reflection during the first five or six years of my life I must have been permanently afflicted with one or other condition. Not only did I suffer from earache and nose bleeds at regular intervals, but I also frequently had urinary infections. This caused discomfort in another part of my body, nowhere near my nose or ears! Just like the cure for my earache, this required another visit to hospital for surgery. However, this time it was only day surgery and the hospital must have been doing "have one get one free", because both Gra and I went in on the same day to be circumcised! I don't remember Mom and Dad fully explaining the procedure to me before I went in to hospital, because I am sure I would have made some excuse like "it doesn't hurt anymore". I can still clearly remember the moment I was anaesthetised that morning. There were several doctors dressed in green overalls and wearing white face masks, staring down at me lying on the operating table. One of them said, "We are just going to give you some gas to put you to sleep," and then proceeded to place this large black rubber mask over my face. I didn't resist or complain, but I can still smell the rubber in my nostrils every time I recall the memory. The next thing I remember I was waking up in the recovery ward with Gra just a couple of beds up from me. Mom and Dad soon arrived to see us, and after a drink of orange squash we were on our way home. Both of us were sick as soon as we got home, it must have been the anaesthetic and the journey. I can see it now: Gra was sick all over the settee but I managed to wait until Dad had fetched a bucket; they were so grateful to me. We both had an early night and certainly I had a good night's sleep without any discomfort or pain.

Things didn't exactly go straightforwardly though. When Mom came into our room in the morning to get us dressed, she was in for a shock. On pulling back the blankets she discovered my sheets had turned from white to scarlet! The dressing had become dislodged and I had been losing blood for most of the night. I imagine it was probably my fault because when I was little I also had this other condition, which Mom and Dad were always trying to cure me of. They would often refer to it as "playing pocket billiards"; apparently I usually got chronic bouts of it when I was nervous during school assemblies and Christmas plays. I think Mom exaggerated it a bit. I don't believe the condition was ever as severe as that of a chap I once worked with. Everyone knew him affectionately as "Jim from Feltham". Anyway, it wasn't long before I was in an ambulance and on my way to the theatre again for an emergency procedure. This time the anaesthetic mask I was given was much different to the one I was given the day before. It reminded me of a silver coloured tea strainer, with a fine mesh covered with a purple cloth; this time the smell was of chloroform not rubber.

Children heal quickly at that age and it wasn't long before I was back at school, with instructions from my Mom ringing in my ears. "If Miss Murphy asks why you have been off school, tell her Mommy has handed in a letter to the Secretary." Of course Miss Murphy did ask me why I had not been in school for a few days. I remember we were all sitting quietly for registration, with legs crossed, in three rows right at the front of the classroom. I was in the middle row and I soon got the distinct impression 'Miss' wished she had never asked. Forgetting everything Mom had told me to say I said, "I have had an operation Miss."

"What sort of operation?" she enquired.

"One down below Miss," I replied. I can see the faces of all my class mates around me now. They all had expressions of "What's he talking about?" I could just tell they didn't believe me, or hadn't got a clue what I was talking about. I turned to them all and said "It's true, I have had an operation down below." I still cringe today when I think about what I said; perhaps I should have done as my Mom asked.

There were plenty of other occasions when I had a 'near miss'; like a split lip on the living room window sill. I was five and I was looking through the front room window. My Dad had just left the house and I was watching him disappear across the green and up the gulley. If I stretched on tip toes I could just see above the sill and out of the window. The sill was made out of typical 1950's tiles, about an inch thick; tiles that you don't get today.

They were red, shiny and as hard as concrete, with edges that were at perfect right angles, making them as sharp as most knives. Trying too hard to see my Dad until he was completely out of sight, I slipped and caught my bottom lip on the edge of the sill; resulting in a cut which went straight through into my mouth.

That wasn't the last time I damaged my lip. Graham, the lad I had the fight with, was once quite a good friend. He lived the other end of our road and we played together regularly, at weekends and after school. We formed a club, with just two members, but with our own 'homemade' member's badge. We would cook baked potatoes and play games, including darts. I suppose it was my own fault, because on this occasion I was too close to the board. The target was resting on the floor and I was standing about three feet to the right of it. I also think Graham was a terrible shot, because his last dart hit me on the side of my face, and ended up going straight through my cheek.

There were other occasions I can recall when it was my head that took a bashing, like the time I was playing cricket during a lunch break at Cranmore School. Being an infant school it wasn't a full blown cricket match, just individuals batting against school pals taking it in turn to bowl an over. There was only one wicket as well. That is three stumps for the batsman and a single one at the bowler's end. It was my turn to bat and for once I was doing really well. Everyone who bowled got thumped out of sight, which was quite unusual for me. I continued to hit out even when Christopher took his turn to bowl. Chris was without doubt the sportiest lad in the school. He went to all of the same schools as me and he was good at everything. Chris even played rugby for the England U16s. In fact many years later his son also played for England, but this time as a full international. Obviously nature must have played a big part in this. You can imagine that when I continued to score heavily from his bowling Chris was not best pleased. I reached a score of 100 not out and stroked the ball into a gap to take yet another quick single. "In!" I shouted as I reached the bowler's end, adding another run to my already huge score. Chris did no more than run with the ball to the other end and as he took the bales off yelled, "You're out."

I ambled back to the batsman's end and said, "Don't be daft, I shouted "In" way before you hit the wicket."

"Yes, but you were out of your crease," he screamed.

"I wasn't, I was in the bowler's crease," I shouted back at him. I was aware of the rules of cricket and I knew I was right, but on this occasion Chris was not going to let it go. He grabbed the bat out of my hand and as I struggled with him, he hit me over the head with it. I ended up spending the rest of the lunch break in the first aid room with a dinner lady. She was trying to stem the flow of blood from a cut down the centre of my head and I had one hell of a headache.

That was the only time I got hurt by a boy at school, but there was an incident some years later when I was clobbered by a girl. Her name was Lynne and she was one of the girls I fancied at junior school. At Shirley Heath School I was quite musically inclined, joining the school choir and recorder club. The latter was quite a select little group, with four of us being chosen out of about 120 pupils who 'learnt' to play the descant recorder. Lynne was one of the other performers who played alongside me during assemblies. We accompanied the rest of the school when they sang hymns and played specialist pieces of music for their entertainment. My favourite piece of music was Mendelssohn's Spring Song. I am not quite sure it sounded as Mendelssohn meant it to, but our music teacher was always very complimentary about our recitals. To be this good we had to practise regularly, mostly straight after school on a Tuesday. Lynne lived in Witherford Croft, which was in the opposite direction to our house, but we would always walk home together for part of the way. Lynne was a lovely little girl, with short fair hair, a lovely smile and a bubbly personality. We always seemed to get on well, so I was the envy of every boy in the school because she was everyone's favourite.

Lynne was a typical little girl of the 1960s; complete with a small vanity case to carry her recorder in. On the particular evening in question she appeared to be really happy; dancing and spinning around like Maria from the Sound of Music, and me her Captain Von Trapp. Unfortunately amid all of the excitement I stepped too close and got struck by a metal foot on the vanity case, as it spun around. Lynne ran off home and left me to explain the large lump just above my right eye, to Mom and Dad. I was too embarrassed to say it was a girl that hit me, so I told them I tripped, after catching my foot in a wire trailing from a fence in the gulley by Bronte Farm Road. The gulley was a short-cut home and the fence was always in a bad state of repair. Dad wanted to complain to the local council, but somehow I managed to convince him that I wasn't too badly hurt and it was not really worth the effort.

You would have thought that with all of these incidents I might have learnt my lesson and been a little more careful as I grew older, but no. There were a number of occasions when I had near misses with cars, like the time we were leaving the carnival in Tudor Grange Park. The pavements were very congested on both sides of the entrance to the park, as the whole of Shirley and Solihull seemed to be leaving the carnival celebrations. Everyone was chatting noisily about the procession, the fair and what a great time they had just experienced. There were cars both entering and leaving the site at the time; I had never known it so busy. I was walking on the outside of the pavement and in the hustle and confusion got jostled off the path towards the passing traffic. Thankfully the cars were only travelling slowly and I got pushed into the side of a car and not under its wheels. All I received was a bruised arm and a telling off from Dad, who said, "Next time you may not be so lucky." It might not have been my fault that time but the next one was, and Dad was there again to save me.

The whole family was walking to Home Farm in Monkspath, to visit Gran. The route took us along the main Stratford Road and I was holding a small blue ball, which I was going to play with in the garden when we arrived. The traffic in those days was far from busy, with only the odd car travelling along the road, in either direction. It just so happened one came along as I dropped the ball into the road. Of course I was unaware of the traffic and without looking darted into the road after the ball. Luckily for me, Dad had those brilliant reflex actions – the ones fast enough to catch flies. He grabbed my collar just before I disappeared under the wheels and then proceeded to give me a right rollicking! Mom and Dad were always instilling into us how important it was to be careful when crossing the road, not to talk to strangers, not to play with matches and to be careful in the kitchen; all of those things necessary to keep us safe.

I think by this time the penny had started to drop and I was beginning to learn my lesson about being careful. However the next incident was not my fault, but was far more life threatening. It happened in mid-September 1965, on the way home from school. I attended Harold Malley Technical Grammar School at the time and it was a few weeks in to my second year there. School finished at 4 o'clock, so the accident occurred at about a quarter past four. I was cycling home along Blossomfield Road on my blue and white bicycle, in good weather conditions and with my school satchel strapped to my back. The last thing I remember, before being hit by a car, was approaching the bus stop a few hundred yards past the Widney Lane crossroads. There was a large queue of people waiting for the next bus. They were literally a few feet away from me, watching me ride by, when everything went black. What happened next is only what I have been told by Mom.

Mrs. Hall, who lived nine doors up from us in Arbury Hall Road, rode past the accident on her bike shortly after it happened. Seeing me lying in the road unconscious she cycled home as quickly as she could to inform Mom. Mrs. Hall told Mom to take her bicycle and to hurry to the scene as speedily as possible. Mom was never the most athletic person I have known but the adrenalin she generated, worrying about what she would find at the other end, got her there in record time just as the ambulance arrived. Mom left Mrs. Hall's bike at a local shop and went with me in the ambulance. The first occasion after the collision I can guarantee remembering was when I woke up in the hospital ward. I do have a vivid picture in my mind of the ambulance going the wrong way up a one-way street, with its siren sounding and blue lights flashing, but that must be a result of Mom recalling her nightmare journey, over and over again. I gained full consciousness after a couple of hours and was lucky to get away with concussion and a few other minor injuries. These were grazing to fifty per cent of my legs and a mysterious three inch stab wound under my right arm, very close to my arm pit. The grazing was made worse because of another of Mr. Collins' ridiculous head teacher's rules. Boys were not allowed to wear long trousers until they were in their third year. We were the only boys of our age in the whole borough who had to wear shorts throughout the year, even during the winter when we had sub-zero temperatures.

I awoke to find myself in a men's ward, full of old men and next to a chap with some 'mental issues'. He insisted on talking to me and showing me his drawings. He didn't talk a great deal of sense but his pictures were rather good; all of them of horses. Being only eleven and so much younger than the rest of the patients I felt quite isolated, although they were all very friendly, even including me in some of their games. One particular elderly gent played draughts with me on a number of occasions and complimented me on my ability. I didn't stay in hospital very long, just three or four days, although it could have been longer. On the first morning the nurse did her tour of the ward, took my temperature and asked me some questions. Questions such as, "Are your bowels open?" She could tell by the expression on my face I hadn't got a clue what she was talking about, so kindly explained it to me. I had to say, "No" the first morning, but the following day said, "Yes", even when they weren't. I was too embarrassed to admit they weren't. In addition to this the nurse had told me I could not go home until I was 'moving regularly'. However she believed me I don't know, because I had not been out of bed and she hadn't brought me a bedpan at any time. It did the trick though because after a little more monitoring I was allowed home.

I was not fit for school yet and required six weeks convalescence. Six weeks off school would have been most lads' dream, but they were probably the worst six weeks of my life. It wasn't long before I was getting the most severe headaches I have ever had. It is how I imagine people with migraines suffer, but these were every day for more than a month. When I tried to concentrate on anything such as reading, doing jigsaws or watching television the pain would start. The doctor prescribed aspirin as frequently as I needed them; I am not sure whether there was anything else available at the time. All I know is they had very little effect. The only relief I got from the headaches was when I was in bed, resting in the dark.

It was during the six weeks off school that I began to learn exactly what had occurred on my way home that dreaded afternoon. The car that hit me was a little Mini, the driver of which said I had swerved out in front of him as he drove past. I don't believe I did, but obviously cannot be 100 per cent sure. What I do know is the design of Minis in the sixties meant the door handle pointed forward in the direction the car normally travelled. The handles also stuck out 'proud' from the bodywork. I believe the driver got too close to my bike and the handle caught me under the arm, resulting in the mysterious stab wound.

Only two months earlier, in July 1965 the British Motor Corporation (BMC) announced that "Following comments by safety experts about the Mini's external door handles, these will be modified on new cars so that the gap between the handle and the door panel will be effectively closed." I believe this decision resulted from similar accidents to mine, when other pedestrians and cyclists were not as fortunate as I was.

To say I was lucky is an understatement, according to the doctors who treated me in hospital. They told Mom and Dad if I had not been wearing a satchel on my back at the time of the accident I would not have survived. They believe I fell off my bike and on to my satchel before banging my head. If my head had hit the ground first I may not have been writing this book today. My Aunty Barb believed I was dead anyway. Cousin Jackie had seen a crowd of people standing around me on her way home from school and overheard someone say, "He looks like a goner to me". When poor Jackie recognised me lying motionless on the floor she must have been distraught, and ran home to tell her Mom. My bicycle had to be scrapped; it appears it hit the bus shelter. There was a Midland Red bus ticket jammed in the end of the handle bars and the front forks were bent to an angle of almost 90 degrees. I do consider myself to be very lucky indeed; another of my nine lives had been used up!

Eventually when I returned to school, still feeling tender and delicate, most of the teaching staff had no idea who I was, or what had happened to me. Some of them thought I was a new boy, while others thought I had been in lessons from the beginning of term. Consequently they had no sympathy for me when I couldn't answer questions in class. The Reverend Williams even hit me on the back of my head for not being able to answer questions in English about a book the class had been reading since September. I never let on to Mom or Dad, because they would have been down to see the Head to make a fuss.

They say every cloud has a silver lining and this accident was definitely no exception. When I returned to school I was able to wear long trousers. My Mom thought Mr. Collins' rule about short trousers was outrageous, so made up some ridiculous excuse about me having to wear long ones to protect my legs, following the accident. I still cannot believe the teachers and school actually 'bought it', but well done Mom.

I may have been accident prone when I was growing up, but it has put me in good stead for later in life. I not only survived all of the accidents and lived to see another day, but I learnt from them as well. I honestly believe nurture has played a big part in making me more aware of the dangers life can throw at you and has resulted in me taking greater care with everything I do. Past experiences proved to be valuable lessons for me to take into life as I grew older; it certainly helped me when I learnt to drive in 1973. Driving is not just about the mechanics of making the car move where you want it to, but perhaps more importantly anticipating the actions of other drivers on the road – expecting the unexpected. I only needed eleven lessons before I passed at my first attempt. I suppose it helped that I took my test on a Wednesday afternoon, when all of the shops were closed for business. It meant there was very little traffic around and therefore, more or less, I only had my own driving to concentrate on.

Another area of my life where these experiences have had a major influence is Health and Safety at work. In recent years, Health and Safety has become increasingly more important. All organisations now have a duty of care to ensure that employees and any other person who may be affected by the company's undertaking remain safe at all times. I have lost track of how much time I have spent over the years on Health and Safety, but it must run into months, not weeks. I have attended courses and taken examinations for Health and Safety at work, risk assessments, lifesaving, firefighting and first-aid; all useful to know, but mostly common sense. Common sense that I learnt from the 'near misses' I experienced while growing up. Most of what I learnt on these courses was never put to good use while I was working, but who knows, there still may be time yet. There have only ever been relatively minor incidents for which I have needed the knowledge I assimilated, although there was one occasion when it was nearly called for.

In the late 1980s, I was working for a large FTSE100 company, as a Data Information Officer, responsible for ensuring the collection and quality of analytical results. It bought me into contact with the company's analytical services at Shrewsbury, including the chemical, biological and microbiological laboratories. At that time the laboratories were run by the Principal Microbiologist, a guy called David. He was an extremely clever individual, with a PhD and an enormous amount of letters after his name, including ICFA, the International Certificate of First Aid. Luckily for one of David's colleagues, he was on hand when they were involved with a very serious accident. The person in question was working on their own in one of the laboratories when there was a significant explosion caused by a faulty gas cylinder. When the explosion occurred, I was working some 25 yards away on one of the company's PCs. The noise was deafening and the whole room shook. Those of us in the data room all thought we were experiencing an earthquake at the time because the glass in the windows vibrated so violently. We were looking at each other in disbelief, for what seemed like an age, until we realised it was something more specific. I rushed into the laboratory to discover complete devastation.

There was broken glass everywhere and a bluish grey smoke filled the air, creating an acrid smell that burned the back of my throat. The next thing I noticed was an individual lying motionless on the floor between two of the work benches. They appeared to have minor cuts and bruises to their face and their normally white coat was charred and in shreds, leaving them barely covered. My head was still in somewhat of a spin, but I was aware that David was already in the room administering First Aid. It took me a second look to realise quite what was happening. David appeared to have turned the patient over and was blowing into the casualty's bottom. Desperately trying to recall my first aid training I realised things weren't quite right. With some hesitance I went over to him and asked, "What are you doing?"

"The kiss of life," he replied.

I knew what the 'kiss of life was'; it was an emergency procedure consisting of external cardiac massage and artificial respiration or 'Mouth to mouth resuscitation'. Just as the name suggests you blow into the patient's mouth.

"Aren't you supposed to be blowing into his mouth?" I retorted.

"Yes, I am," he snapped, "but have you smelt his breath?"

Clearly I knew the theory, but still had a lot to learn before I could put everything into practice.

*Dad - Private 14376712*

*Mom around the time she met Dad*

*Dad on leave in Cairo*

*Mom and Dad's Wedding day, 25 June 1949*

*What a bonny little boy – wrapped up well from the winter's chill!*

*Me at about 18 months old*

*Gra, me and Sue in the front room*

*Enjoying an ice-cream with Gra,*
*Margaret McGuire and Sue.*

*Gran and Grampy came to tea on my third birthday; December 1956*

*Everyone around the tree, Christmas evening in 1956*

*Christmas morning with Sue and Gra; a special time in 1956*

*Christmas card from Miss Murphy*
*during first year at school - 1958*

*Walking hand in hand to school with Gra.*

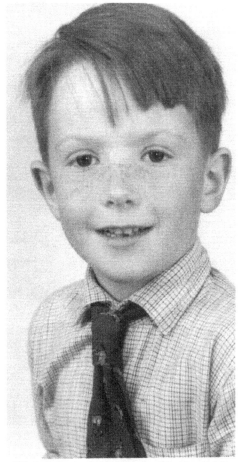

*What a haircut, - look at the size of that 'cowlick'!*

*Me and Sally; a faithful friend*

*Days out in the park at Stratford were our summer holidays- Great times!*

*In the park at Stratford with Dad*

*A steam locomotive, passing under the foot bridge in Earlswood woods.*

*The foot bridge in Earlswood woods; just as I remember it.*

*Uphill near Weston Super Mare – First 'real' holiday with Mom and Dad.*

*Brothers Gra, Lol and Jon.*

# Chapter 6

## TIGHT LINES

I consider myself to be very lucky in more ways than one. In the previous chapter I wrote about how I was perhaps fortunate to reach adulthood without too many scars to show for it. I consider my best luck is to have had three male role models during my childhood years. It is often reported today that there is an increasing number of boys who do not know what it is to have a 'man' in their lives. Many children go to bed at night without saying goodnight to their father because they do not have one or they are not around. Apparently one in four households in Britain is a single parent family. That means there are about two million single parents and three million children living in one parent families. Another statistic is that of these single parents, more than 90 per cent are women. This implies there are nearly 1.4 million boys living without a dad and hence a regular male role model.

The majority of these boys live with a woman and more than likely are taught by a woman at school. When do they see and interact with a positive male role model? How do they learn what it means to be a man; from television, films, or on the street? No matter how great a mother is, she cannot replace what a father can provide to a child. Traditional stereotyping suggests mothers are typically nurturing, soft, gentle, comforting, protective and emotional, whilst fathers tend to be challenging, loud, playful and physical; encouraging risk taking. Children need this balance of protection and reasonable risk taking in order to develop into a rounded individual. If a positive male role model is not present in the life of a child, there is emptiness in this area. Research shows children who live in this environment are more likely to be involved in criminal activity, premature sexual activity, achieve less at school and participate in potentially harmful activities. This is not to say it is the fault of mothers, because children in single parent families run by men have similar issues and difficulties while growing up. Having a family and running a home is rewarding, but without doubt is hard work. I firmly believe that it is best tackled by a couple in a partnership together; supporting each other and passing on their individual values and principles to their offspring. Sadly in today's society everyone seems to be too busy. There is never enough time to do everything needed to be done and it is the children that often miss out. I wonder how many children, even in homes where both parents are present, miss out on meals with their parents, a bedtime story or even a goodnight kiss, because their dad is working late. Regrettably we are living in a culture where emotional and spiritual fatherlessness is becoming the norm.

I mentioned having three male role models when I was growing up. Clearly the most important was my Dad, but my Uncle Les and Grampy came a close second. I have already spoken about Dad, the strong character he was and the times we spent together doing simple activities; things that didn't cost anything but his time. So this chapter is devoted to my Uncle Les and the influences he had on my life.

I have always considered myself to be the son my Uncle Les never had. He had two daughters Jo and Jackie, whom he dearly loved, but he never had a son to take fishing, or to go and watch a football match with; just someone to share and pass on those male passions for sport and the outdoor life. Luckily, out of all of his nephews, Uncle Les chose me to share those passions with. I think it was because I was the eldest nephew on his side of the family. No matter what the reason, I am glad I was the one.

Uncle Les was very different from my Dad. Not only did he look very different, but he also had very different values, principles and qualities. He was a little shorter than Dad, not as slim and certainly had far less hair. Not just on his head either. Les had very little hair on his chest and his legs were as white as milk and as smooth as a baby's bottom. His hair was very similar in colour to his Dad's and the style too. It was short and thinning on top, a style that showed off his ears to good effect. I often heard him being referred to as 'FA Cup' ears. He had a good sense of humour like Dad did, but it wasn't as corny as Dad's. It was more your usual 'joke telling' humour; he could tell a good story and deliver the punch line correctly with decent timing. He was always another great source of jokes for me to tell at school.

Whereas Dad was domesticated and could turn his hand to anything, Les was probably the exact opposite. When he split up from my Aunty Barb, I always felt he found it difficult to cope on his own with the everyday domestic chores and cooking. I got the impression he could make a cup of tea and a sandwich, but that was about it. I never saw any artistic side to him either. He was more of an engineer, comfortable with mending a bicycle puncture or changing a wheel.

I cannot remember where he took me first, to St Andrews to see Birmingham City play football, or to Swan's pool to dangle a worm or two and catch fish. The football matches cost nothing to take me to, because Les would always sneak me in by taking me through the turnstile in front of him. It didn't really matter because we always went in the 'Railway End' and it was standing terraces only. Outside the ground before the match was always very exciting. Les would park the car in a side road somewhere in Small Heath. Getting there by car was an experience for a start. Although Dad had a driving license, we could not afford a car, so a ride in Uncle Les' car was novel and special. Once parked and before Les could get out of the car there would be two or three kids tapping on the window shouting, "Look after your car mate?" Les would always say, "If it is still here when I come back and it is in one piece, there's a shilling waiting for you." Each lad would make a killing on match day, with half a dozen cars parked in their bit of the road. When we approached the ground there were vendors selling programmes and club colours in the form of scarves and rosettes. Or there would be some old guy trying to get Les to buy me a wooden rattle by spinning it around ferociously and making as much noise as he could. The rattles consisted of a thick wooden cog wheel attached to a handle and two wooden flanges that alternately hit the teeth of the cog when the handle turns. The rattle worked by holding the handle and swinging the whole mechanism around. The momentum made the board click against the gearwheel, producing a clicking and rattling noise.

The 'Blues' weren't really my team. With Dad coming from London he always brought me up to support the Spurs. Nevertheless, each time I went to a match I enjoyed the game and atmosphere. In the early sixties the ground was usually packed. I would not go as far as saying full, because they could always squash in a few more on the terraces. Whenever the ball came down our end the whole crowd would move forward to try and get a better view. Half the time you would miss the action due to being pushed down three or four steps towards the front. Then as the ball disappeared up the other end, everyone would make their way back to somewhere near their original position in the stand. Les would often try and get there early so we could stand in front of one of the barriers, thus avoiding me getting crushed in the excitement. At half time I loved to stand and look around the ground, watching for the flickers of light as spectators lit up a cigarette or pipe. I always thought it was incredible that there was always someone striking a 'Swan Vesta', somewhere in the ground throughout the whole 90 minutes.

I remember players like Jimmy Bloomfield, Johnny Schofield, Terry Hennessey, Graham Sissons, Bertie Auld, Mike Hellawell and Malcolm Beard. The manager was Gil Merrick, who only the season before had been in the squad as a goalkeeper. Probably the two most memorable games for me were in the FA Cup against Arsenal and Chelsea during the same season. Blues won both matches and the crowds were phenomenal. There were over 50,000 people in the stadium on both afternoons and those were the official figures. What if they had counted every child smuggled in by their dad or uncle?

Leaving the ground was fun. I remember Uncle Les saying, "Stay as close to me as you can and if we get separated we'll meet by the programme stand." There wasn't much hope of me trying to do anything; I just went with the crowd. Being smaller than the adults, I could see very little but smell a lot, generally with my nose pushed in places I would rather it had not been. Coming out of the gates the masses were so large we were packed like 'sardines in a can'. On one occasion I can remember lifting my feet completely off the floor and getting swept along by the crowd. I went to St Andrews quite regularly and enjoyed watching them play some good football, but I didn't become an ardent fan. At this age I hadn't been to White Hart Lane or even seen the mighty Spurs play, but I still supported them. After all they were my Dad's team; why would I support anyone else?

I don't think football was Les' favourite pastime – without doubt that had to be fishing. By my early teens he was probably going at least once a week, if not more, and I usually went with him. I am not certain, but I believe at the time he was a relative novice himself. He must have got the 'bug' from his dad. Grampy was always telling me tales of the times he went fishing, the monsters he caught and the even bigger ones that got away. Les and I learnt to fish in a small private pool in Earlswood, which belonged to Pete Swan's parents. Pete was a longtime friend of Les and Aunty Barb. His mom and dad lived in a property in Wood Lane, a few hundred yards away from Earlswood Woods. I don't remember whether it was a cottage or a bungalow – my memories are only of the exciting times we went fishing there. I do remember though that it was a typical country residence with a large garden running downhill towards what can only be described as an exquisite pond.

The excitement started way before we arrived on the bank. Mom would awaken me early, give me breakfast and make me a packed lunch to take. This was all before six o'clock, the time Uncle Les had promised to pick me up. He was not always the most punctual of people, so I usually ended up waiting for him in the front garden, with butterflies in my stomach. On the earlier occasions I would stand at the end of the path listening and watching for his car to appear around the corner. When I got to know about his timekeeping I would more often than not play with a ball to pass the time away. Every time we went fishing it seemed as though it was a lovely day – dry, warm mornings and blue skies. During the first couple of years I never remember it raining and only once did I ever get cold.

The car Les drove in the early sixties was a large, blue Ford Consul, so there was plenty of room for our tackle and lunch. In fact I didn't have any tackle; Uncle Les always provided me with his spare rod and line. Swan's pond, as we always referred to it, was only a ten minute drive away, along the country lanes. I remember uncle Les always went the back route so that he could approach from the far end of the lane. This was somewhat out of our way, but coming from this direction it meant the last 100 yards was downhill. Les always stuck the car in to neutral, turned the engine off and coasted the last bit of the way, so as not to disturb Pete's mom and dad during their Sunday morning lie in.

We would then creep down the garden, marching to the dawn chorus, undetected by the occupants of the house.

My recollection of the pool is it was almost square in shape, having sides about 30 yards long. The water could be fished from three sides only; the far bank being a thick hedge of trees and hawthorn. There was a large willow tree to the left, on the nearside bank and to the right and far side of the pond were large large lily pads. We did not fish from this bank because the lilies were quite invasive, leaving very little clear water to cast in to. I would occasionally walk around to that part of the pool though, to stretch my legs when bites weren't coming quite as quickly as I would have liked. This wasn't that often as I would usually sit quietly, perched on my grey wooden stool, watching my float like a hawk watches a mouse. The depth of the pool ranged from a couple of feet up to about four feet and it contained a selection of perch, roach, skimmers and carp. They were not huge fish, but there were plenty of them to be caught. I usually fished close to the willow tree, between two clumps of reeds. For 12 months or more I fished with my line tied straight to the end of a ten foot rod, a bit like a roach pole, but much smaller. I wasn't impressed, I wanted a reel like Les, but he insisted it was for the best.

I realised the day I started to use a reel why uncle Les started me off in this way. If he hadn't, he would never have got any fishing done himself. The first time I fished with a reel, Les spent more time trying to untangle the line from the back of my reel than I did with my float in the water. I clearly recall sitting on my little stool at the water's side, watching the red and yellow tip of my float, against the green of the water. If you have never been fishing it is hard to explain the anticipation you feel when the float begins to bob up and down as a fish investigates your bait and then the excitement as it suddenly disappears from view. You strike, lifting the rod upwards, not knowing whether you were quick enough, until you feel the resistance of the fish trying to make its escape.

The first fish I ever caught was a tiny perch, probably the first fish most anglers catch. This is because they are an aggressive predator that will eat almost anything an angler dangles in front of it, including insects, crustaceans, flies, larvae, worms and all fish fry. In my view it is one of the most beautiful looking fish. It has a flat-sided greenish body, which becomes white at its belly. It has bright red to orange pelvic fins, two dorsal fins with six broad black vertical stripes down the sides. This is where it gets its nickname 'Stripey' from. Its body is distinctively rough to the touch, which makes it easy to hold, but when unhooking a perch you need to take care to avoid its row of sharp pointed spines along the dorsal fin. Being aggressive predators, they are notorious for swallowing the hook, and will often require the aid of a disgorger or forceps for unhooking them. This is where uncle Les always proved useful. Unhooking a fish at the age of seven is difficult anyway, but taking the hook out of a tiny perch, which has swallowed your worm almost down to its tail, is almost impossible. This is why we always sat close to each other, just so my Uncle could unhook my fish and put another worm or maggot on for me.

I was a quick learner and it wasn't long before I was using a reel, tackling up, putting my own bait on and unhooking my own catch. This meant we could go and fish in Earlswood Lakes and the local 'cut' or canal. We were lucky, living in Shirley, because we were close to Earlswood and never far away from the canals at Lapworth, Rowington and Lowsonford; all excellent locations with plenty of fish to catch. I have lost count of the number of occasions I have been fishing, the majority of them with Uncle Les, but I can count on one hand the number of times I have come away with a 'dry' net. Even on days when I didn't catch anything or the fish weren't biting particularly well, I always enjoyed myself. Uncle Les not only taught me how to fish, but he also made me aware of the environment we were fishing in. He would point out, birds, insects, flowers and wildlife living along the towpath. Sitting quietly on the bankside, early in the morning, we saw the usual fauna like squirrels, blackbirds and robins, but would regularly see what you might say are rarer species, such as kingfishers and water voles. Sometimes a vole would swim out from the bank, right beneath my feet and make its way across to the other side, its little head just peeping out of the water. They are extremely good swimmers, using water to access vegetation and avoid predators, and inhabiting burrow complexes in the banks of water courses. In the sixties, water voles were a common and familiar sight in our countryside, but recent habitat loss has diminished their population by over 90 per cent. On the canals where I last saw a water vole, much of the bankside has now been reinforced by replacing reeds and natural vegetation with corrugated metal panels; hardly conducive to homes for water voles.

When I reached my teens, Les and I decided to cast our lines further afield and joined the Red Lion Angling Club in Earlswood and Wavis Engineering AC. There was generally a contest or two every month during the season, typically in the big Midland Rivers, such as the Avon, Severn and Trent. At this point I really needed to start having my own tackle. I couldn't go on using Les' spare rods and tackle, so I saved up and bought my own with money earned from a little Saturday job. Everything was so expensive though, in particular the old wicker fishing baskets or creels. I couldn't afford everything, so Dad volunteered to embark on one of his special projects and made me a 'wooden' creel. I have to admit, it was pretty special. No one else had one like it! My new fishing 'box' was everything a budding 'Sir Isaac Walton' needed. It was very sturdy, had a lovely grey painted finish and a leather carrying strap just like the shop bought ones. The only slight negative was, as per Dad's special projects, it was 50 per cent bigger than any creel I had ever seen and it weighed an absolute ton.

The first time I used it was quite an eventful day, in more ways than one. Les and I were fishing in a contest, somewhere on the river Great Ouse. If my memory serves me correctly it was on the Relief Channel, a few miles south of King Lynn. It was quite a journey, so rather than go by car the club hired a coach and all members travelled together. The coach started in Birmingham and picked up club members at various locations on its way to Widney Lane shops. This is where Les and I got on, the last stop before East Anglia. Les had told me to meet him at the top of his road at a quarter past six. This would give us fifteen minutes to walk the last part of the way together, in time to meet the coach. I set off at about six o'clock and struggled along Cranmore Boulevard, with the strap of my new fishing 'box' cutting into my shoulder. Approaching Northlands Road I could see Les leaving his house, laden with all of his tackle and 'weighing in' scales. It was perfect timing. We arrived at Widney Lane just before half past six, with the coach already waiting for us. I was completely shattered. I had walked approximately one mile from home, but with dad's fishing 'box', it seemed more like a marathon. "Where have you been?" they all said with some disgust. "You're late, we have been waiting since six".

"Oh, that was Malc," Les quickly replied. "He was late. I have been waiting for him at the top of the road for half an hour." I stared at him to show my disbelief in what he had just said, but I was too tired to put up any defence. Les was the Club Secretary and had booked the coach and made all of the arrangements. He should have known what time we were supposed to leave; at least you would have thought so. After putting my tackle in the boot, I climbed on the coach to find a seat for a well-earned rest. Before Les had even found a seat the coach was pulling away to the depths of East Anglia.

Three hours later it was all forgotten and we were at the venue, standing around the back of the coach to pick up our tackle. We were just about to set-off for the bank, when the coach driver said, "Whose tackle is this?" pointing at a creel and rod-bag. Everyone looked at each other in horror as they realised we had left Frank at Widney Lane shops. While waiting for Les and I, he had decided to pop into the newsagents to buy a paper and a packet of cigarettes. We knew this when we found his boots on the coach where he had been sitting. Believe it or not we had only gone and left him, miles from home in his carpet slippers. I smiled and thought to myself, justice had been done; as Secretary Les was going to take responsibility for this 'cock-up'. Taking the blame for making them wait probably wasn't too bad after all!

Everyone had a great day fishing, catching plenty of big bream and soon forgetting about poor old Frank. Mind you Frank probably didn't feel too bad when he discovered the coach had broken down on the way home in the middle of nowhere. We were stranded for around three hours while we waited for a mechanic to repair the coach. I had no problem falling asleep, while Les and four others played cards on the back seat. You may feel it would have been a little awkward with so many playing and without a table, but the ever resourceful Les found a solution. "We can use the 'Portmanteau' in the boot," he said with excitement. For the next five or six hours Dad's special project was a huge hit, while I was worrying about how I was going to walk home with it after such a tiring day.

I usually did reasonably well in contests, considering I was the only junior in the club. I had some noticeable results, including a first place at Wyre Piddle and a third on the river Severn at Hampton Loade; both of which got me a mention in the Birmingham Sporting Argus. Even some of the lads at school noticed the article in the paper. Of course I took great delight and every opportunity to tell them my win was at 'Wyre Piddle'. On the way to this particular contest we dropped one of Les' friends, Charlie, at a gravel pit near to the venue. Having won the contest, when we stopped off to pick him up on the way home, I had a smile as wide as my face. That is until we saw what Charlie had been catching. He had a net full of large tench, probably totalling over 100 pounds in weight. Neither of us had ever seen such a huge catch and I had not even seen a tench before. It is one of the most distinguishable of fish – an olive green body, small, teddy bear like, red eyes and powerful tail and fins.

That was it, as soon as Les clapped his eyes on this net full of tench our following Sunday was mapped out for us. Plans were soon in place to arrive at the crack of dawn, torch in hand, so we could tackle up and be ready to catch tench as the day began. Tench are renowned for feeding at either end of the day, away from the heat of the midday sun. Mom was working as a waitress at the Plough at the time and Saturday evening shifts were a regular feature for her. After cashing up and clearing tables in readiness for the next day, she would arrive home about one o'clock on Sunday morning. "Ideal," said Les. "Get your Mom to wake you when she gets in and I will pick you up around two." It sounded like a plan.

The following Saturday I had an early night in order to grab a few hours of sleep before our day of fishing for tench. It hardly seemed as though I had been asleep more than a few minutes when Mom woke me. There was barely time to get dressed, prepare my lunch and have a quick bite to eat before Les pulled up, for once earlier than planned. I cannot tell you how keen and excited he was. It took me back to how I was when he first started taking me fishing. At two in the morning there was hardly a car on the road, so with Les driving like the legendary Stirling Moss, we were on the bank of the gravel pit even before the rabbits had gone to bed. Luckily it was going to be a lovely sunny day and light from an almost full moon filled the night sky. It was a good job, because we had a real difficulty tiptoeing our way around the ex-quarry trying to find the best spots to fish. Thank goodness we remembered our torches; even with them it was a struggle to thread the line through the rings on our rods and to tie on our hooks. It was a bit of a logistical nightmare – holding the line in one hand, the rod in the other and the torch between my knees. I have absolutely no idea how Uncle Les managed.  He was slightly bow legged and was reputed to be unable to 'stop a pig in an alley'. He must have managed somehow though. After I had finally tackled up, I walked up the bank to chat to him while I waited for the sun to rise.

It was still so dark I had to shine my torch to actually see where he was. He was perched on the edge of his creel, staring out into the darkness. "How long do you think it will be before the sun comes up and we can start fishing?" I said quietly.

"I have cast in already," he whispered back.

"It's still too dark, I can't see where I am casting," I said. "Besides that I wouldn't be able to see my float if I got a bite."

"I haven't worried about that. Tench are so powerful, if I get a bite it will probably pull the rod in," he countered.

"Where did you cast and how deep are you fishing?" I asked.

"Oh, about five feet, and just out there to my right." He pointed with the cigarette in his right hand, so I could visualise just where he was fishing. We chatted for about ten minutes about tactics, rig set-ups, bait and how we hoped to catch a bagful, just as Charlie had the week before. We both peered into the mist lying on top of the water, as Uncle Les lit up his second cigarette of the day. It was a race to be the first to spot exactly where his float had landed. Perhaps a tench had swum off with his bait, just like Les had suggested; that's why we couldn't spot it. Then I noticed his float with its fluorescent red tip out in the direction he had gestured. "I wouldn't fish there if I were you," I said.

"Why not, where is it? I still can't see it," he replied.

"The only thing you will catch there," I laughed, "is a flying fish. It's up in the tree." Les had only been sitting for fifteen minutes, with his float hanging from a tree, ten feet above the water! I left him to it and went back to my peg to cast in, chuckling all of the way. It reminded me of the popular Aesop's Fable about 'the hare and the tortoise'; more haste, less speed. It was something I never let Les forget, often relaying the story to others at our weekly club meetings at the Red Lion.

Les and I had many great days out fishing together, always having plenty of laughs and numerous tales to tell. None more so than on our holiday to Tenby in Wales with Les' family and my sister Sue and her husband Don. For the three lads it was a great opportunity to have a week of fishing at Bosherston Lakes, a large freshwater lake fed by small streams and natural springs. The lake supports rare freshwater plants, and there is a healthy population of otters, which feed on the eels, pike, perch, roach, rudd and tench that live in the lake – exactly what we were hoping to catch. For Les and me it was a magical place to visit, not just for the fishing, but for the flora and fauna as well. Bats hunt for insects over the water and over 20 species of dragonfly and damselfly live there together with numerous birds including heron, kingfisher, little grebe and moorhen.

We were staying in a cottage only a few miles from the lake, in a fantastic location. The cottage was one of two in a block, with both properties having to share just one bathroom. Aunty Barb and Sue went off with my two nieces to the beach each day, while Les, Don and I pitted our wits against the occupants of the Lake. The lake is only about three or four feet deep and is covered in lilies, for which it is so well known.  During the week we all caught plenty of small roach and rudd: two very similar looking types of fish. That was until Les caught a perch and a decent sized one at that. It was about a pound or more in weight, so I walked along the bank to take a better look at it. He took his keep net out of the water to show me and sure enough it was a lovely specimen. Lying amongst the tiny roach and rudd it looked even bigger than it was, its bright red fins standing out against the silver of the smaller fish. "Nice one," I said, "what did you catch that on?" I didn't get chance to take in the answer, because as he threw the net back into the water he caught me with his left arm and knocked me down the bank. Fortunately for me, and Les, I was quick to react and managed to scramble up the side of the bank. However, not before my right leg had taken a dip in the clear, cold water of the lake. "What did you do that for?" I said, emptying the water out of my shoe.

"I never touched you," he replied, trying not to laugh, but clearly not succeeding very well. I hopped back to my peg, shoe and sock in hand, leaving a trail of drips from my sodden jeans.

I never let any incident like this stop me from fishing, so I cast in again, hoping to outdo Les. I sat with one bare foot for the rest of the day, reeling in small rudd with some regularity. It was about tea-time when four lads from Wigan walked past. Having packed up for the day they were on their way back to the car park. Just like us, they were down there on holiday. We met them several times and chatted on a number of occasions about our angling exploits; that is successes, or lack of them. Just as they were approaching my peg I caught yet another rudd. This time though, as occasionally happens, the fish wasn't hooked particularly well. I lifted it out of the water and swung the fish towards me, but it came unhooked and dropped to the floor. When this occurs I am certain the fish can sense a chance to escape, because they usually flap about frantically, making their way towards the water's edge. Almost with a reflex action I flicked my foot out and lightly placed it over the escaping rudd. Just as I was picking it up I heard this Northern voice say, "Hey lads, take a look at this. Those Brummies are so skilled they even unhook fish with their toes." I half smiled and turned around to explain how my precious uncle had pushed me in, but it was too late. They were already several yards away, having a good laugh at my expense. Anyway we were more serious anglers than they were – we were going to fish on until dusk.

Some hours later, just as it was getting dark and about the time we were thinking of packing up, Les hooked yet another small rudd. While he was reeling it in, it was grabbed by a small 'jack' pike. Pike are even more ferocious than perch. They are almost prehistoric looking with long, slender bodies and a large head and jaws, containing extremely sharp teeth. They have a great camouflage from their olive green bodies marked with short, light bar-like spots, waiting in the shadowy depths for an unsuspecting fish to pass by. If anglers want to catch one, they generally use wire traces to prevent their line from being broken, as it rubs against the pike's rough upper jaw.  Les was lucky, because the pike was conveniently hooked in the corner of its mouth, with the line in no danger of being broken. The instant he had this small pike on the bank, yet again our future was mapped out for us. "Tomorrow, let's go to the beach with the girls during the day and then come fishing for pike and eels in the evening," Les said excitedly. I recognised the excitement in his voice. It was similar to that day we saw Charlie's monster bag of tench. Just as before, plans were soon in place to arrive just as it was getting dusk, torch in hand, so we could tackle up and be ready to catch pike and eels as the night began.

It was another lovely day, so the evening was warm, still and clear, with the light from an almost full moon filling the night sky. We set our rigs up to fish on the bottom, with a larger than usual hook and some of the previous day's catch as dead bait; ledgering was the chosen method.  This meant we didn't need to see a float if we got a bite. We just watched the line as it was taken straight off the reel. We had a great night's fishing, catching plenty of eels and as unusual making sure we had plenty of laughs. We managed to reel in some big ones too, unlike those we were used to catching. I caught the heaviest at just less than four pounds. It was around three feet long and its body was as thick as a man's wrist; a real beauty according to Les. It was so large and such an unusual catch, Les wanted to take a photograph of me holding it. To be honest so did I; it would be great showing it off to all my school mates. Unfortunately, in the late sixties instamatic cameras weren't particularly great and the flash facility was even worse. It looked like we were going to have to return them to the water without capturing them for posterity. That is until Les had another of his bright ideas. "I know," he said excitedly, "let's take them back to the cottage in a bucket, and take a photograph in the morning." I was as keen as Les to have a photograph to keep, but was more of a pessimist. "That is all well and good, but where are we going to keep them overnight? I asked him. "If we leave them outside the bucket is likely to get knocked over by a fox or something. It is not fair to the eels."

"We can put them in the bucket and then in the bath, back at the cottage," he replied resourcefully.

Again always thinking about problems, I countered, "What about the family in the other cottage, won't they mind?

"They will never know," he said. "We can take the photographs first thing and return them to the stream in the garden, before they are even up." Despite my best judgement and knowing how my aunty would react, I went along with his plan.

We carefully took three of the largest eels back to the cottage and stood the bucket in the shared bathroom, setting the alarm clock for six the next morning. This would allow us plenty of time to complete Les' plan. I slept rather well that night, dreaming about how the monster eel had taken my bait and then shot off across the lake before I hauled it on to the bank. Les was at my side when I landed it, screaming at me, "Oh my god, look at the size of it, it's huge." I must have relived the event and caught the eel half a dozen times during the night. After the final time though, Les sounded different somehow. I couldn't quite make out what he was saying and he seemed to be screaming more than usual. In fact he was screaming so loud it woke me up. I lay there thinking about how envious the lads at school would be until I realised the screaming was still going on. It didn't sound like Les either, it sounded more like a woman. Then horror of horrors, my Aunty Barb discovered the woman from the cottage next door had got up early to have a bath. Regrettably for us, our three eels had knocked the bucket over and were swimming up and down the bath, much to the lady's shock when she switched on the light. Les had to go around and apologise with his tail between his legs, and he had a regular ear bashing from my aunty for the rest of the holiday! Still we got the photographs we wanted and set the eels free at the bottom of the garden to fight for another day.

This wasn't the first holiday I went on with Les and Aunty Barb, they also took me on my first real holiday. I mentioned previously that Mom and Dad could not afford to take the family away on holiday when we were younger, so we only ever went out for day trips. When I was aged ten, Les and Barb booked a week's break on the west coast of Wales in a self-contained flat in Borth, near Aberystwyth. They knew Graham and I were not going to have a summer vacation again that year, so invited us along. Secretly, I think Les wanted someone to go fishing with him. If you have never had the pleasure of visiting Borth, let alone spent a week there, then you are exceptionally lucky. It may have changed now, but in 1964 there were just a few houses along the front facing a featureless beach. I don't believe there were any shops or pubs, just this row of old grey properties looking out at the equally grey sea. The only good thing about Borth was you could get away from it quickly and into some very pretty countryside. One of my favourite days out was to Devil's Bridge in the Rheidol Gorge, a world famous tourist attraction 12 miles from Aberystwyth. The unique waterfalls have attracted thousands of visitors there since the 18th century, including William Wordsworth who wrote about the "Torrent at the Devil's Bridge". I have clear memories of Devil's Bridge, just because of the falls and the fact I saw my first ever red squirrel there.

Mid-week Les and I went on our one and only fishing trip. I think my aunty rationed Les to just one trip in the week, because she had to put up with him going fishing almost every weekend. She rarely went out to the cinema or for a meal with Les, so she was determined that fishing would not spoil the holiday. The venue was Caersws, a small village on the upper reaches of the river Severn; the best part of forty miles from Borth and halfway back towards England. I suppose the journey took about an hour or so, which meant Les needed at least a couple of cigarettes during the journey. We must have been halfway there when he asked me to pass him a cigarette and the box of matches out of the glove compartment. Without thinking, I took a cigarette out of the packet, struck a match and lit up before handing it to him, having a tentative 'puff' before doing so. He wasn't best pleased, and instructed me never to do it again. I was a little put out by his reprimand, but soon forgot about it when we got back on to talking about fishing and football. We had a thrilling day, during which I saw my first brown trout and grayling. I struggled with fishing such a fast flowing part of the river, but enjoyed watching Uncle Les catch plenty of fish.

A few days later we all went out together on a drive around mid-Wales, taking in the vistas, playing in woods and rambling alongside babbling mountain streams. This was altogether a wonderful day for me, everything I loved doing as a child. There was only one thing that spoilt it, and it happened as we were driving back to Borth. We were on the main A487 Machynlleth to Aberystwyth road, travelling towards our holiday flat – me in the front and the others in the back. Les said to me, "Malc, can you get me a cigarette out please?" Without thinking, I took a cigarette out of the packet, struck a match and lit up before handing it to him, again having a tentative puff before doing so. Well that was it, Aunty Barb nearly hit the roof. "Stop the car, stop the car," she screamed, "I cannot believe you have taught him to do that." Despite my uncle's fervent protestations, she just kept shouting at him. "How often does he light your cigarettes for you: all of the time? Stop now, we are all getting out of the car." By this time Les had pulled up at the side of the road. Aunty Barb, Jo, Jackie and Gra immediately got out and without looking back, started to walk the last five miles home. I just sat in the car, sinking into the front seat very sheepishly and feeling just a little bit guilty. After all, Les had told me off earlier in the week, so it wasn't really his fault. Although with hindsight perhaps he shouldn't have asked me a second time. Five minutes later realising there was still a long way to go, Aunty Barb decided to accept Les' explanation. However, it wasn't easy, particularly as Les found it difficult to hold back his nervous laugh.

A few years later Uncle Les and Aunty Barb split up and went their separate ways. At the time I regularly thought back to this incident and hoped it in no way had contributed towards the break-up of their marriage. I am sure it didn't, although Les going fishing on a regular basis probably did. I don't think him taking me along made any difference, because I am certain Les would have gone without me anyway.

# Chapter 7

## BEST IN SHOW

Home Farm (where Mom was born) holds many happy memories for me. Not just because it is where I spent numerous wonderful days with my Gran and Grampy, but because it was a fabulous environment for a child to grow up in. I was so envious of my Mom. The memories I have of Home Farm are endless. The more I sit and think about the times I have spent there, the more I remember. Unfortunately there will not be room in this book to recall everything. Therefore any close family who may read my book and were lucky enough to experience life at Home Farm will have many more memories of it than I have been able to put to paper here. I am sure they will reminisce about times, people, objects and occurrences that I cannot even recall. Hopefully what I have written will jog memories and kindle other thoughts about what happened in 'times gone by', at this truly memorable place.

From the age of about eight, come rain or shine, I would visit Gran and Grampy almost every Saturday. I had been to visit them many times as a youngster, but at eight years old Mom and Dad decided I was old enough to travel there on my own. Initially Mom would put me on a number 150 Midland Red bus at Cranmore Boulevard and ask the driver to make sure I got off at the correct stop a mile up the road, opposite North's newsagents. Mom had already told Gran which bus to expect me on, so she would be at the garden gate, waiting for me to arrive.

In the evening Gran would reciprocate, with Dad waiting for me at the other end.

Home Farm was a typical double fronted Edwardian house, set in around three quarters of an acre of garden. It was surrounded on all sides by tall mature hedging, comprised of mainly hawthorn and ash trees. The house itself could only be viewed, in full, from the gate, which was at the end of a long cinder path. The path split the garden in two almost equal parts and led right up to the front door. On either side of the path there was a narrow strip of grass about a foot wide, each one opening out into a 15 foot, square lawn in front of the house. In the summer the garden was full of colour from flower borders on each side of the path and vegetable patches beyond them. When it came to his garden Grampy was a creature of habit. The borders were planted exactly the same every year; I can still recall the detail today. He planted blue ageratum at the front, followed by mixed nemesia then bright red salvias. After that there were asters against a backdrop of large, 'cactus' dahlias. The latter comprised five regular varieties, a red, yellow, white, orange and a purple and white bicoloured variety, called Edinburgh. Everything was planted with military precision, using a string between two sticks to ensure straight lines and a measuring stick to guarantee consistent distances between both rows and plants.

The vegetable patches on either side were produced exactly the same, only changing each year to comply with a strict crop rotation. There were 'Polestar' runner beans grown up young, six foot, ash whips, cut from the surrounding hedges. Dwarf

French beans, 'Tendergreen' or 'The Prince' were in abundance, hidden under the leaves but hanging in enormous bunches. There were 'Kelvedon Wonder' peas grown amongst twigs also collected from the hedges, along with 'King Edward' potatoes and 'Tender and True' parsnips. The young 'Webbs Wonderful' lettuce and 'Greyhound' cabbages would be protected from sparrows and pigeons by lines of cotton attached to specially made row markers. The rows of 'Autumn King' carrots, 'Boltardy' beetroot and 'French Breakfast' radishes would stand as straight as a die, like rows of soldiers taking part in trooping the colour. Sprouts, onions and broad beans would complete the full complement of vegetables grown. Maybe I recall everything through rose coloured glasses, but I never remember Grampy having a crop fail.

To the left as you entered the garden there were loganberry bushes growing in the shade of a large apple tree. The tree was enormous, standing about twenty five feet high, with its branches and fruit always hanging well out of reach. The apples were small and sweet, much like 'Gala' apples you can buy today. To the right, bordering the far side of the vegetable plot were half a dozen Damson trees, which did not fruit every year, but when they did, the fruit would hang like huge bunches of black grapes. At the end of the vegetables on the right and in front of the lawn stood cold frames, where all of the dahlias started their life. These were flanked by old fashioned roses, in standard and bush form. Very much portraying the age of the plants, the colours were pale and weak, but their fragrances could still fill your head with intoxicating odours as you walked past. Just before the lawn to the left was a dwarf 'Egremont Russet' apple tree, which only ever had a small amount of blossom and even less apples. I only remember ever seeing a couple of apples on the tree, but its distinct 'nutty' flavour remains one of my favourites even now.

To the left, behind the tree was the entrance to a small, but beautiful rock garden, at the centre of which was my favourite part of the garden: an ornamental pond. The rockery was approached from the lawn and was surrounded by a small horseshoe shaped path, allowing you to view the pool from three sides. The rockery was raised behind an eight inch wall, which fringed the path, allowing visitors to sit just above the water's level. The first thing you noticed as you approached the rockery was a small, ten by eight inches, concrete plaque, with a poem engraved upon it. The inscription read:

> *The dawn of the morn for glory,*
> *The hush of the night for peace,*
> *In the garden at eve' says the story,*
> *God walks and his smile brings release.*
>
> **Anon.**

I have sat at the side of the pond and read those words so many times they are etched deep into my memory. It may also be because I feel they portray my feelings about the garden at Home Farm so well. The garden was never more peaceful than when sitting at the edge of the pool, on a warm summer's day, scouring the water's surface for signs of life. Most of the pool was filled with an oxygenating weed and a lily pad, which threw up an endless supply of pink flowers. It was just the far end of the pond that remained clear; the spot where Grampy would drop a pinch of biscuit crumbs every morning. I always marvelled at the way in which the surface tension of the water would disperse the crumbs in every direction, as soon as they touched the water. I didn't have to wait long before half a dozen goldfish rose from the depths ready for their breakfast. The feeding frenzy would be closely watched by frogs, with bulging eyes, peering just above the water from beneath a lily pad. Water boatmen were oblivious to what was happening as they raced each other around the pond.

When I was fourteen, Uncle Les added a dozen crucian carp to the pond, with compliments from one of our fishing trips. Crucians are a medium sized member of the carp family that don't grow very large, like their relatives the common and mirror carp. The young are a golden bronze, with distinctive orange fins: very attractive and ideal for Grampy's pond. The fish were soon at home, frequently feeding on the biscuit, slowly slipping to the surface with mouths open wide ready to suck in the crumbs. I knew what crucians ate in the wild and realised biscuit crumbs were not going to be enough, so I started to feed them small pieces of bread from the kitchen and worms from the garden. Much to my delight I soon found they were willing to eat straight out of my fingers. Within twelve months they were becoming very tame. All I had to do was wiggle my finger at the water's edge and they would swim up to discover what was going on and start to gently nibble my finger. Within a short space of time I discovered I could even pick them up out of the water, without any resistance whatsoever; for me this was a magical feeling.

To the far side of the opposite lawn stood a large 'Bramley' apple tree, about ten feet in diameter and fifteen feet tall. It is without doubt the most prolific apple tree I have ever come across, bearing several hundred large fruit each year without fail. Each apple on its own could weigh up to a pound in weight. You could always tell when the apples were ripe and ready for picking. They would turn a speckled yellow colour and develop a thick greasy wax all over. When they reached this condition, given the slightest of twists, they would fall off easily into your hand. They stored brilliantly as well, keeping for many months on newspaper placed on the floor of one of the bedrooms. They were almost sweet enough to eat raw, but were at their best in one of Gran's celebrated apple pies. That is as long as you could avoid the cloves she insisted on adding to the stewed fruit. If Grampy left the picking too late in the season, you had to be careful of wasps, which were eating their way through the over ripe fruit. Grampy regularly put out a wasp trap on the lawn. It was a Victorian bell shaped container made from glass, in which he put sugared water, or jam. The bell stood on four legs and its only entrance was from underneath. Once inside the bell the wasps were too daft or disorientated to find their way out. I was always fascinated by the dozens of wasps trying to escape through the sides of the jar, only to eventually fall into the water and meet their sticky end!

Beyond the Bramley tree the garden was, for as long as I can remember, always wild and overgrown, with brambles and ferns.

As a boy it was an excellent environment to explore. Once you were at the top of the garden there was a path which circumnavigated the house. This was a source of entertainment in itself, just running around the outside of the house or chasing or being chased by Graham. At the back of the house the garden was very much smaller and surprisingly nowhere near so ordered. In fact, I would even go as far as saying it was quite overgrown and untidy. There was a large detached coal house, a lean-to shed, the remnants of a pigsty from the war years, a well-used timber-framed greenhouse and the dreaded 'Dunny'.

Originally Home Farm did not have any services connected, and the only one it received before it was demolished was electricity. There was no gas and water was always fetched from a pump 'out the back' while the toilet was a tiny brick built building at the bottom of the garden. All of the bedrooms contained a chamber pot or 'gazzunder'; there was no way anyone would get to the toilet and back unscathed during the night. For me and, I suspect, for my brothers, sister and cousins it was a nightmare to use during the day, let alone the night! For those of you who have not been lucky enough to experience Home Farm's toilet facilities, it was like a 'portaloo' but far worse. The toilet can best be described as a bucket underneath a wooden bench with a hole in. The building itself was about three feet by five feet and once the door was shut, it was as dark as night. If you were brave and spent more than two or three minutes in there, your eyes did eventually become accustomed to the low level of light with a minimum amount creeping in underneath the door. I don't think I ever spent long enough in there for my eyes to become adjusted to the light; I could not hold my breath for longer than a minute. Light wasn't the only thing creeping in either, there were spiders galore, which, admittedly when the door was shut, you couldn't see. If all of this wasn't bad enough, we had to put up with 'Bronco' toilet paper – very similar to greaseproof paper, but much shinier. I suppose using it wasn't too bad. It was certainly a lot better than using sheets of newspaper when Gran's supply of 'Bronco' ran out! Of course this toilet didn't have the technology of a portaloo and it had to be emptied every week by the 'Jam pot men'. They usually called to collect the bucket and swap it for a 'clean' one, on a Tuesday morning. Only once did they catch me while I was in there – what were the chances of that happening?

I am sure you can understand why I tried to make sure I didn't need to use the Home Farm facilities. I have to admit though, boys were luckier than girls, because if we only wanted a 'number one', we could stand and use the designated place for peeing in the garden. This was to the back and right of the main house in the ruins of a previous property. The far corner was where Grampy stored his horse manure for the garden and the rest of it was used as an open-air urinal. There were always plenty of nettles around, which I would do my best to flatten. It never really did any good. In fact I often felt they thrived on the attention we all gave them.

To the left, separated from the main garden by a hedge, was what Gran and Grampy always referred to as the Fordrift or Fordrough. I have recently discovered it means 'a medieval farm track', which would make sense. It was a twenty feet wide strip of grass land, stretching the whole length of the garden. I often used it as a cricket pitch, because of its location and size, whereas Uncle Les and his friend used it as a car park and garage. Apparently it was an ideal place for getting the car off the road and being able to work on it. When you finally couldn't get the car to work at all, it was somewhere safe to leave it. For as long as I can recall, there were two old cars parked up close to the house: an old model-T Ford belonging to Les and a flashy soft-top sports car belonging to someone called Ken. Those cars were both driven to Weston-Super-Mare and back, by me, on more than one occasion (sadly only in my imagination).

The house itself was pretty standard. It had two small reception rooms at the front, one being the main living room and the other the 'back room', which was not really used. It contained a green leather suite and a sideboard, with an aquarium sitting upon it. I only ever went in there to look at the goldfish and to borrow some games or books out of the sideboard. They were games which I have not seen since, such as Totopoly and "Does Grandfather Sleep with his Whiskers Under or Over the Sheets?" Totopoly was a board game made by Waddingtons, based on the events leading up to, and during, a horse race and the latter was a card game whose rules I didn't get to learn. Whenever I did venture into the back room it always had a distinctive musty smell, even during the summer months.

If I wasn't outside in the garden I would usually spend my time in the main living room. It had a three piece suite, a dining table and four chairs and a television in the corner by the window. For me the most interesting feature was the fireplace, which many years before would have been the main focus of the house. It was a small open fire with an oven above and enclosed warming shelves to the side, which at one time would have been used for cooking. When I was little Gran already had a 'Belling' electric oven, so I only ever remember her using the fire surround for putting stale bread in. After several days the bread would be baked hard and ready to mix with and supplement the dog's food. At the side of the hearth was a fireplace companion set, comprising the usual things: a small brush, shovel and poker, plus an extendable toasting fork. On cold winter's evenings, when the fire was roaring, Gran would let us use the fork to make toast. It wasn't ever perfect – generally over done, but with lashings of butter on it always tasted pretty special. Whenever we picked up the fork, Grampy for some unknown reason would say, "Who stuck the fork in George's eye?"

Above the fireplace, nailed to the wall just below the ceiling line, was a dragonfly. It was about six inches in length and had clearly been up on the wall for many years, because although complete and still in perfect condition, it was devoid of any colour. I had not seen a dragonfly before, so would stare at it for ages, wondering what it would have been like in real life. I didn't get to find out for at least another twenty years. Despite spending many days in the countryside and numerous mornings sitting on the canal bank fishing, not once did I ever see a dragonfly. I felt it was because farmers in the 1960s used herbicides and pesticides recklessly, without feelings or regard for the flora and fauna. Since the decline of their use, dragonflies and damselflies are a regular sight wherever there is water. This even includes my old back garden in Solihull Road. Southern Hawkers and several types of damselfly, both blue and red, could regularly be seen there throughout the spring and summer months.

The kitchen at Home Farm was not my favourite room in the house, mainly because it was cold and dark, and contained the 'bogey hole'. This was a very dark and scary cupboard under the stairs. I cannot even tell you what Gran stored in there, because I was too frightened to look. The kitchen had a red tiled floor and a beamed ceiling, from which large meat hooks hung. This was a reminder of Mom's childhood days when Grampy would hang up sides of bacon, obtained from the pigs he kept. There was a tiny window in the corner of the kitchen, covered by a wooden shutter, which when opened and looked out towards the dreaded 'Dunny'. Underneath the window stood the washday boiler, into which Gran would add her 'Dolly blue' and clothes. Thursday was always washday, and yes washing did take all day long, generally from morning through to night. To the right of the boiler was the old oven, a proper hole in the wall oven, very similar to the pizza ovens one often sees in Italy. Needless to say, I never saw Gran use it at all, unless perhaps for storing things in. A Belfast sink and wooden draining board were located on the far wall, under a small glass window overlooking the backyard. There were no real storage cupboards as we have today, just low level shelving hidden by plastic curtains.

Off the kitchen to the right, as you came through the door from the living room, was the dairy. This had to be the most remarkable room there was. As Gran didn't have a fridge, the dairy was the place where she kept all of her food fresh. On opening the door there were two or three steps down into the dairy, the majority of which was set below ground level. The room was 'L' shaped; the part missing being taken up by the hole in the wall oven in the kitchen. On all sides of the wall there was what I can only describe as one long continuous, three feet wide concrete table. The table was solid, apart from eight or nine arches, which were perhaps four feet wide and two feet deep. I imagine the arches went right back to the walls. I didn't know for certain, because I never looked too closely; I wasn't sure what was living in them. Everything below ground level was covered in large red terracotta tiles. I knew it was ground level from the window on the far wall. It always appeared to be strange from the outside, having a window that was level with the grass. It did serve its purpose though, because even on the warmest of summer days, milk, bread and meat would all stay cool and fresh. Just like the 'Dunny' and the 'Back room' this was another place I did not spend much time in. When Gran asked me to fetch the bread, my feet barely touched the floor. I was always scared of what might come out from the cold darkness of the arches!

There was a door in the corner of the main living room, which opened up to reveal a set of very narrow, hazardous stairs. The steps took a sharp 90 degree turn to the right, meaning each individual step narrowed to a point at the right hand side. When the door was closed, there was very little light, making climbing the stairs extremely precarious.  If you managed to successfully negotiate the staircase, there were three bedrooms at the top. Needless to say, the bedrooms were not somewhere I went very often either. Gran and Grampy slept in the front bedroom, the back bedroom was for the lodger and the third one, to the side of the house and above the dairy, was for the apples. The two rooms used for sleeping both contained a fireplace and a 'gazzunder', jug and washing bowl as standard. Gran's room was the best but scary nonetheless, particularly when her dentures were left in a glass of water on the bedside table. When you are not much taller that the table itself, looking at teeth through glass, is not a pleasant experience. The glass and water always seemed to magnify the contents significantly so much so it invariably left me wondering how Gran ever managed to get the dentures in to her mouth.

I hope I have managed to portray my range of feelings for Home Farm. The fact I loved the enchantment of the garden, but was unsettled by the mysteries of the house. The house had too many dark corners and held too many fears for me; never more so than after dark. With no street lights anywhere near to the house, unless it was a moonlit starry night, outside was pitch black. When home time was imminent I had to summon up all of my courage to leave. It wasn't too bad if Mom or Dad were with me, but on my own the 400 yards to the bus stop was worse than any ghost train at the local fair. Walking down the cinder path towards the main Stratford Road was the easier part, but stumbling along the grass verge of the main road was when it got worse. With very few cars on the road, rarely was there any respite from headlights. It only took a couple of minutes but often seemed much longer, when I saw shadows and heard rustling noises in the hedgerows. Warm damp evenings were exceptionally eventful, when you would hear the occasional crunching of a snail's shell underfoot. Despite my misgivings about the house and an uncomfortable journey home each week, at nine o'clock the following Saturday I would always be very keen to get back to Home Farm. Between these visits on a Saturday and fishing on Sundays, many of my weekends were always busy.

My memories of Gran were of a diminutive, elderly lady with short grey hair, who never seemed to stop moving. Gran permanently seemed busy: cooking, cleaning or looking after her grandchildren. Regardless of her small size she was always a very strong character, rarely succumbing to sickness. I can only recall one time when she was ill and confined to her bed. Even when she was well into her seventies Gran rode her bicycle everywhere, cleaned houses to earn extra money and looked after her grandchildren on a regular basis. The one part of Gran's life I will always remember, as clearly as anything, is her bike. Gran always had a flowery plastic rain hat tied over the back wheel to prevent her from getting splashed in the rain. Gran was always on the go, but still had time to take in lodgers. They were usually students from horticultural college, on work experience at the local garden centre. This was 'Sydenhams' (now known as Notcutts), located a couple of hundred yards down, on the opposite side of the road, towards Stratford-upon-Avon. It was very handily positioned for them, and they came in useful as Grampy got older, often doing a bit of 'rough' digging for him.

I say as he got older, but in all of my memories Grampy was always old. I suppose at the time of my earliest memories he was already in to his seventies. He was not a particularly tall man, I suppose around five feet eight or nine. He had short balding hair, swept across the top of his head, a little like Bobby Charlton, if you can remember his hairstyle. His hair partly hid the many freckles on the top of his head, but you rarely saw them because he seldom went anywhere without his flat cap. When out and about in the garden, greenhouse or shed he would usually wear a light brown 'lab' coat. In the right hand pocket he always kept his silver and mother of pearl cigarette case and in the other pocket his trusty penknife. These two essential accessories went everywhere with him. Grampy had a very distinctive manner in the way in which he took out one of his Park Drive cigarettes. He would click the case shut and then tap the end of the cigarette on the outside of it, before eventually lighting up. This was done religiously every time he wanted a smoke. Grampy didn't always finish his cigarettes. There was many a time I would sit and watch as he fell asleep in his armchair, letting his cigarette burn slowly in his mouth. It was often stuck to his top lip with the ash longer than the cigarette that remained. I could see quite clearly the red embers close to the rest of the cigarette and the ash hanging precariously, ready to drop at the slightest movement.  His steel penknife was always in use, whether it be to cut lettuce, sharpen sticks or peel apples.

Grampy was almost always in the garden or the greenhouse. I should know, because wherever he went I would follow, close behind. Whether it was down the garden to lift a bucket of new potatoes for dinner, or into the greenhouse to prick out seedlings, I was never far away. I would even follow him outside, to stand behind him, while he 'watered the nettles'. It was almost as though we were attached by a piece of elastic, so much so I was often referred to as 'his shadow'. Grampy taught me all he knew about gardening. I would help out with planting seeds in the greenhouse, pricking out, potting on, taking cuttings and bedding out. He gave me my own piece of the garden to grow vegetables, showing me everything I needed to do to obtain crops just like his. He really was a stickler for doing jobs correctly. I had to use a line to ensure straight edges when rough digging and he would check I had removed every last weed, before I could rake it flat.  Raking was an art in itself. Everything had to be as flat as a snooker table and the soil was broken up with the back of the rake to ensure a good tilth suitable for sowing tiny seeds in. Rows were in regimented lines, a set distance apart, and seeds were sown at depths of pinpoint accuracy. It might sound relatively easy, but the patch of land I was given lay at the bottom of the garden, towards the road. It hadn't been cultivated for years and was full of 'twitch' grass and dandelions. If you left the smallest piece of root from either of these plants, they would soon be back with a vengeance, strangling the tiny seedlings you had created.  I had a fairly large plot, big enough to grow potatoes, carrots, peas, lettuce, carrots, radishes, beetroot and dwarf French beans, all of the same varieties Grampy grew.

Every Saturday as I walked up the path, I would stop alongside my plot to see how it had changed in a week. The first job was to spot whether seeds planted the previous week had started to poke through the soil and then I would measure how tall the peas had grown in seven days or how much the beetroot had increased in size. If you have never planted seeds before and anticipated their growth, it is hard to explain the excitement when you first spot seedlings bursting through the soil or compost. Even now, fifty years on, I still get enthusiastic about the first sighting of new seedlings. I will often stand in wonderment, marvelling at the spectacle and miracle of nature. You can imagine, fifty years ago, the pride of a nine year old, harvesting the crops he had grown and skipping home with them to Mom and Dad for the family to eat. The crops that I grew did so well, there were always more lettuce and beans than we could eat as a family. Any extras were sold to Mr and Mrs Fleming who were close neighbours, making me a few extra pence in pocket money each week.

During the spring Grampy and I would spend many hours pottering around in the greenhouse. It was a typical Victorian lean-to greenhouse, built up against an outside wall of the old property in the garden. The lower part of the structure, up to the height of the benching, was made of wood. The rest was glass in a timber frame. Grampy started off all of his seeds in the greenhouse, in homemade potting compost; there were no bags of John Innes or peat based compost to use. Later I would watch intensely as Grampy pricked out tiny seedlings, always seemingly with a half smoked Park Drive cigarette hanging from his top lip. When spring was over and the many trays of bedding plants were in place in the borders, the greenhouse would be filled with tomato, cucumber and pelargonium plants. Growing plants must have been in the family, because Grampy's Dad, my Great Grandfather, was a keen horticulturist as well. Mr Arthur Carter was Honorary Secretary of the National Viola and Pansy Society in the early 1900s and was awarded a First Class Certificate from the Society in 1922 for the viola 'Mrs A Carter'. This was his own seedling, a variety known as a 'fancy viola'. It is unobtainable today, but apparently was a stunning dense violet purple, with ground marble and striped French grey. Grampy's brother George followed in his father's footsteps, becoming Secretary of the Society for about thirty years.

I believe 'showing' plants and vegetables must have been in the Carter blood, because Grampy often told stories about his own experiences of 'showing' vegetables. He never really talked about any prizes or success, but more about how he grew and prepared the vegetables for entering into the show. The two stories that stick in my mind most strongly are his endeavours to produce prize tomatoes and runner beans. For those unaccustomed to the rules and objectives of showing vegetables, there are a few important pointers to ensure success. Most vegetables are shown in pairs or groups of a larger size. Generally whatever you show it is not just the size that counts. More important is consistency between each item: uniformity in size, shape and quality. Above all the vegetables must be fresh. A good judge will always check the freshness of an exhibit by snapping a bean to ensure they are not 'stringy' or cutting through a beetroot to see if it is 'woody'. Grampy used to explain how he went to great lengths to ensure this consistency. He recalled how he would wrap tomatoes in silver paper, so they would ripen simultaneously on the vine and how he grew runner beans down tubing hung from the canes to make sure they were straight. He may not have realised it at the time but I took in every word he said and every sentiment he portrayed. This was to prove extremely helpful to me later in life, when I showed produce and flowers in a local village show.

After spending most of the day in the garden, Grampy and I would retire to the living room to watch the wrestling on TV, or play dominoes together. He taught me to play 'Newmarket' and my favourite 'Fives and Threes'. Winning the latter game required not only logic and guile for getting rid of your seven dominoes first, but also numerical skills to work out the scores. The objective of the game is for players to attach a domino from their hand to one end of those already played, so that the sum of the two end dominoes is divisible by five and/or three. One point is scored for each time five and/or three can be divided into the sum of the two dominoes. For example six at one end and three at the other makes nine, which is divisible by three, three times and hence is worth three points. Double 5 at one end and 5 at the other makes 15 which is divisible by three five times and divisible by five three times and hence worth eight points. The running total score was kept on a cribbage board, with golf tees used as markers. I think I enjoyed this game more because of the arithmetic skills needed and because of the terminology used. There was 'Big Emma' for double six, the 'Working man's three' for five, four and 'one for his knob' for playing your last domino, before the other player. After a steep learning curve, competition between us was always very tight. We would usually match each other point for point, with Grampy forever saying "Damn the man who is fust", whenever we were level pegging. Even clearing the dominoes away was fun when we played 'Put em in the box'. If we weren't playing games I would spend time building towers that Grampy had shown me how to construct. The easiest was balancing all 28 tiles on two legs in a structure which I always thought looked like The Tower of London, but the ultimate was balancing them precariously on just one tile, standing on its end.

If you think this is clever, Grampy taught me something even more amazing: how to balance the point of a needle on a pinhead. All you need is the needle, pin, a cork and two dining forks. First you stick the needle into the bottom of the cork. Then place the two forks into the side of the cork, one on either side, with the handles pointing downwards towards the needle. After that you will find it easy to balance the point of the needle on the pin head, with the forks acting as counter balances. I suppose having a similar effect as the pole used by a high wire artist. The other party trick he showed me was one I have not done myself and is slightly cruel, something that would be unacceptable today. Using his penknife Grampy fashioned a dumbbell from a match stick and two small pieces of cork. After catching a wasp in his handkerchief, he stuck a needle through the hard shell on its back and then placed the needle into a cork. This gave the impression the wasp was standing upright on its back legs, like a soldier in a yellow and black striped uniform. When offered the homemade dumbbell, the wasp grabbed it with all of its six legs and began to juggle, as though it were an accomplished drum majorette. I must say it did look astonishing, but I have to admit it is not something I would ever try and repeat. Dad always taught me to be respectful of all life and to treat even the tiniest of creatures with kindness. This is why I will not kill spiders. I am not fond of those large ones, with huge hairy legs and beady eyes that just seem to appear from nowhere when the weather gets cold. Just like Dad used to, I will catch them in a glass and put them outside. I have a feeling it doesn't do a great deal of good, because how many times have you taken the same actions, only to find the same spider back in the house a few days later? It is almost as though they have a homing instinct and know exactly how to get back 'home'.

If we weren't playing dominoes there was always time for storytelling and party tricks. Usually the stories were about Grampy; stories which Mom and Dad said were exaggerated for effect. I am not sure who to believe, but I like to think Grampy was telling the truth. Perhaps some of the fishing tales were embellished a little, but doesn't every angler do that? Uncle Les always did! I would sit and listen intensely about how Grampy used to fish the 'cut' in Hockley Heath, the very same canal I fished years later. He could walk from Home Farm across the fields at the back of the house towards Illshaw Heath. While the sun rose Grampy fished for roach with hempseed, using horse hair as line. Anglers stopped using horsehair for line, long before I started to fish, so I find it incredible that they ever managed to catch anything with it at all. I recall hearing one tale many times, it was of Grampy catching a huge bream the size of a meat dish. To catch it he used a piece of bread paste as big as his thumb nail. Grampy would indicate an approximate size of the fish by pointing the finger on his left hand and using his right index finger, laid part of the way up his left arm. It was usually placed somewhere near his elbow, occasionally lower, but more often than not higher. Mom and Dad said it wasn't as big as Grampy remembers, but I am not so sure. Today there are many bream in the local canals weighing around four pound or more; I have even recently caught some myself. He may have overstated the truth on occasions, but in this instance I don't feel he did.

At breakfast time my Gran would walk across the fields herself and take him a warm bacon and egg sandwich, wrapped in greaseproof paper. This was dedication, but my Gran was a traditional housewife of her time. She made sure she looked after the men in her family, first and foremost. I know this only too well, as my Mom often recalled how she felt her brother Les was Gran's favourite. If there was an extra piece of apple pie in the dish after dinner, she would say, "You can't have that, I am saving it for Les." I believe this is why Mom tried not to have favourites amongst her children, making sure we were all treated the same. I am not sure Gra would agree with this, as quite recently he told me he was the only one of us children not to go on a school trip. It obviously sticks in Gra's memory and caused him some hurt. Perhaps he should write his own book; who knows we may get a whole new perspective of life in the Day family!

Another interesting story Grampy relayed many times gave me an insight into how generations have changed. Between 1935 and 1937 Grampy was employed to help install the aquariums at

Dudley Zoo. I am not sure how much work was done in the 30s, but Grampy used to recall how he would spend time each day polishing his spade until he could see his face in it. Then he would cook bacon and eggs on it over a brazier, all washed down with a cup of tea made by pouring boiling water over a spoonful of condensed milk and tea leaves. Gran would send Grampy off to work each day with everything he needed for his cup of tea, wrapped in greaseproof paper. It sounds pretty disgusting to me now, but when I was small I always wanted to try it out for myself. Grampy must have been used to drinking this type of tea, which probably explains why he had some other rather strange tastes in food. Grampy was never happier than when he was eating a jar of pickled walnuts, a pig's trotter or a plate of tripe and onions. I have stood and watched him many times while he ate a plate of tripe, usually without his teeth! This shouldn't have been a surprise because he always told me, "The thing I like about tripe is, you don't have to chew it." Never mind the taste eh!

Grampy did not have the best of health when I knew him. He had developed lead poisoning earlier in his life, a consequence of the lead paint he used as a sign writer and interior decorator. By all accounts he was seriously ill and off work for a couple of years. I am certain this also had an impact on his health later in life. In the early 1960s Grampy developed trigeminal neuralgia. Neuralgia is pain in one or more nerves, caused by a change in the neurological structure or function of the nerve. Lead poisoning is known to affect the peripheral nervous system, especially motor nerves. In the case of trigeminal neuralgia the affected nerves are responsible for sensing touch, temperature and pressure sensations in the facial area, from the jaw to the forehead. Grampy's disorder caused him short episodes of excruciating pain, usually lasting for a couple of minutes and generally on the right side of his face. Grampy described the occurrences as "sharp stabbing pains; like lightning shooting up his cheek". Simple actions can trigger an attack, such as eating, talking, making facial expressions or washing the face. With Grampy it appeared to be the sensation of a cool breeze on his face, which meant at the time he had to wear a scarf whenever he ventured outside. The attacks occurred "out of the blue" and would then disappear as quickly as they came. Apparently neuralgia is more difficult to treat than other types of pain because it does not respond well to normal analgesics. I can remember being scared, seeing him with his head in his hands and tears running down his face, not really knowing what was happening to my precious Grampy. After a couple of years of suffering he had surgery to the nerves in his face and the neuralgia disappeared as quickly as it came on.

Not all of my memories at Home Farm were centred on my grandparents – I had many great times on my own, as well as with Gra and Cousin Jo. I spent many happy hours exploring the garden and surrounding fields, searching for wild flowers, birds and butterflies, probably much like Mom did when she was young. In early autumn the garden was always full of colourful butterflies, flitting from one Michaelmas daisy plant to another. One year I was lucky enough to see a spectacular and rare Swallowtail butterfly amongst the hedgerows, down by the gate. Mesmerised by its beauty I can remember chasing it through the garden, trying to get one last glimpse of its vibrant colours and wonderfully delicate tails. Autumn also allowed me to throw 'apples on a stick'. With the apple tree down by the gate, it was so tall there was no way of picking the ripe fruit. I could only wait for the fruit to fall from the tree, which meant most of the fruit became bruised and unusable. If you were useless at throwing, like I was as a child, you could still get the apples to travel huge distances. This was done by piercing them on to the end of a stick, around two to three feet in length. The stick was flicked quickly from behind your back and over your shoulder. When the stick stopped, the apple would carry on in a forward direction. The trick was to get a 45 degree angle of trajectory. If you got it right and the speed of your arm was quick enough, the apple would disappear over the hedge, out of the garden past the Fordrift and into the field, some one hundred yards away! On the other hand if you didn't get the point of release quite right, or if the apple wasn't fixed to the stick properly, it could go anywhere to the front, back or side. Gra found this out to his cost on many occasions, with a half rotten apple whizzing past his ear, as I tried to break the Home Farm world record.

I don't ever remember my 'favourite' brother ever being injured from our games, but there was one other time when he remembers getting hit. Apparently we were throwing one of Grampy's turnips over the hedge, to and from the garden into the Fordrift – Gra on one side and me on the other. The hedge was so tall and dense, there was no way of knowing when or where the said turnip was going to appear. The rules were, before letting go we had to shout "coming over", so the other was prepared for the huge root vegetable dropping from the sky. Gra has consistently professed that on this particular occasion I deliberately forgot to say the magic words and he ended up in tears with a large lump on his head. I have no recollection of this whatsoever, so there are only two possibilities. Either I have blotted the incident from my memory bank as a self-survival mechanism, or Gra was trying to get me into trouble once again! Personally I tend to think it is the latter; it seemed to me at the time that Gra was always trying to get Mom and Dad to think the worst of me.

I have already mentioned the football games down on the green, when I supposedly told everyone else not to let him play. Also there was the time when we were washing our hands upstairs in the bathroom, ready for Sunday lunch. We were both standing side by side, sleeves rolled up, soaping our hands as we had been taught. Suddenly, out of nowhere Gra whispered, "Splash me, go on splash me." Of course being the good little lad that I was, I refused. This didn't stop my little brother though, because he came back at me saying, "Malc, splash me, splash me, go on splash me." After about the third time of asking I got fed up with his persistent wittering and splashed him as requested, only to hear him say, "I am going to tell Mom and Dad of you." My heart sank – the ungrateful little beggar! I had done just as he had begged me to and now he was going to "dob" me in. Fortunately as quickly as my heart had sunk, it rose again once I heard Mom's voice shout out, "Oh no you don't my lad, I heard you. I have been listening at the top of the stairs." For once Mom and Dad believed me, but only because they had witnessed exactly what had happened. Every other time the decision has always gone in Gra's favour.

The wonderful days spent at Home Farm and the wonderful times spent with Grampy have shaped my life forever, not least in respect of my love for gardening. After I left home and married Heather, I immediately began to take a pride in my own garden. When we first got married and lived over at Hartshill, in Warwickshire, I even took on an allotment and grew vegetables, so that we became self-sufficient. Every year, in September, the 'Hartshill Allotment and Garden Society' held a 'Flower and Vegeatable Show' at the local 'Stag and Pheasant' hostelry. Yes you have read it correctly and no it isn't my misspelling. Each year the schedule of show categories and the posters advertising the show had it as the 'Flower and Vegeatable Show'. This was despite my many years of complaining, even when I was Chairman of the organisation. Wishing to be an active member of the Society and to support the local show, I decided to exhibit some of my produce after the first twelve months. I entered carrots, parsnips, beetroot, onions, beans, potatoes, marrows: every category I could. For five months I had also been growing a fuchsia in my little greenhouse. The greenhouse was only six feet by six feet, quite small, but all we could afford at the time. I had bought the fuchsia as a small rooted cutting from 'Fuchsia man', who lived opposite us in Charnwood Drive. I remember it well, it was called 'Perry Park', a white and lavender blue single. The 'Fuchsia man' gave me some advice on how to get the best out of it and when to stop 'nipping out the growing shoots', in order to have it flowering at its best, in time for the show. When it came around to show day, the fuchsia was almost a perfect sphere, approximately three feet in diameter and covered in hundreds of perfect blooms. I was ready to display my pride and joy at the show, but it was so large I had to take the side out of my greenhouse, because it wouldn't fit through the door. That evening when we were all gathered in the bar at the Stag and Pheasant for the results, there was a buzz in the air. All of the old experienced gardeners were standing around waiting to see who had won. If I recall correctly the two top prizes for the most points in the show and the Best Garden went to Bert Wilson. He was like most of the allotment holders in the village: retired and with plenty of time on their hands. Mind you I was not expecting what happened next! The prize for the 'Best Exhibit in Show' went to me and my massive fuchsia. That was just the beginning, because the following year I won 'Best Novice' and in the following two consecutive years I won Best Garden in Hartshill village. Hopefully Grampy would have been very proud of what I achieved, mainly thanks to him.

This success undoubtedly has to be an example of nature encouraged by plenty of nurture from Grampy. His enthusiasm for horticulture, attention to detail and insistence on having everything precise and orderly has definitely left its mark on me. I don't feel it was just gardening he influenced in my life either. The many stories about his fishing exploits had to have an effect on my love of angling.

# Chapter 8

## OPPORTUNITY KNOCKS

This chapter is about the more artistic side of my nature and my ability, or otherwise, to entertain through the arts both visual and performing. I suppose my introduction to the performing arts was at Cranmore Infant School when I was cast as a shepherd in the Christmas nativity play. It was hardly a leading role, but when I wore my brown dressing gown and a chequered tea towel on my head, I really looked the part. The icing on the cake was when Mom allowed me to take Gra's little woolly lamb on the day of the play to clutch under my right arm. This first time that I trod the boards was only a non-speaking part, but the next time I was given the opportunity to make an even bigger impact on the audience with a speaking part. It was in my final year at Shirley Heath Junior School in a play that involved a king and amongst other parts, five pixies. I was the 'white' pixie who had to portray a sense of fear during the production. I must say I was completely the right child to be cast in this part, because I was definitely petrified. I was undeniably an introvert, never liking to be the centre of attention. I can still remember my part as clearly as the day we performed it to the rest of the school. I was dressed in white tights, a white t-shirt and a white 'Noddy' hat made by Mom. My only line was, "I'm not scared of you", spoken while cautiously approaching the king and then retreating into the arms of the 'Brown' pixie played by my school pal Ron. Learning my line and plucking up the courage to deliver it in front of an audience was quite an ordeal for me.

While at school I was not very outgoing and always found it difficult to stand up at the front of the class and talk to the rest of my school friends. This was despite the fact almost daily I would stand amongst them and tell them a joke or funny story. I once used this to my advantage. It was on one occasion, in an English lesson at Harold Malley Grammar School, when everyone was asked to talk to the class for five minutes, on a subject of their own choice. When it came to my turn I had chosen a topic specifically to take the attention away from my inadequacies at public speaking: I spoke about rhubarb. It might seem a strange thing to talk about, but remember I was a keen gardener and just introducing the title to my class mates made them laugh. I remember my opening line quite clearly. It was intended to involve the class and put myself at ease, by doing 'what I did best'. "I am going to ask you to guess the title of my talk, but first I'll give you a clue. What is long and pink and used for stuffing tarts?" This was typical schoolboy humour of the 1960s, which made all of the lads in class roar with laughter. However, when I took a sideward glance at 'Miss' I could see she was not impressed and immediately knew I was in for a 'good hiding'.

I feel this was a key moment in my life, the moment when I realised what worked for me while speaking in public. The most important things are: to know what I am talking about, involve the audience and to add some humour. I have used this format frequently since that day, at weddings, anniversaries, leaving dos, seminar presentations and training sessions at work. Rarely has it let me down. I am definitely not the type of person who can 'blag' their way through a situation. Unlike some people, I always have to know what I am talking about. Furthermore I only ever speak if I have something to contribute. I am not one of those annoying people who always have to say something, just so others don't forget they are present.

I have said how at an early age I disliked getting up on stage and acting, but as I grew older I became quite accustomed to role play, particularly dressing-up in women's clothes! It was as though something had changed in my life, something which made me overcome my fears and embarrassment of play acting. I would like to think this is the point of my life when I discovered my metrosexuality, but I actually believe it was all started by my sister Sue bullying me. It was one Christmas, when I was aged about twenty and the whole family were at Sue's house on Christmas Day afternoon. There were probably about twenty of us altogether, including Uncle Les, his new lady friend and Heather, whom I had been going out with for just less than a year. While tea was being prepared everyone got tired of the games we were playing and the atmosphere fell a little flat. It was at this time that Sue made me dress up in her wedding dress, high heels and fur coat. After pinning up my shoulder length hair under a wig and applying some foundation and "lippy", I was forced out of the back door. Sue's plan was for me to knock on the front door and pretend I had come to see Les. It all worked rather well, with me ending up on Les' lap, much to his shock and embarrassment. It was several minutes before anyone in the room 'twigged' it was me, when they spotted my rather large slippers under the dress. Even Heather hadn't got a clue at the time.

Ever since then, realising that if done properly I could remain undetected without anyone recognising me, I have on occasions dressed up as a woman for charity. Probably the most dramatic was dressing up as a gangster's moll for 'Children in Need' along with two colleagues from work: Sean, as a second moll and Ash as the gangster. In just an hour and a half, at Corley motorway services on the M6 motorway, we collected over three hundred pounds. We would have stayed longer but the cold, damp, November weather wasn't conducive to tights and a feather boa! Before we left to come home I visited the gents' toilets to relieve myself. I made sure I went into a cubicle because I realised just what a logistical nightmare wearing tights can be! It took me approximately ten minutes to get the job done and make myself respectable; I shall never moan about women taking so long ever again! It was all made worthwhile by seeing the shock on the other men's faces, as I opened the cubicle door and wiggled my way to the exit.

Other creative pastimes I have been interested in have been drawing, painting, knitting and cooking. The last two areas are probably down to my Mom and Dad making us earn our pocket money. In a way I think I get my metrosexuality from Dad. He was always cooking Sunday dinners and baking; a lemon Madeira cake was his speciality. He wasn't scared to do knitting and embroidery either. Back in the 1950s these were usually considered to be hobbies women took up. No one would have dared to call Dad a sissy though! Even today I get great satisfaction from cooking and quite enjoyed knitting, when I produced pairs of booties and several cardigans for Kerry, my own daughter, when she was born.

Drawing and painting was something I didn't realise I was good at until I reached the age of 16. Although perhaps I should have tried it earlier seeing as Grampy was a decorator and sign writer by trade. The fifth year at Harold Malley was when I took my GCEs. Yes I do have that right, examinations taken used to be General Certificates of Education, until the Tories combined them with Certificates of Secondary Education (CSE), in the late 1980s. One of the subjects I was taking was Art and I was doing sculpture as my chosen topic. There were only a few of us doing this area of art; everyone else had preferred to take the History of Art. I definitely didn't want to do this because I was never any good at 'normal' history, so I was bound to be rubbish at this as well! Taking sculpture had its advantages. Our art teacher, Mr Malpas, affectionately known as 'The Walrus' because of his size and droopy moustache, told us, "Those doing the sculpture option will not be having a mock examination in January."

However on the day of the mock examinations, mine and the other three names were up on the list of attendees, along with everyone else. We were forced to sit down under examination conditions and answer a previous year's paper. When the invigilator said you may start and I turned the paper over, my heart sank. There were questions such as "Explain what a rubber kidney is used for?", "At what temperature should you have the kiln for firing a pot?", "Describe how you would make a teapot handle from clay." and "Write about the times and life of Joan Miro". These topics weren't ever on my radar. 'The Walrus', bless him, had never taught us any of the theory, we had just made models in class. After five minutes, I wrote at the top of the paper, "I can answer none of these questions. We have not covered these or any other topics in class." I then got up and walked out. The other three did at least try and put something on their papers, but received the same mark as I did, a big fat zero! One of them, my friend Mal, had stayed in the examination for nearly two hours and still was given no marks. By the way if you are thinking Mal stands for Malcolm it doesn't. Many people have thought the same, but it does in fact stand for 'malnutrition', because he was so painfully thin! Mal was also double-jointed. He would often sit on his stool in physics, with his right foot tucked behind his neck. With him sitting in front of me I couldn't concentrate on lessons properly, which is probably why I failed my physics GCE twice, despite obtaining 95 per cent in the practical examination.

Getting back to art, 'The Walrus' got the sack a few weeks later to be replaced by Mr Mathews. He was a really talented artist and decided to put everyone in for the same examination: 'drawing and still life'. Mr Mathews was so passionate about his subject, he inspired us all. He gave us regular art homework, which was unheard of, and we all began to enjoy the subject. In a matter of only a few weeks we were producing some great drawings. I went on to obtain a reasonable grade and continued to draw until I got married. There were many things I stopped doing when I got married... enough said.

I have already mentioned being a member of the school's recorder club, with Lynn, in a previous chapter. The whole class had an opportunity to show their potential and join the recorder club when we were all given recorder lessons. Only those who picked up the technique quickly were asked to continue. That was me, Lynn and a couple of others, whose names escape me! The chosen few were given extra lessons after school and I certainly practised regularly at home in order to improve and learn tunes off by heart. We were always playing in assembly, which made us feel quite special. I learnt to read music, which was a big advantage when I moved up to Harold Malley. My new grammar school had an excellent reputation for music at the time, with an exceptional brass band that played concerts at the local Civic Hall. I looked forward to joining the band, perhaps playing something like a trumpet or trombone. The school had its own supply of instruments, which were loaned out to boys while they were pupils there. I was hoping to get one of those. Sadly, for me, all of the school's own instruments were taken and of course there was no way Mom and Dad could afford to buy one. I remember going in to the local music shop and obtaining a catalogue of instruments for sale. I spent hours looking through it. Staring at the entry level trombone, hoping and wishing. It cost £30, which was far too much for me to even consider buying. Saving up my pocket money would have been a waste of effort. By the time I'd have saved enough, I would have left school long ago. My only hope was for Dad to win the pools – not much chance of that then.

After the disappointment, I had to be satisfied with continuing to play the recorder. The school's recorder group, never quite had the celebrity status of the school band! My biggest fan was Gran, who always said I was so good on the recorder I should be appearing on 'Opportunity Knocks'. I don't ever remember playing the recorder in front of her, so how she knew I was so brilliant is beyond me, but she clearly meant what she said. Opportunity Knocks was a television talent show originally hosted by Hughie Green, with the winning acts decided upon, not by a panel of experts, but by the viewing public. It was one of the first shows to do this, way before 'X-Factor' and 'Britain's Got Talent'. A large part of the show was gauging the reaction of the studio audience by using the 'clap-o-meter'. This didn't count towards the final result, but gave an indication as to who might be the favourite to return the following week. Previous participants included such huge names as Su Pollard, Paul Daniels, Darren Day, Mary Hopkin, Bonnie Langford, Les Dawson, Little and Large, Frank Carson, Bobby Crush, Max Boyce and Pam Ayres. How my Gran thought I could compete against such eminent entertainers used to puzzle me, until Heather and I became grandparents. When your grandchildren are born the bond is quite special, like no other you have experienced before. It must have been like this for Gran, almost believing I could achieve the impossible.

Many of you will recognise the participants listed as going on to be really famous, but I am sure for every one of them appearing on Opportunity Knocks there were many other talented people who never made it. For example the pianist Bobby Crush made six winning appearances on Opportunity Knocks in the early 1970s and received the Variety Club of Great Britain award for 'Best New Artist' of 1972. However around the same time there was a similar talent, local to Solihull, who also could have found fame and fortune, but did not have the same opportunity. I first came across him in the Red Lion public house in Earlswood, where we had our weekly angling club meetings. I didn't ever get to find out his name, but being only 18 inches tall he was easily recognisable. I am certain his height, or lack of it, had a lot to do with why he was less successful than Bobby Crush. Thankfully things are improving and people with disabilities today have greater opportunities than forty years ago.

This tiny man came into the Red Lion every Thursday evening, our club night, with a friend and played the keyboard all night. He was accompanied by what appeared to be his friend or manager. The friend would set up his keyboard for him, act as compere and manage his drinks. I say manage his drinks because the guy was so popular with everyone in the bar that they would buy him his favourite tipple for playing their requests. He was so versatile, an unbelievable talent. He could play any genre of music and whether it was classical, music hall or pop, he held everyone in the pub spell-bound. He did not need any sheet music either and rarely was there a tune he didn't know. One evening I asked his friend for a request and got talking to him about his companion. He told me he had come across the guy about four years earlier, recognised his talent and the rest was history; they had been playing the pubs ever since.

It wouldn't be very politically correct today, but I made some remark about his size and was told he had grown since they first met. "When I first met him he was only a foot tall," his friend said. I was intrigued as to how such an unlikely couple had come together, so asked where they had met. "It was quite a chance meeting," he replied. "I was walking locally in Earlswood Woods, early one morning. I remember it clearly because the weather was absolutely atrocious, it was cold and wet. The rain was coming down in stair rods." Not trying to second guess what was coming next I kept quiet. He carried on by saying, "I was walking down towards the private lake, when I saw an elderly lady carrying a large wicker basket, amongst the bracken. She looked so weak and frail and I thought at the time, this is no place for you to be, in this dreadful weather. I approached her and asked if I could help at all." Apparently the conversation that followed was very difficult, because the old lady was extremely hard of hearing and the friend had to keep repeating himself. The old lady told him she was gathering wood for a fire to keep her warm. I couldn't see where the story was going, so asked him to explain further. He continued, "The old lady was so grateful to me, she said no one else had ever bothered to help her before. When we had filled her basket the old lady said she would grant me a wish. Only one wish, but it could be anything I wanted." Still confused, I remember saying, "And?"

"And that's when I ended up with a 12 inch pianist," he said. Bobby Crush, eat your heart out!!! (*This definitely works better when read aloud!*)

Dad always loved piano music; the piano forte was probably his favourite instrument. I don't necessarily think it was Mom's though, particularly after one Saturday afternoon when Dad came home from Birmingham with a pianola, complete with boxes full of rolls of music. A pianola, also known as player piano or autopiano, is as the names suggest a 'self-playing' piano. Our pianola was operated by large foot pedals, which activated a pneumatic mechanism. This in turn operated the piano keys via pre-programmed rolls of music, in the form of perforated paper. Mom may not have been keen, but Dad and I loved it. Dad managed to work the pedals perfectly, but me being significantly smaller found it quite difficult. The pedals were so hard to move I had to grip the underneath of the keyboard and almost stand on the pedals, just to get them moving. The speed at which you moved the pedals dictated the speed at which your chosen tune was played. Some of the shorter pieces were easy for me, but longer tunes almost came to a halt when I got overcome with fatigue.

Each of the rolls came with the lyrics printed down the side of the perforations in the paper. Once I became proficient with the pedals I could sing along with the words as well. There were literally dozens of melodies to choose from, but just three stick in my mind. They were, "I'm happy when I'm hiking", "Roses of Picardy" and "Spring Song", the very same tune I loved playing on the recorder. I suspect Mom not only hated the pianola, but also the singing that went with it. We used to play on it for hours and regularly formed an orderly queue to wait our turn. Our singing was actually quite good. By all accounts Dad had a lovely voice. I am not sure if it was the same time he was drunk and slid down the piano, but Gran always said he had the best amateur singing voice she had ever heard. However, I cannot recall him ever saying anything about Gran putting his name forward for Opportunity Knocks!

I must have inherited my voice from Dad, because Mom rarely sang. Probably the only time was when she had to sing as a forfeit, at Christmas. Like Dad, I have the voice of an angel. I was in the school choir at Shirley Heath and even got selected to join the St James Church Eucharist choir. I was ten at the time when Mr James Allen, the organist at the church, came to school looking for recruits. From my year there were three of us chosen, me, Derek and Ron of Brown pixie fame (my first acting part). At the time Mom was heavily involved with the church, particularly with the Women's Institute, so as far as I can remember I was actively encouraged to join. Choir practice was every Friday evening from about six o'clock until eight, above Mr Allen's shop in Shirley. He was the local chemist, so we would meet upstairs just before six, in a store room amongst bars of soap, tubes of toothpaste and boxes of condoms. Luckily choir practice was next door, otherwise I don't think we would have ever concentrated properly. I always looked forward to Friday nights, not because of the singing, but because the girls' practice was after ours and they would be waiting as we came out. While the average age of the boys in the choir was around 12, the girls were quite a bit older, probably 16 or 17 and there were some stunners. Having said this, I was scared silly of girls right up until the age of about 18. I put it down to going to an all-boys grammar school. A year after I became a chorister, Gra joined the church choir as well, so every week we were able to spend some 'quality' time together.

Sundays were a nine o'clock start for the church service, which meant we had to be there by about 08:30. I would go straight to the vestry and put on my purple cassock, white ruff and surplus. Everyone tried to get there early because there was only a limited number of each. If you were late you may not have had one at all, or worse still had to wear one that was far too large for you. The older members of the choir would always do their best to make sure everyone was suitably attired. However there was many a time one of us would trip up in front of the altar, because we were wearing cassocks that were far too long for us. All of this effort and humiliation generally went unrecognised and unrewarded. The Evensong choir, at the same church, got paid for their services. Not a lot I admit, but it was around five shillings per week. They even got paid extra to sing at weddings. If we were asked to sing we got nothing in return and we could never understand why.

I stuck it out at for approximately four years and in all of that time I rarely missed a practice or a service. Not having summer holidays like most families, Gra and I were the only ones that attended every Sunday during the summer. I did miss quite a few weeks towards the end of my time in the choir, but that was when I got knocked off my bike and was suffering from severe headaches. Choirboys singing can be unbearable at the best of times, but when your head is thumping it is not recommended. I did return after six weeks, but this was probably the catalyst for me leaving. Despite all of our family involvement with the church, not once did anyone from the church send a card or enquire after my well-being, let alone come and visit me. That's Christians for you!

I think when my time in the choir was over, I suddenly changed my favourite genre of music. Out went the Hallelujah Chorus and Jerusalem and in came Tamla Motown and Reggae. I was growing up quickly and began listening to Radio Caroline, a pirate radio station. It was not the easiest of things to do, as the reception was often very poor. You could spend five minutes tuning your radio in to somewhere between 252 and 259 metres longwave, only for it to disappear again a couple of minutes later. A few years later Radio 1 was established, which was a huge improvement. It was conceived as a direct response to the popularity of offshore pirate radio stations, such as Radio Caroline, which had been outlawed by an Act of Parliament. Radio 1 was launched at 7:00 am on Saturday 30 September 1967. I don't remember the occasion at all, but I do remember the following Monday morning. Monday was the only day I caught the bus to school, because first period was swimming lessons at Tudor Grange Baths. This was further away than school and it was an early start. This particular morning I was waiting at the bus stop when 'Sir' pulled up and asked me if I wanted a lift. During the short journey to the Baths he got quite excited, asking me, "What do you think of Tony Blackburn and the new Radio 1 station?" I had to admit I knew nothing about it. After all, we didn't ever have a newspaper in the house and we definitely didn't listen to the BBC Light programme. How would we have found out? Once 'Sir' had told me about it though I started to listen on a regular basis, usually while doing my homework in the evening.

My taste in music was always very different to most of the lads in my class. They were always listening to 'The Beatles', 'Rolling Stones' or something heavier like Black Sabbath. Motown and Reggae was more 'girlie' music and was looked down on, which meant you never let on to your classmates. I think I was attracted towards this type of music because you could generally understand the words and it had a beat that you could dance to. I can recall many occasions when I danced to my Reggae music from 'Tighten up Volume 1', in the kitchen. The kitchen had linoleum, aka 'lino', as a floor covering. I wasn't allowed to wear out the carpet in the living room by constantly dancing on the same spot. At the time, an acquaintance would keep me up to date with what was being played in the local clubs, frequented by 'skinheads' and 'top townies'. His name was Ray. An unreliable sort and a scrounger, but nevertheless someone you could not help but like. He was always broke and constantly trying to find ways to make money. He would often invite you out to the local pub, only to get to the bar and announce he'd got no money. I never really minded buying Ray a drink because he knew I liked Reggae and Motown, so would often tell me which singles to buy and from time to time sold me an LP or single. I have no idea where he got them from; it was usually better not to ask. Often I didn't even know or like the songs, but I would buy them anyway because I felt sorry for him, or was it because I was too soft?

One evening Ray came around for a chat and told me they were playing a new single in all of the clubs. He was so enthusiastic about it I just knew I had to get this record as soon as I could. The single was by Prince Buster, it was on his own label and was called 'Big 5'. Mom could tell I was really excited about it, so being the kind Mom she was, offered to get it for me while she was out shopping in Birmingham. Later that day she returned triumphant, with a copy of 'Big 5' in a paper bag. In the late sixties they used to make special paper bags for single records; just the correct size. "Have I had trouble getting this record for you," she said, looking quite exhausted from her efforts. "I must have been to a dozen different shops and none of them had got a copy. I was beginning to think I wasn't going to get one," she added. "And when I said I was desperate to obtain a copy, they looked at me quite strangely and said they wouldn't even be getting any copies in."

"Thanks Mom," I said, "I am really grateful."

I remember Sue was in the kitchen at the time when Mom asked if I knew what all of the fuss was about and could she listen to the record to find out what was so special about it. Of course I couldn't tell her, because I had not heard it either. I had only wanted to buy a copy on Ray's say so. If they were playing it every hour in all of the top clubs, it must be good. I opened up the stereogram and put the record on the turntable and stood back, ready to dance and listen. Wow, when the tune started it was awesome: a fantastic beat to dance to. I could now see what all the fuss was about. My delight lasted no longer than the first verse, because when the chorus of "It will be pussy versus cocky tonight" rang out, I wished the ground had swallowed me up there and then. Sue went as red as a beetroot and I thought Mom was going to explode. "No wonder everyone gave me strange looks when I said I was desperate to obtain a copy," she stuttered, "I cannot believe you let me go out and buy it for you." I tried my best to protest my innocence and to blame Ray, but she was having none of it. So I awkwardly grabbed the offending single and skulked upstairs out of harm's way to listen to the rest of it. I found out later why Mom had found it difficult to buy. The single was deemed too offensive and hence taken off the shelves. Thanks to Mom though, I still have a copy of a very rare '45'.

I suppose it was how good a song or tune was to dance to that influenced whether or not I bought it. My sense of rhythm was evident from an early age, when I was asked to play the tambourine and to take part in dancing around the maypole at Cranmore. The maypole has long since gone at Cranmore, but it was something I always enjoyed. The pole was around twenty feet high with many brightly coloured ribbons attached to the top. Pairs of boys and girls stood alternately around the base of the pole, each holding the end of a ribbon. We had to weave in and around each other, boys going one way and girls going the other. This continued until the ribbons were woven together around the pole and we all met at the base. However I was often irritated by other children who couldn't dance to the beat or were uncoordinated, which resulted in the ribbons getting tangled around the pole. I don't think 'Miss' ever managed to get the whole class to meet successfully at the base of the pole.

There are also more complex dances for set numbers of more competent dancers than we were, so we didn't even try them. They involved complicated weaves and unweaves, that are not particularly well known today. However, such dances are still performed every Mayday in some country villages and at special events, often organised by local Morris dancing groups. A number of years later, spurred on by dancing around the maypole at Cranmore, I did apply to become a Morris dancer. Morris dancing is not just about dancing around the maypole, but it includes all sorts of English folk dance. The dances are usually accompanied by music and are based on rhythmic stepping-cum-skipping and the execution of choreographed moves. Morris dancers wear bell pads on their shins, which jingle as they dance, adding to the atmosphere and excitement. I think it was the waving of implements such as sticks, swords and handkerchiefs during the dances that first attracted me to it.

At the time I believed I wasn't quite as good at dancing as I imagined, because like most applications I have ever submitted, I was unsuccessful. It was only when I passed my teens that I discovered the truth about why I never made it. I have been told that it was most likely the medical that I failed. Initially I didn't believe it. After all I was young and fit and had only a few months earlier passed my medical at an RAF interview with flying colours: A1, G1 and Z1. My eyesight and hearing were perfect and I had no disabilities that I knew of. Yes I had caught the usual childhood diseases, like German measles and chicken pox but no more than any other child. And I couldn't imagine my bike accident made any difference, or having my tonsils out or being circumcised. Then I was told it was the latter, the fact I had been circumcised as a young lad. Apparently, "You have to be a complete prick to be a Morris dancer." How lucky was I?

# Chapter 9

## THE SPORTS ARGUS

Dad, above anything else, loved his sport; whether it was football, boxing, horse racing, greyhound racing or darts. It didn't always go down well with Mom, because she thought sport was pointless and absolutely hated anything to do with it! Saturday afternoon for Dad was usually spent in front of the TV, watching Dickie Davies and World of Sport. Therefore, for Mom the living room was always a 'no go' area until after six o'clock. Dad watched the horse racing avidly, urging on his meagre bets and accumulators and then finished the afternoon with listening to the football results and checking his pools. The full classified results were usually completed by five o'clock, just half an hour before the first *Sports Argus* hit the shops. The Sports Argus was a Saturday sports paper printed on distinctive pink paper and published locally in Birmingham, between 1897 and 2006. It was for many years the largest-selling sports newspaper in Britain and had up to 40 pages of results and reports on every sport imaginable. This included a regular angling column with 'yours truly' getting his own special report one week. This happened after I won a club contest and caught my first barbel on the River Severn. Needless to say, this was all Uncle Les' doing, him being Secretary of the Red Lion Earlswood Angling Club. The Sports Argus was proud of its reputation for getting its first edition onto the newsagents' shelves, within an hour of the final whistle. The final edition as a standalone newspaper was published on 13 May 2006. Although its circulation at the time was good, it was constantly losing money each year. This was partly due to the increased number of matches shown on television. In order to fit in with TV coverage, not all football matches kicked-off at 3pm on Saturdays afternoons.

You would have thought an afternoon of sport was enough for any man, but Dad had to have a copy of the Sports Argus at the earliest opportunity. This is where I came in. Every Saturday, at half past five, Dad would persuade me to fetch a copy for him. This was achieved by timing how long I took to run to the newsagents, in Marshall Lake Road, and back again. On the count of three I would be off, haring up the gulley and along Cranmore Road to old man Lewis' shop. It was almost as though Mr. Lewis was expecting me, because I rarely got time to catch my breath before I was out of the shop and on my way home. There were rare occasions when the shop already had customers and I had to wait my turn. Frustrated, I would be champing at the bit, anxious to get my hands on the pink newspaper. Once my mission was accomplished, I was out of the shop and on my way home. Approaching the bend in the gulley, I would catch a glimpse of Dad standing on the front door step in his slippers and watch in hand, waiting for me to sprint for the line. The shop was roughly a quarter of a mile away, but even aged around nine I could easily be there and back, with the newspaper, within three minutes.

Along with aiming to put golf balls into flower pots, this was my first introduction to taking part in sport. With Dad's love of everything sporty it wasn't surprising that I soon developed his passion. Throughout my school years I tried almost every type of sport there is and with the exception of tennis, was generally of above average ability in anything I played. I was not exceptional at anything, but usually accomplished at everything. I suppose you could say "Jack of all sports, master of none"! I represented my school at rugby, cricket, football, hockey, running and high jump. I have played darts for a local pub, table tennis for Accles and Pollock (a company I worked for), swum a mile for charity and once took part in a diving display at a Solihull Lions swimming gala. I often think I was pretty poor at tennis, thanks to my Dad. He taught me to be left handed, when holding a golf club or cricket bat, therefore holding a racquet in my right hand was not ideal. I didn't feel as though I had the power or control of other players, probably because all of my power and control were in my left hand.

Being left handed was an advantage for me though when I played hockey. The first time I played in a games lesson at Harold Malley, I spent ten minutes in the equipment store cupboard looking for a left handed stick. Why wouldn't I – I always used a left handed golf club. It wasn't until the games master came looking for me to find out what was keeping me that I discovered there are only ever right handed hockey sticks. If they accommodated both left and right handed players the umpire would not be able to establish when players hit the ball with the back of the stick, a foul according to the rules. When I started playing it took some getting used to. Again, just as in tennis, I didn't have the power or control that other players had. When my stick was in its correct position, to my right, my left hand was in front of the stick and below my right hand. This was far from ideal, but I did cope with it really well. The advantage I had was when I played reverse sticks: when it is to the left of you and you are hitting the ball with the very end of the stick, as opposed to the larger flatter part. Most players have great difficulty in even hitting the ball in this position, let alone controlling it. For me it was easy. It was just like hitting a golf ball, except the ball was much larger.

I played for the school on a regular basis, making the left wing my own position. The teacher didn't have much of a decision to make. In my first game I scored our only goal, in a one all draw, against Blossomfield Men's Hockey Club reserves. The ball came screaming across from the right wing and I was there to thump the ball in to the back of the net, using my natural reverse stick action. The crowd went mad and the opposition stood in amazement at how hard and accurately I had struck the ball in this manner. It was my only moment of glory, because although I played many games for the school and helped the team to win on numerous occasions, that was my one and only goal. Despite this every week I was proud to run out onto the pitch to represent my school. After all, this was the only sport in which I had the correct footwear, even if the trainers were coated in polyurethane.

Playing hockey for the school was a bit of a double edged sword as it meant I couldn't play football for the school. It was either one or the other and as far as the school was concerned hockey took precedence over football. In fact at 'the Malley' football was bottom of the pecking order, with rugby top of the pile. This meant the only football I played was on the big green with the lads from the local estate near my house. Dad loved football as well and his favourite team was Tottenham Hotspurs. With Spurs achieving the League and Cup double when I was seven, I didn't take much persuading to support them as well. Yes Les took me to see live football at St Andrews, home of Birmingham City, but I only went to watch the match; Spurs were the only team I have ever followed and supported wholeheartedly.

Following success in the home competitions, Spurs became the first British team ever to win a 'European' cup, when they won the European Cup Winners Cup in 1963. Playing in Europe was something new for all British clubs and travelling abroad was not as easy as it is today. There was no way Dad and I could have ever afforded to visit White Hart Lane in London, never mind Holland, Spain or France. There wasn't the TV coverage like we get today, so Dad and I had to be satisfied with listening to matches on the radio. That was not easy either! Some evenings Dad would spend twenty minutes, or more, trying to tune the radio to the correct station. One game in particular I remember listening to was a match in Portugal against Benfica. It took an age to find the right station and when we did it was really poor sound quality. There was a significant crackling on the commentary, and to make matters worse it was in Spanish. We still enjoyed the excitement though. Dad had his left ear and I had my right ear pressed close to the transistor radio on the kitchen table, with its aerial fully extended! Spurs were denied, what appeared to be, two perfectly good goals on the night. Both were ruled out for being off-side, despite the fact for the second attempt two Benfica players were on the goal line. Regardless of this, I was well and truly captivated by their style, flair and passion with which the Spurs team played. Without doubt, I was going to be a Spurs fan for life.

I have stayed true to Spurs throughout my life and have in the last five or six seasons been privileged and lucky enough to watch them both home and away on numerous occasions. In fact after a wait of eight years I finally achieved my dream of having a season ticket at White Hart Lane. The enjoyment and excitement I have experienced at recent matches has been heightened by being accompanied on many occasions by my son Matt. He is probably a more enthusiastic fan than I am and undeniably will remain a true 'Lilywhite' for the rest of his life. They say sport brings people together – I can vouch for that, having spent many a great moment with Matt down at 'The Lane'. I know for certain Dad would have been so pleased and proud to see us carrying on his legacy and tradition of supporting Spurs.

With all of the sports I have played, I have not had any real instruction, apart from swimming. If I had joined a club, or been given special tutoring, I wonder whether I could have been exceptional at even just one of these sports. Sadly I will never know, because Mom and Dad could not afford for us to join clubs or have proper lessons.

The only exception is when, at an early age, Mom and Dad insisted we all learnt to swim. They continually impressed upon us the need to be able to swim, saying that being able to swim could save your life. I am sure you are thinking how lucky I was to have Mom and Dad pay for me to have swimming lessons when they could barely afford to feed or clothe us all. You may change your mind when I tell you they could only afford it if I was given swimming instruction when the local baths wasn't busy. When I say not busy, I mean really not busy, like when there was nobody else in the swimming baths at all. I expect you cannot imagine any swimming baths nowadays having just one person in the pool when it is open. However, when I first learnt to swim I can say, with hand on heart, I was the only one in the water.

Back in the early 1960s Solihull Council only owned an outdoor lido, located at the back of Malvern Park. During February and March this is where I received my individual swimming tuition. I swear one morning when Mom and I arrived for a lesson, my instructor was breaking the ice on the main pool. The pool surround was made of blue painted concrete, so my feet were frozen before I even put a toe in the water. For half an hour Mom would wait for me, sitting on the side in her coat, hat and gloves, with a scarf tied tightly around her neck. While I splashed around in the icy cold water, wearing just a tiny pair of thin red trunks, she watched on in relative comfort. At the age of eight or nine I was as thin as a rake, with barely an ounce of fat anywhere about my body. I went in looking as white as a sheet and came out more like a wind up Smurf. Every week I finished the lesson shivering and blue from the cold, my teeth chattering like a pair of Spanish castanets.

Mom wasn't all bad, because after quickly wrapping me up in a towel there was the usual flask of hot tomato soup, ready to bring me back to life. On exceptionally cold days we would stop off at a little 'olde-worlde' black and white café in Drury Lane, where Mom treated me to a hot chocolate and a jam tart. I am not sure she could afford it, but I think she needed it more than I did. Mom would often say, "I feel cold just watching you." It may have seemed cruel at the time but I believe I learnt to swim very quickly that spring, purely because it was in the lido. I knew the sooner I learnt to swim, the sooner the lessons would stop. Later that year I joined the Solihull Swimming Club, and within a few more years I had earned my gold personal survival badge and several lifesaving certificates.

I suppose my most successful and prolific sport has been running. I think racing to fetch the Sports Argos on a Saturday evening was when I first realised running might be a sport I could be good at. Not necessarily sprinting, but certainly longer distances. I suppose you could compare me to the tortoise in the Aesop's well-known fable about 'The Hare and the Tortoise'. Speed wasn't my forte, but endurance was. When younger, I was often referred to as 'Duracell'; I had a copper top and went on forever. I joined the school cross country club run by Mr. Tipping. He was so impressed with me I represented the school at a Solihull schools cross-country event. The one and only race I competed in was a bit of a disaster for me, because conditions on the day were dreadful. I think it must have rained all week and the course was waterlogged and extremely muddy. Everyone stood around the start, standing inches deep in mud and anticipating the whistle to begin the race. I looked around me and all of the other runners were dressed for the occasion, wearing cross-country spikes on their feet. Whereas I was wearing a pair of black hockey plimsolls, the very same shoes I took with me to the school's Mountain Centre. If you can remember, they were the ones Dad had coated with polyurethane, supposedly making them waterproof. Just like walking boots, running shoes weren't good for my high instep and strangely shaped feet. It was either the hockey shoes, or not run at all. When the whistle blew to start the race I was left on the line, slipping and sliding around like Bambi on ice. My plimsolls had about as much grip as spiders have when walking up a pane of glass. I did make up numerous positions over the next four or five miles, but finished well down the field. After running around the course taking three steps forward and two back, I decided it would be better if I didn't represent the school again or wait until I could afford a pair of spikes.

Unlike all of my school pals, I always looked forward to the inter-house cross-country race. I never actually won the event, but regularly came in the top three. I suppose it was down to my fitness. I had a natural ability but never really trained on a regular basis, whereas others who were members of local football clubs trained hard and were super fit. This put me at a distinct disadvantage, which was evident towards the end of a race. This is when I would start to flag and get pipped at the post. The only race I ever won at school was the thousand metres steeple chase. I believe I won because the steeple chase is a combination of middle distance running and high jump, another event I was above average at. Either that or none of my class mates wanted to represent our house in this jumping event.

After leaving school I forgot all about running until a friend of mine ran the Birmingham Half Marathon in the late 1980s. We all went as a family to cheer Mick on his way to the finish at Cannon Hill Park, in Edgbaston. We waited for him just down the road from the Edgbaston cricket ground and were dismayed to see him in such distress with still more than six miles to go. By the time we first saw him he was walking, sweaty and red faced, looking extremely tired and dejected.  With so much at stake I could not see Mick give up, so I accompanied him for the rest of the race, joking and encouraging him on towards the finish, running some miles and walking others. Just before the finish, I had to slip into the crowd leaving Mick to take the applause and recognition.

A few weeks after the event I decided to buy a decent pair of trainers and began a strict training regime. Six months and six editions of Running Fitness magazine later I ran the Heart of England half marathon in Atherstone, finishing in a respectable time of 1 hour and 37 minutes, for the 13.1 miles. That was it, I had got the bug and was already planning my next race and target time. For anyone thinking of participating in semi-serious running I would recommend buying copies of Running Fitness or Runners World. They are full of great advice and inspirational words on many topics to ensure a successful run. They certainly helped me with kit, choosing the correct running shoes for my gait, training schedules and hydration techniques – all guaranteed to help you cross the line relatively unscathed and injury free.

The second competition I entered was a Bristol half marathon at a time when the race started up on Clifton Downs by the suspension bridge. The route of the course took you downhill for the first mile, alongside the River Avon and then back up the side of the gorge, through a housing estate, to the finish. On this particular day it was relatively warm and sunny, far from ideal distance running conditions. Therefore I ran around the course with a large water bottle to prevent dehydration. Not everyone had planned as well as I had, or anticipated the need to drink plenty on route. By the time we were running through the housing estate and back up the gorge, people were already beginning to slow down and even walk.

At ten miles I was still going strong when I came upon a girl in her twenties really struggling to stay upright. She was unsteady on her feet, taking large steps from side to side and clearly not feeling at all well. As I approached her, she stopped to catch her breath and take a drink of water. It was evident she was dehydrating – I had once seen an example of this on television. It was a clip of Dorando Pietri, an Olympic marathon runner, taking part in London 1908. Pietri was a 5ft 2in pastry chef by trade and looked much younger than his 22 years. On entering the White City stadium for the last 400 yards of the marathon Pietri paused momentarily, as if physically blown backwards by the wall of noise that had suddenly struck him. Then he started to teeter around the track, having to be picked up five or six times and eventually having to be helped across the finishing line. Needless to say he was disqualified for being assisted during the race.

This girl reminded me of a female Dorando Pietri; she was struggling and was going to require assistance if she wanted to complete the race. Still focused on my race and determined to achieve a personal best, I ignored her plight, put my head down and continued up the hill. Then maybe only a minute later the same girl came past me, running in exactly the same fashion as before. I remember looking across at her and thinking, "Blimey, you're never going to finish." What I hadn't realised was that although she was almost running backwards, she was still travelling faster than I was. Then a strange darkness came over me and I heard someone shout, "Watch out, he's going over!" just as I passed out.

Some minutes later I still couldn't see anything, but remember someone shining a light in to my eyes and saying, "It is okay, you have become dehydrated, collapsed and you are on your way to the St John Ambulance tent." Ten minutes later I came to, in what looked like a field hospital from World War 1. There were probably fifty or sixty other runners lying on camp beds, set out in rows, in a large white canvas field tent. Five minutes later and after a glass of water, I was allowed to leave and make my way back to the finish, to try and find Heather, Kerry and Matt. Just as I left the tent Heather arrived, desperate to find where I was and anxious for my safety. Before leaving for home we had a somewhat subdued picnic, with me feeling rather delicate as though I had one enormous hangover, but without having had the pleasure of getting drunk!

Heather at this point was adamant I was never going to run again, but having mastered the half marathon I was now ready to complete a full one, the whole 26.2 miles. Clearly there was only one marathon to run. If you wanted to prove yourself and gain inspiration from the crowds, it had to be London. Getting a place in London was not as easy as it sounds. Even if you applied early and paid the £16 entry fee, you were not guaranteed to get a place. I filled in my application form in the September of 1991, in anticipation of obtaining a place for the April 1992 marathon. At the time, applications outnumbered places on offer by two or three to one and this was despite there being about 30,000 runners starting the race. For the average applicant the probability of being given a place was about one in three. However, some categories of applicant were guaranteed a place on the starting line. 'Elite' runners – those who had run 'fast' times within the previous 12 months – were automatically accepted, as were runners with places for the 1991 race who could not make it that year because of injury. All other applicants were put into categories, depending on their age, gender, occupation and predicted finishing time. If I had been a seventy year old, ex brain surgeon, then I would have been almost certain to have gained a ticket. But being a 37 year old office worker hoping to finish in three and a half hours (the most popular time) the probability dropped to about one in ten. For this reason December approached without a great deal of expectation for taking part the following April. Around about my 38th birthday (December 6th) and much to my surprise, I did receive a letter confirming my place!

That was it! Once I had been accepted the motivation was unbelievable. Early morning runs before work, in the cold and dark, were no effort at all. Likewise, I was ready for the long slow Sunday morning run every week, come rain or shine, without fail. By Christmas I was running almost every day, 25 miles per week, including ten miles on a Sunday. This increased weekly until three weeks before the race, when I was running 45 miles per week and had three or four twenty milers in my legs. I was training really hard and particularly on a Sunday morning, I would get back home exhausted and ravenous for some carbohydrates. I believe it was that year when Heather and I went to Kerry's parents evening at Sharmans Cross Junior School and were embarrassed by one of her English essays. The class had been asked to put themselves in someone else's position and to write a piece of work as though they were that person. Kerry chose Heather and her story began something like this. "It was Sunday morning and I was asleep in bed, when something awoke me. "Urgh, what is that awful smell? Oh it's okay, it is only my husband coming back from his early morning run!" You can imagine how we felt talking to her teacher afterwards, especially when she asked, with a smile, what we thought of her excellent writing skills? She never said anything, but I had the distinct impression she was trying to make sure I was seated as far away from her as possible, with Heather strategically placed between the two of us.

I went on to run in the London marathon that year and in fact in three other races at the same distance, in subsequent years. I was proud of myself for completing all of them, raising significant sums of money for various charities and running reasonable times. Having said that though, I don't feel I am cut-out or built for running this ultra-event. On each of the four occasions, I have 'hit the wall' at about 22 or 23 miles into the race. 'Hitting the wall' is a condition caused by the depletion of glycogen stores in the liver and muscles, which manifests itself by sudden fatigue and loss of energy. I am pleased to say, each time I was able to finish the race by taking a brief rest and taking onboard carbohydrate-rich energy drinks. I am not sure why this happens to me. It seems to be I get caught up in the euphoria of the atmosphere in this truly brilliant event. Running in any race, once the gun goes it is difficult to hold back and restrain yourself from setting off too quickly. You have completed all of the training, you feel great and forget that there are still 26 miles to run. I cannot recommend taking part in this race more highly though. The whole weekend is magnificent and the crowd and other runners are inspirational. It is also quite humbling when you pass a fellow competitor at 21 miles, who started some hours before you, but has run around the course with crutches and just one leg. I can recall becoming quite tearful as I passed this particular guy. The crowds were deafening as they cheered him on and shouted words of encouragement, in recognition of his remarkable achievement.

London may be the best marathon in the world, but for your average runner it is not conducive to a good time, or personal best. I have usually crossed the line in a time somewhere between three and a half and four and a half hours. This is probably the worst time to finish, because this is the most popular time, with perhaps ten runners finishing every second. It is even more congested at the start and during the race itself.

Once the gun has gone off to start the race, it takes some runners half an hour to cross the start line. I remember one year when I had to stop and walk at the 15 mile marker, just because there were so many runners and the course was too congested. It was for this very reason I decided to run my last marathon in Rotterdam.

There are usually only about 11,000 runners and like London the crowds are excellent. This amount of participants is enough to ensure you don't have to run around on your own, but there is always plenty of room to be able to keep to your planned schedule. I said I decided, but perhaps it was more arm twisting from my mate Julian (a work colleague) with whom I trained at lunch time. Unlike me, Julian was built to run. He is younger and shorter than I am, but built like a whippet; all muscle and no fat. To say he was a better runner than I was is an understatement. His half marathon times were nearly ten minutes quicker than mine and he was aiming for two and three quarter hours for the Marathon; a time I could only dream about. This was an incentive for me. We ran regular hill and interval sessions together, with me always doing the chasing, so it pushed me to better my performance. On top of this, Julian's humour and laughter were infectious, which meant we had many hours of fun, running around the streets of Elmdon and Solihull.

We were not the only ones to go out running before work and at lunch time. Andy, Phil and Sallie regularly came out with us whatever the weather. Andy had been an above average club runner at Loughborough University who at one time trained with Hugh Jones. In 1982 Hugh Jones became the first British man to win the London Marathon, finishing in a time of 2:09:24: serious running. Andy wasn't quite that good, but had a best marathon time of around 2:40:00 and a half marathon time more than twenty minutes faster than mine. When running with us his best days were behind him, although he was still substantially better than I was, but not quite as fast as Julian. Sallie worked in my section at Severn Trent, had strawberry blonde hair and freckles, often reminding me of a younger version of Patsy Palmer. I encouraged her to take up running because she was an excellent tennis player at county level and wanted to build up her fitness and stamina. Sallie took to running like a duck to water, which is ironic really, because one of Phil's running partners once told her she had a lovely bottom. He said he loved running behind her because her bottom reminded him of a couple of duck eggs wrapped in a white handkerchief. While out running a few days later she told me what had been said, so I dropped back to run behind her for a moment, only to report I could see what he was saying. However, I felt "it looked more like a couple of ostrich eggs wrapped up in a tablecloth"! Needless to say Sallie was not best pleased, but could not stop herself from laughing along with the rest of us.

With fewer runners in the Rotterdam marathon Julian and I easily managed to obtain a couple of tickets for the 2001 race. Once more I got really excited; it was just the incentive I needed. This time I was determined to try and achieve my target time of three and a half hours. I upped the mileage significantly, running every day for something like six weeks, peaking at more than sixty miles per week for three consecutive weeks. If I didn't run my target time this year, I never would. On top of the rigorous training, Julian and I also had to plan our trip to Holland. We were travelling over by car, via a ferry on the Friday, registration was on Saturday, with racing on Sunday and returning home on Monday, after appropriate celebrations. Julian was taking his car, so agreed to book the ferry, while I agreed to book a twin room for three nights in Rotterdam. All I can say is thank goodness for the internet. What did we do before computers? It was so easy finding a suitable hotel close to the race registration centre with good reviews. We shared the driving and made excellent time arriving at the hotel mid-afternoon; perfect timing for getting access to our room. I cannot recall the name of the hotel, but it was very central, so we soon found it with just a couple of minor detours on the way.

We booked in with the receptionist, who spoke perfect English, and took the lift up to our room on the top floor ready for a well-earned rest. The room was fairly basic, almost dormitory like in fact. The decoration was dull and the beds and bedding were, to say the least, uninspiring. However, it was functional, we had both seen worse rooms and we urgently needed to rest before race day. So we put our bags down and slumped on to the beds. We had been lying there for all of two minutes talking through our race plans and hopes for the weekend when our nostrils sensed one of the worst smells I have ever known. It was on a par with the outside loo at Home Farm, but here there was no getting away from it! A quick investigation in the bathroom pinpointed the problem to the shower; it really was disgusting. The shower looked clean, but the smell from the shower trap was unbearable. To cut a long story short we went down to reception to complain after the receptionist refused to respond to our telephone call.

All of a sudden the guy on reception appeared to forget how to speak English and was not very helpful at all. After five minutes of arguing and gesticulation he gave us the key to another room, saying, "You can have the 'ooh' room." "What room?" we asked. His reply was even more muffled than the first time, so we gave up and set off to find it, the smell of the original room still strong in our memory. There was no room number to go by, but it was on the second floor and he intimated we would know which room it was when got there. We exited from the lift and I spotted the right door immediately. The painting on the door in front of us matched the 'Scooby Doo' key fob I had in my hand.

When we turned the key and opened the door we discovered there were no windows – the room was pitch black. Neither Julian nor I were expecting to see what we found inside when we eventually found the light. There was a small, and I mean very small, en suite to the right hand side, but at least it didn't smell like the last one. To the left the beds had been boxed off behind a panel designed to look like the front of a dog's kennel. Hanging up to the left, just outside the opening was a gold studded lead with a silver dog's bowl on the floor below and a box of 'Bono': very aptly named. To the right was a leather muzzle, clearly not meant for a dog, unless your dog had a head the size of a man's. Everything inside the room was decorated with doggy artifacts: wallpaper, bed linen, the lot! Even the picture frames on the wall contained pictures and certificates from 'Crufts' and its American counterpart. After a few moments, when both Julian and I had taken everything in, we just fell about in fits of laughter. I was literally rolling around on the floor holding my stomach, which was aching from so much laughing. I even continued to laugh after I pulled a muscle in my back as I contorted around the room. Sitting in the car for six hours had taken its toll and the fetish 'dog' room had been the straw that 'broke' my back.

After composing ourselves, we eventually decided there was no way we were going to stay in the room any longer than was necessary. We collected our bags and set off around the city to find somewhere to stay. Easier said than done with me struggling to straighten up every time we got out of the car. We felt as though we were Mary and Joseph, not Malc and Julian. We were there for the marathon, not the census, but everything else seemed very familiar. We travelled around the city, stopping at every hotel where Julian would ask if they had a room for us to stay in. He explained that we were desperate to find somewhere, because with my back strain I needed to find a place to rest. Alas at every hotel we tried, the answer was the same, "there is no room at the inn". Following hours of searching and with the light fading fast we finally discovered an Ibis hotel a short train ride away from the city centre in a very nice location, with plenty of bars and restaurants close by. These were essential facilities if we were to carbo-load and stay well hydrated in preparation for the big race ahead of us.

Without boring you with the detail of the race, once again I hit the wall at 23 miles, but managed to finish in the respectable time of 3:30:21, just a few seconds outside of my target time. Having run three half marathons, each under one and a half hours, all of the theory says I should have been able to run 3:20:00. If I had managed to avoid the wall just once I am sure that would have been possible. With my best running days far behind me now, I will never know what could have been. Given some encouragement in my youth and being able to join an athletics club as I grew older, without doubt I would have achieved greater things. I may not have represented my country, but my PBs would be significantly better.

# Chapter 10

## HAROLD MALLEY

At the age of eleven I took what was known then as my '11+'. This was a standard examination, involving Maths, English and verbal reasoning questions, taken by most junior school pupils. The outcome of the test determined whether or not you were 'bright' enough to attend one of the borough's two Grammar schools. If you passed the 11+ you could choose which school you attended, so Mom and Dad took me to the open days at both Tudor Grange and Harold Malley Grammar Schools. Tudor Grange concentrated on the classics, including Greek and Latin, while Harold Malley was the local Technical Grammar School, focusing more on the sciences and technical subjects, such as engineering and woodwork. Once inside the latter school there was no way Dad was going to let me go to any other school. I have to admit the laboratories and workshops were pretty impressive. The engineering workshops in particular wowed Dad. He said the lathes and drilling machines they owned, were better and more modern than those he had used when he was working at the BSA. I think Dad thought if I was going to follow him into engineering then Harold Malley would give me a great grounding. Consequently, unlike my closest friends at junior school, I put down Harold Malley as my first option. Fortunately, I passed my 11+ and was offered a place at the school of my choice.

I suppose I was a bit like a black sheep, because along with Derek, I was the only lad from the Cranmore estate to go to

Harold Malley. All of the other lads in my year came from the better off areas of Solihull, so it was a case of having to make new friends. That wasn't too difficult because although I wasn't well spoken and lacked the social skills of my peers, I did have something they didn't – humour. All of those jokes Dad and Uncle Les told me came in handy for getting the attention of my classmates. Again similar to most things in my life I was an average scholar, probably only excelling in one subject, which was Mathematics. Maybe I could have done better but there was little or no encouragement from Mom and Dad. I always felt they thought studying was secondary. While it was important to be able to read and write, exams weren't going to help me later in life. I am certain the type of job they envisaged me doing after I left school was not going to require biology, history, geography or French; engineering and woodwork would be far more beneficial.

In September 1964 I started at Harold Malley to begin my Grammar school education. There was no hiding on the way to school because of the distinctive colour of our uniform. It was compulsory to wear a white or grey shirt, charcoal grey trousers and a very vivid purple blazer! This was completed by a purple and grey striped tie and purple cap, which had to be worn at all times, to and from school. If you were caught by prefects not wearing your cap, you were kept in detention after school. Therefore, I developed eyes in the back of my head on the way to school in order to stay out of trouble. You can imagine I stood out like a sore thumb on the local estate, because almost without exception all of my mates wore black, a far better colour. Having said that, I did quite enjoy being different. After all Mom had brought me up to look different from everyone else, what with the black and white checked trousers! On top of which the purple looked great against the warmth of my burnished chestnut coloured hair!!

During the winter we were supposed to wear a light grey raincoat to keep dry, but they were not very fashionable, so everyone did their best not to wear them. Besides that, having to wear shorts until you were in year three (aged 13), if you wore your mac it looked like you had nothing on underneath it! If the weather was wet I would generally run from tree to tree all of the way to school, just to keep out of the worst of the rain. Often I wished I could wear the raincoat, because when the blazers got wet the smell was dreadful. They smelt really 'fusty'. It was something to do with the material they were made from.

Harold Malley was an all-boys school, with girls going to Harold Cartwright a completely separate building close by. We were a four form entry school and there were, at times, forty lads in my class alone, far larger than they have today. The four classes formed different houses, named after famous castles in Great Britain. There was Harlech, Windsor, Kinsale and Edingburgh, with me being in the latter. I have a feeling that pupils were not allocated randomly to each form, because there is no way we could have had so many bad apples in our class if it had been. Over the next five years we got a reputation for being the bad boys, so much so we used to joke that we were in class 3E, 'E' for ignorant. I soon made friends with some of the more refined lads in the class, those that didn't get into too much trouble. However we often all got tarred with the same brush and received the same punishments as the 'not so desirables'.

Trouble began right from the start of year one in French lessons, with the very aptly named Mr. French, or 'Bog brush' to his students. For some reason only our class was taught French, the other three all had to learn German instead. Anyway, Mr. French was a young, smartly dressed teacher with short spikey hair: hence the name. Without exception, every day he wore a light, almost white, lightweight jacket. He would enter the class room and say "Bonjour mes eleves", before starting to teach us how to say various phrases, relevant to everyday life. There were three particularly despicable lads who sat at the back of the class every day: Simon, Ron and Dave. They were not interested in learning French and would mess about something mercilessly. Dave was without doubt the worst pupil in the class, a pupil who answered every question he was asked with the same answer, "Il pleut". Once the teaching part was finished 'Bog brush' would give us work to complete in our exercise books. While we sat writing nicely with our regulation fountain pens, he would walk up and down the classroom, between the desks and chairs, answering any questions. Whenever he passed Simon, Ron or Dave they would 'riddle' the back of his jacket with ink. 'Riddling' is carried out by flicking your fountain pen in a downwards motion in the direction you wish the spots of ink to go. Of course it only took a visit to the staff room by Mr. French for him to discover 1E had just ruined his 'nice' jacket.

Thankfully the Deputy Head, (Big Bad) Mr. Hobday, soon put a stop to this horrid practice, which meant us having to move on to a new prank: 'fart machines'. This was something I could participate in, because although disruptive it was just a bit of harmless fun. A 'fart machine' was usually made out of pieces of Meccano. Three straight pieces were bolted together to form the shape of a small five or six inch bow saw. Instead of a saw between the two ends, a strong thick elastic band was attached, with a small washer threaded onto it. Before 'Sir' entered the classroom the washer would be wound up to its maximum capacity and the 'fart machine' primed inside an exercise book, which had to be sat on immediately. At strategic times of the lesson, you just had to slowly lift one cheek off the exercise book to allow the washer to spin around and make a rasping sound against the pages. Some days there were six or more pupils with these contraptions in any given class. Once someone had discharged their 'fart machine' Sir would look up to see an almost entire class of lads finding it difficult to contain their amusement. He would enquire as to who had made the noise and ask what everyone thought was funny? He never suspected me of 'letting rip' in class because I always portrayed an air of innocence by having that gift of being able to keep a straight face.

Our reputation was so bad we attracted special attention from 'The Acorn', Mr. Collins, our Headmaster. He insisted we have the strictest form tutors possible, to try and keep us restrained. Both Mr. Williams and Mr. Goodson had fearsome reputations, but for some members of the class it seemed to have little effect. In our second year we had a new teacher for Physics, a Mr. Jawah, who was probably the first black teacher in

Solihull. The same few lads at the back of the class, who regularly caused trouble, climbed right inside the laboratory cupboards. The cupboards were huge, large enough to fit the largest of pupils, particularly as the only apparatus kept in them was one solitary Bunsen burner per cupboard. They spent a whole double period inside the cupboard, shouting, "I'm in the cupboard," along with obscenities offensive to Mr. Jawah. He eventually left the room in tears, leaving slides to melt in the school's projector.

The next day we were kept in at playtime and hauled in front of Mr. Collins. He went berserk and insisted upon the offenders owning up, which was never going to happen. He was adamant unless he found out who the offenders were we would all be kept in detention until further notice. Then one lad meekly put his hand up and asked to speak. It was Roger, a 'goodie two shoes', who never got into trouble and was a bit of a 'know-all'. He stood up and bravely but very foolishly said, "Please Sir you could be wrong. Mistakes are made even in the highest courts of law." All of a sudden a deathly silence fell across the whole room. You could have heard a pin drop. The silence didn't last for long though, because when 'The Acorn' had prised himself off the ceiling, he dragged poor Roger out to the front and told him to be outside his office the following morning along with a friend for a witness. The next time we got changed for games Roger could not hide six distinct, black weals on his backside from where Mr. Collins had administered six strokes of the cane. We all felt sorry for Roger because he seemed to have taken all of the wrath and anger from the Headmaster. The class only received one day's detention and the incident was barely mentioned again. The fact that shortly afterwards two of the main offenders were sent to Borstal for six months for stealing from a large department store in Solihull may have also had something to do with it.

Perhaps the worst episode in my class' history was in 1970, the year we all went on a school trip to France to enhance our chances of passing our French O' Level examinations. I think the whole class went along, including me, together with a dozen A level students from the Sixth Form. By this time in my life Mom and Dad had started to have a little more money in their pockets, which meant they could afford for us to have holidays at last. It coincided with Mom starting work at the Plough as a waitress. Great for us boys, but too late for Sue whom I don't ever remember going on a family holiday. Additionally, I had already been working part-time at the Plough (a steakhouse restaurant) for two years and therefore was able to contribute towards the cost. The whole class was excited by the trip, with three days in Paris and four days in St Malo on the northern coast of Brittany. I can recall staring at one of the Geography atlases, not daring to believe I would be travelling across the channel to a foreign country at last. Up until then, the farthest afield I had ever been was Uphill, near Weston-Super-Mare. This was our first family holiday together: Mom, Dad and the four boys. Sue, who was sixteen, had left school and was working for a living already. Back then I thought Weston was southern England and Nottingham was in the North. I knew this because I had been there several times, by coach, fishing on the River Trent.

Regarding the French trip, there are three incidents that stick in my memory like limpets do to a rock. Two were in Paris, the other when we were at St. Malo. One of the highlights of our visit to the French capital was a trip up the 'Tour Eiffel'. The whole class made it to the top and being nearly 900 feet above the ground, the views were spectacular and breathtaking. Surprisingly, despite the height, it is not that scary. You are so high up, it doesn't look real. I suppose we had been up on the top floor, taking photographs and admiring the scenery for approximately five minutes, when suddenly the whole area became flooded with Gendarme and security guards. They were all there looking for the person who had stupidly thrown an orange over the safety barrier. Luckily it hadn't landed on any unsuspecting passersby, but the word soon made its way up to where my class were enjoying the sights. Clearly we were prime suspects: fifty, English school children, aged between 14 and 17! The teachers quickly rounded us all up and ushered us towards the lift to make our way down and out of trouble. The Gendarme had a pretty good idea it was one of us, but they had no witnesses or CCTV camera footage to prove it. The culprit was, according to reliable sources, Simon. He was, to say the least, a strange character that was frighteningly obsessed with the Nazis and SS.

This was not the last time he misbehaved that week, because on the last evening in Paris, along with two other lads, he went out 'on the piss' to the local bars. The rest of the class were all tucked up in bed by half ten inside the dormitory style rooms of the Parisian Hostel. Simon and the other lads got back to the

Hostel after midnight, long after the doors had been locked. They were all well and truly drunk and created quite a fuss outside the front door. The elderly man on reception eventually let them in, but not before they had verbally abused him. Unfortunately for me and eight others, they were all three supposed to be sleeping in our room. We all started by keeping our heads under the blankets, pretending to be asleep, but it didn't last for long. Simon did no more than open a window, threw an apple across the courtyard and then proceeded to urinate from the second floor. He must have drunk quite a few bottles of beer during the evening, because as it splashed on the floor below it sounded like the 'Niagara Falls'. Four of the older sixth form lads soon entered our room and restored some sort of order, but we didn't get a great deal of sleep that night. Luckily for the teaching staff, we were scheduled to be leaving the following morning. If we hadn't the owners said they would have kicked us out anyway.

The third is a happier memory and is about something positive I recall from my week in France. To be perfectly honest I am not a huge fan of the French. My opinion of them is pretty low because in general they come across as having an attitude of "Je suis 'ok' Jaques", or as we say over here "I'm all right Jack". The original saying was "I'm all right Jack, pull up the ladder". Apparently when a man had got safely on board ship by climbing the ladder from the sea or from a lifeboat he would say this, meaning don't bother about saving the rest of the men because I don't really care about them. This is the very same attitude the French seem to have: we can have their tasteless French Golden

Delicious apples and tough mutton, but they won't have our delicious apples or succulent lamb. What's more, our government usually lets them get away with it!

Apart from a trip to Mont-Saint-Michel, we didn't really enjoy our time in St Malo. There wasn't an awful lot to do for a group of teenage boys in this pretty dismal seaside town, only marginally better than Borth in mid Wales. The highlight of our stay was the little creperie located opposite the hotel. It was run by a typically French looking, grey haired old lady, who spoke no English. This was fantastic, it allowed us to practise our French and gave us an excuse to supplement the terrible food we were given at the hotel. The crepes were cooked fresh, while you waited, and they cost just a few French francs: the chocolate, confiture or lemon and sugar ones were the most popular. When we weren't out on trips there was always a steady queue outside her shop. My class, who were only at O level standard, usually kept words to a minimum, saying something like "Une crepe, avec confiture, s'il vous plait". This was in complete contrast to the older sixth form lads who wanted to study French at a higher level. They would show off their linguistic skills, by having 'complex' conversations with the old lady and holding up the rest of us in the queue. That was until one of them, whose name was Richard, made a massive faux pas. I suppose you could say he made himself look "a right Dick". He entered the shop while four of us were waiting to be served and pushed his way to the front of the queue. He started mouthing off in French and excused his behaviour by saying he was dying of hunger. Well that is what he wanted to say; "Je meurs de faim." However, he wasn't thinking quite straight and it came out as, "Je faim d'amour". When the old lady's face turned the colour of the strawberry jam, we could tell he hadn't quite got it right. What he actually said was, "I hunger for love". The old lady and the rest of us saw the funny side, but 'Dick' slipped away quietly and never returned all week.

Back at school it was hardly surprising we played up and got into trouble, because frankly many of the lessons we had were boring and none more so than English. English lessons were mostly taken by the Reverend Williams, supposedly a man of the cloth, but not someone who set a fine example to his pupils. At least twice during a 40 minute lesson, he would disappear into his stock room for five minutes at a time to have a cigarette. With our class having a poor reputation, he had to leave the door open slightly to hear what we were getting up to. That meant the smoke would drift slowly out into the classroom, like smoke signals from a Red Indian's camp fire. When he was teaching it wasn't brilliant either. Probably the only thing I ever learnt from him was the meaning of 'victuals'. We were supposed to record the meaning of words we were unsure of in a special exercise book and for some bizarre reason it is the only word I ever wrote down. I don't believe the Reverend had any 'Great Expectations' of me, because I only ever read the first chapter of this classic Dickensian novel. The only book I read from cover to cover was Laurie Lee's 'Cider with Rosie' and that was only because one of my mates told me there was a saucy chapter towards the end.

French lessons with Mr. Williams were far from interesting as well; it is no wonder I was regularly getting told off for looking out of the window. The pattern of teaching appeared to be learn a passage from your text book for homework and write it out from memory in class the next day. I was reasonably proficient at this. I could memorise the words with ease and regurgitate them out at will, but I had not got a clue what they all meant. Then there were the art lessons I have already mentioned, where we learnt virtually nothing for four and a half years from 'The Walrus', and managed to pass our O levels thanks to only four months with Mr. Mathews. Physical Education was only slightly better. During the winter Mr. Green would send us all off on a cross country run around the cold, wet and muddy playing field, while he stayed in the warmth of his office. At least he watched us during the warmer months, even if it was from a deckchair while he was sunning himself. I believe he only kept himself fit by giving boys the slipper for misbehaving or disobeying his orders.

Most lessons were in complete contrast to Music, when believe it or not we all had fun. Everyone was taught by Mr. Price, affectionately known as Fred, who was an excellent teacher. Anyone who could teach the whole school how to sing and play musical instruments to a standard where each year we performed at the Solihull Civic Hall, must have been special. Towards the end of the summer term, the whole school took part in an extraordinary concert. Solihull Civic Hall would be packed full with parents who had paid to listen to the choir, brass band and various soloists. They were always very popular and raised significant amounts of money for the school PTA.

That isn't to say my class always behaved like little choir boys in Music lessons, because we didn't. I remember many times when Fred had to hand out an ultimatum to one of my classmates: "Do you want a detention or corporal punishment boy?" Without exception everyone chose the latter, because it was far less painful than staying behind after school and it generally caused amusement amongst the rest of the class. Fred would call the offender out to the front of the class and would be foaming at the mouth, without a lie, uncannily similar to how camels do when they are attempting to cool themselves down. It did look pretty disgusting, but was always a source of laughter and ridicule. He would then ask the boy to bend over and proceeded to hit the boy with the flat of his outstretched hand. Fred's inimitable words still ring loudly in my head, "This is going to hurt me boy, more than it is you," which were followed by more of a push with his hand than a hit. It was always as much as we could do to keep a straight face. I never had to go to the front of the class in Music; it was probably the only lesson I didn't though. However, I did once get Mr. Price irate and was responsible for him foaming at the mouth on one particular occasion.

Fred asked us to bring in a piece of music or record, which the whole class could listen to and then discuss. The idea was to guess which musical instruments were used and what key it was played in; anything that would involve us all and start us talking about music. I suppose I could have been really bad and taken in Prince Buster's 'Big 5', but that would have been too much, so I took in a much safer option. The single was Jane Birkin and

Serge Gainsbour's "Je t'aime... moi non-plus" (French for "I love you... me neither"). It was number one in the UK singles chart in 1969, but was banned in several countries owing to its explicit sexual content. Birkin, who was Gainsbourg's lover at the time, said she "got a bit carried away with the heavy breathing". There was media speculation, as with an earlier version recorded with Brigitte Bardot, that they had recorded live sex. This is unlikely to be true, because Gainsbourg told Birkin, "Thank goodness it wasn't, otherwise I hope it would have been a long-playing record." The single had a plain cover, with the words "Interdit aux moins de 21 ans" (forbidden to those under 21). I am not sure exactly how I came across my copy, perhaps I asked my Mom to buy it for me? You can imagine the look on Fred's face when the song started playing. To his credit we did listen to the whole four minutes twenty two seconds of it, but he soon skipped on to Glyn's "Sugar, Sugar" by the Archies.

This was the type of trouble I was always getting into; I wasn't so much naughty, as cheeky or mischievous. Most of the time it was my wit or quick thinking sense of humour that got me into trouble. This has occurred throughout my education, my work life and even to this very day. Wherever I go there are always two other people with me, both of them invisible to everyone else around me. They only appear when I have a funny quip, retort or comment to make, which is generally most of the time! The exact moment I have a funny thought, a little man appears above my left shoulder, saying, "Go on, say it." Almost immediately, the second man appears on the opposite shoulder saying, "Don't say it, it is not appropriate". Torn between the two of them, I invariably always listen to the little guy on my left, occasionally regretting it as soon as I have opened my mouth. I have more than a few examples when this happened from my time at Harold Malley, unfortunately far too many to record here. For example the time when our Chemistry teacher asked the class if anyone could remember the alternative name for Copper Carbonate. We had only been talking about it the week before, so I immediately put my hand up. The answer was supposed to be 'Malachite', a blue-green powder we had experimented with in test-tubes during the previous lesson. Sir pointed to me and said, "Day, can you tell me?" I am not sure how long it was before I replied, but straight away up jumped both little men, one on either shoulder. The one whispering in my right ear, "Succumb to your better judgment" the other screaming in my left one, "Go on, just say it". Of course I always knew which one was going to get their own way, every time he was louder and more persistent. "Mala-shite, Sir," I said with confidence. Luckily for me he thought it was just my pronunciation that was poor, while my classmates knew better and were rolling about in fits of laughter.

Engineering Workshop, Theory and Practice (EWTP) were particularly boring lessons. These were the lessons during which I usually got into trouble, because there was nothing else to occupy my mind and stop it from wandering. We were taught by Mr. Jones, who was a truly nice guy; it was just that his subject was tedious and uninteresting. There are two memorable occasions when I said something out of place, for which I received corporal punishment in the form of a T-square. For those not in the know, a T-square is a large wooden instrument used for drawing vertical and horizontal straight lines in technical drawing, one of the subjects in EWT&P. Incidentally it gets its name from its resemblance to the letter 'T'. During the first instance, which is clear in my memory, the class was standing around the blackboard in an engineering workshop while 'Sir' drew shapes for us to guess what they were. They were all geometric shapes, such as a Kite, Parallelogram, Rhombus or Octagon, all except for the last one which he drew to try and catch us out. This happened to be his attempt at drawing a polygon, which in geometry terms is *a flat shape consisting of straight lines that are joined to form a closed chain or circuit.* Sir was smiling all over his face, as guess after guess proved to be wrong, making him smugger than usual. All of the time I could see exactly what he had drawn and my two little men were once again arguing it out, one on each shoulder, as to whom I should listen to. I don't need to tell you which one won. Suffice to say, when I was asked the question I replied, "It looks like a pair of knickers to me Sir." My classmates all hooted with laughter, but Sir must have got out of the wrong side of bed that morning, because my bottom soon felt the pain of his anger.

No one other than me could be blamed for that particular occasion, but the other definitely fell at the feet of my Dad. We were in a port-a-cabin having our weekly Technical Drawing (TD) lesson located at the back of the girls' school opposite. Exactly where it was is not critical to the story, but having our TD lessons over at the girls' school did compensate somewhat for the tedium we had to put up with each week. During our eighty minute lesson, the girls generally changed rooms at least twice, making for a pleasant distraction, as they walked up and down the staircase. On this particular day Roger, the class swot, asked Sir what the engineering term 'ball race' meant. Mr. Jones did his customary thing and threw the question out to the class. There was a deathly silence that befell the class, because none of my fellow students had a clue. I knew though, because my Dad had told me, not too many months before. Was this the correct stage on which to share my knowledge? One little man said "Yes", the other "No": who should I believe? Not wishing to disappoint the little fella on my left and hoping to make my classmates laugh, I put my hand up, straight in the air. My chest pointed outwards and upwards, proud that I had the answer nobody else had even attempted to guess at. Relieved someone was about to give an answer Mr. Jones said, "At last someone with a bit of intelligence. Day can you tell the class what a ball race is please?" "Yes Sir," I hastily replied before the little man on my right shoulder could speak again. "It's a Tom cat with thirty yards start on the vet." Sir had a job to make himself heard over my classmates, as they fell about in fits of laughter. Unfortunately for me he didn't mind waiting. After he had threatened half of the class with a detention he quietly informed me to be outside of his office, at lunch time, with a friend for a witness. By the end of the day, once more I was experiencing an uncomfortable, warm feeling from my rear.

I often contemplate about what Mr. Jones told the rest of the staff at lunchtime that day, and how they all reacted to my joke. Were they offended by what I had said, or did they privately have a chuckle behind the closed door of the staffroom? I like to think they saw me as a window of light relief in the otherwise humdrum of school life and the antics of the really bad boys at the school. I am not sure it did anything to enhance the content of my school reports though. My grades were generally average or above, but with comments like "cheeky" and "could do better", Mom and Dad were never too impressed. I say not too impressed, but possibly it was more not too interested. I hope I am not doing them a disservice when I say this but I don't remember them ever taking a great deal of interest in my school work. There was very little support for my studies and probably even less when it came to homework. At Harold Malley all pupils were expected to complete a homework book each day and have it signed by a parent each week, to confirm we had put in the effort recorded. I don't recall Mom and Dad ever checking to see if I had completed what was expected, or that I had answered the Maths questions set for me. In fact it was frequently a struggle to get them to even sign the book at all. I admit I should have done more studying and perhaps then I could have obtained better grades, but there was no real motivation or encouragement from either of my parents.

I honestly believe I got on well with most kids in the class. There were one or two strange ones who either played robots at playtime or spent their breaks in the physics laboratory being 'radio hams'. Needless to say most of them went on to study at Oxford or Cambridge. Given any opportunity the rest of us played football in the playground. Just like on the big green, goalposts were jumpers or satchels, but because we were not allowed to play with balls we had to use a 'boggit'. A 'boggit' was generally about four inches in diameter and was comprised of a pair of old socks bound tightly together using yards and yards of brown sticky tape. Our boggits were not always perfectly round, thus making them difficult to control and pass during the match. They didn't do much for your shoes either, with the toes coming off worst. At the end of every day our mostly black shoes would have toes that were white from scuff marks.

Playtimes were the only occasions when I played with my classmates, because all but two of them lived in the 'better' parts of Solihull. My evenings and weekends were spent with lads from the Cranmore Estate, either on The green playing football or cricket, or at the local youth club, participating in trampolining, five-a-side football and darts. The Youth Club closed at about eight o'clock and there were no alternative places to go to other than our local hostelry. Hence at the age of fourteen I had my first taste of beer! Our local was the George and Dragon, on the corner of Blackford Road and Stratford Road. We only ever had the one drink, usually sitting on the steps at the front of the building, looking out for any passing policemen. I am not sure whether it was true, but my mates always said I looked the oldest and therefore sent me in to purchase the beer. I didn't mind, in fact I felt pleased they trusted me to carry out this important task. (I was used to going into pubs anyway – Les and I had to attend the weekly Angling Club meetings at the Red Lion in Earlswood.) One of the lads would come in with me to help carry two out of the four glasses, but I always recall them looking rather sheepish. Besides looking older, I had a part-time job and could therefore afford a better pint than everyone else. They had to do with the dregs of the barrel, M&B Mild at 1 shilling and 11 pence, while I regularly drank a pint of 'Double Diamond', at 2 shillings and a penny (equivalent to 10 or 11p today). Although I had a reasonable relationship with the lads from the estate, I always felt there were a few of them that had feelings of resentment. From things that were said I believe some of them felt aggrieved that they went to work and paid taxes, while I was still at school.

These visits to the pub at night may account for the not very high marks at school and just barely enough, efforts at homework. The only lesson I ever excelled in was Mathematics and that was because I found it relatively easy and therefore didn't need to put in too much effort. Eventually I managed to pass seven GCE O levels and asked to stay on at sixth form to study for my A levels. Mom and Dad found it difficult to understand why I would want to! Don't misunderstand me, they never stopped me from furthering my education, but they rarely showed any real interest or gave me any encouragement. After all, I was the first family member to stay on at school to study for any type of further education. That was as far as it went though. Almost without exception, everyone who stayed on to take A levels at Harold Malley applied to University at the end of the two years. My two years in sixth form were without doubt the best years of my school life, but I knew that was the end. There was never any thought or consideration about going to university because regrettably there was no way Mom and Dad could afford it!

Mr. Townsend (bless him), was my form tutor at the time and he became quite concerned about what I would do with my life after I left 'Malley'. He was also my Maths teacher, so suggested I went into teaching. Feeling that I was not too impressed with the idea, he arranged for me to see the school's career advisor, 'Fat Sam' Radford. I spent five minutes talking to him before he asked me to complete a lengthy questionnaire. The questionnaire was a multiple choice, question and answer booklet about my likes, dislikes and attitudes to life. I remember there were sixty questions in total, all with five answers to choose from. I had to stick a pin in the answers that best suited my opinion and had twenty minutes to complete the lot. When twenty minutes were up, Sam unfolded the booklet, held it up to the light and noted that the pin holes spelt out the words 'Pig Farmer'! This was supposedly going to be the most suitable career for me, based on how I had answered the questions. There wasn't much call for pig farming in Solihull, so 'Fat Sam' arranged for me to see a horticultural employment agency in Warwick. They were very helpful and found me an apprenticeship to apply for. It was at the Research Centre in Luddington, near Stratford, with the prestigious Royal Horticultural Society. I became really excited about the interview and they were suitably impressed by my knowledge of vegetables and flowers and my enthusiasm for gardening. The many hours spent at Home Farm with my Grampy and tending to my own vegetable plot had given me a distinct advantage over all the other applicants.

I was so excited when I got home, being able to tell Mom and Dad they had offered me this fabulous opportunity to learn a trade and do something I really loved. It wasn't long before my excitement was abated with Mom bringing me back down to earth as she explained the reality and practicalities of what I wanted to do. With starting pay at just less than fifteen pounds per week, there was no way I could afford it. My options were find accommodation near to Stratford, or travel twenty miles each way on the bus each day. The former was too expensive and, did I really want to devote up to an hour getting to work every morning? Hindsight is a wonderful thing: perhaps I should have taken less notice of Mom and let my heart rule my head. Yes it may have tested my commitment to horticulture, but dreams are rarely achieved without hard work and some sacrifice. If I had accepted an apprenticeship with the RHS, who knows where I may have been today? I could have been a gardening legend like Percy Thrower, or a television celebrity like Alan Titchmarsh. One thing is for certain, my life would have been very different than it is today. It may have been better and more successful, but I doubt whether I would have been happier. It is unlikely I would have ever met Heather and consequently Kerry and Matt would not be here today. Therefore despite some regrets, I would change nothing! After Gran and Mom's Headteacher stopped Mom from going in to nursing when she left school, she maybe should have known better. Having said that, Mom may have cajoled me into declining the apprenticeship opportunity for all of the wrong reasons, but I am pleased she did!

# Chapter 11

## ITALIA '72'

With an apprenticeship at an RHS Research Centre having had 'weed killer' poured all over it by Mom, I still had no plans of what to do when I left school. So when in early 1972, my final year at Harold Malley, I discovered an advertisement in the Sunday Mercury for vacancies in the Royal Air Force, I knew I was destined to be a pilot. The roles were for non-commissioned officers and having had a Grammar School education I soon received a letter inviting me for interview at RAF Biggin Hill, in Kent. It was the most comprehensive assessment I have ever had, comprising a full day medical, a full day of aptitude tests and finishing with a two hour formal interview. It involved staying over for two nights, which meant we were all being scrutinised and evaluated for around sixty hours. The scrutiny even continued while we relaxed in the bar during the evenings, having a drink and playing darts. The medical was extensive, involving a full body screening, including comprehensive sight and hearing tests. The aptitude tests were just as thorough, with written tests as well as practical activities to check our reactions and hand eye coordination.

When it came to the interview, I believe I performed to the best of my ability. However, I did find some of the questions to be quite personal and searching, as they tried to establish my background and knowledge of current affairs. The only four questions I recall being asked were: "What does your Dad do for a living?", "What newspaper do you read?", "Which political party do you support?" and "What are your views on support for the current famine in Biafra?" The first three were easy to answer: I am not sure that Canteen Assistant, the News of the World and Labour were the answers they wanted to hear, but I knew they were all correct. Dad did what he did, he bought the Sunday newspapers and the values and principles I inherited, or he exposed me to, meant I would never vote for anyone else.

The last question was a little trickier, because I presumed there was no right answer. I knew about the famine in Biafra, but had no idea as to what had caused it. Having just 'Googled' it, I now know the Republic of Biafra was a secessionist state in south-eastern Nigeria that existed from 30 May 1967 to 15 January 1970. The creation of the new country was amongst other things a cause of the Nigerian Civil War, also known as the Nigerian-Biafran War. After two-and-a-half years of war, during which a million civilians had died in fighting and from famine, Biafran forces agreed to a ceasefire and Biafra was reintegrated into Nigeria. I can recall the famine reports on the BBC television news, which were very graphic and upsetting; showing children starving and emaciated. Not surprisingly, Biafra was regularly a topic for non-politically correct jokes in the playground. Not being aware of the cause of the famine I probably gave pretty poor answers. I recall waffling on about tackling the root causes and not just the symptoms. I remember saying rather than providing food and first-aid, we should concentrate on making Africa self-sufficient, thus ensuring famine would not happen again. I felt we were saving the children, for them to go through the same difficulties five or ten years' further on in time.

At the end of the three days we were all given a de-brief on our performance and told whether or not the RAF would be taking our applications any further. By the time it got around to being my turn, there were just two other lads left; everyone else had been given the thumbs down and had already left for home. I cannot remember the rank of the officer who spoke to me, suffice to say he had a handle bar moustache and spoke with a 'plum' in his mouth. He was very positive towards me and starting by saying, with clarity and deliberation, that I had passed the medical A1, G1 and Z1. This meant I was fit to work in the air, on the ground and out in the tropics. He continued with the fact I passed the aptitude test with flying colours, having reactions and the hand-eye coordination to be a pilot. At this point my pulse started to race, as I thought about how I would react when he told me I had been successful. I remember thinking I should stay calm and dignified, suitable for the occasion. Finally, he moved on to the outcome of the formal interview. I recall his very words, even now forty plus years later. "We all thought you were a fine chap, but not the sort we are looking for."

On the train home, trying not to be too disheartened, I thought about why they didn't want me in the RAF. Was it because my Dad wasn't a doctor, lawyer or General in the armed forces? Perhaps I only read 'tittle tattle' in the News of the World and not about proper current affairs, or maybe because I was my father's son and would never vote Tory? It did even cross my mind that it was because I was a 'Ginger' nut! I desperately tried to imagine what colour hair Biggles had. Biggles was the nickname of James Bigglesworth, a pilot, adventurer, title character and main hero of the 'Biggles' series of adventure books written by W. E. Johns (1893–1968). While I had been desperately trying to avoid taking out any books from the school library, all of my mates had been avidly reading this popular series. If only! Perhaps it was none of these reasons and I was never meant to be a pilot after all. A few years later when I met Heather, she informed me her Granddad used to be a Wing Commander in the RAF and if I had used him as a reference, things may have turned out differently. It was a case of not what you know but more about who you know. Whatever the reason, the only thing I would have changed about my life is the Sunday newspaper I read. As for the rest, I can honestly say I would not have changed one thing about my Dad and what he stood for.

With my career in the RAF not taking off and there being no possibility of furthering my education, I started to think about what I should do when I left school in June. The decision I made was quite unexpected, out of character and completely down to my school mate Dave. He was the smallest boy in our year, but had above average intelligence and was a 'footie' fanatic. His team was Leicester City, but he idolised Johan Cruyff, a former Dutch international, widely regarded as one of the greatest players ever. Cruyff won the Ballon d'Or, often referred to as the European Footballer of the Year award three times: in 1971, 1973 and 1974. This award is presented annually to the player who is voted to have been the best player over the previous calendar year. Johan Cruyff is best remembered for the 'Cruyff Turn' a trick of evasion he perfected and had named after him. To make the move, Cruyff would look to pass or cross the ball. However, instead of kicking it, he would drag the ball behind his planted foot with the inside of his other foot, turn through 180 degrees and accelerate away leaving a bemused defender. It still remains today one of the most commonly used dribbling tricks in the modern game. Dave would spend hours in the playground each week, trying to emulate his hero and together we spent many an hour practising our 'keepie uppie' skills. We perfected, no, invented, new ways of catching the ball. None of them were very elegant, but we certainly had great fun practising them.

Dave was much better off than I was, because his Dad ran the local music shop in Shirley. He would often bring to school a 45rpm single record that I wanted, once I had given him the money. There was no friend's discount, but it just saved me the trip and bus fare into Shirley. I am not sure he approved of my taste in music, because he would often say, "You don't want to buy that, it's rubbish!" Dave's Dad was in the fortunate position of being able to take Dave and the rest of his family on exotic summer holidays. I remember in the summer of 1971 they spent a fantastic holiday in Dubrovnik, part of the former Yugoslavian republic. It may not be exotic by today's standards, but it certainly was forty years ago. While I was dodging the rain for a week near Beer in Devon, Dave was on a sun drenched beach of the Adriatic, chatting up foreign girls.

In the September he returned to school full of stories about his wonderful holiday and how he had become pen pals with a great looking girl from Vukovar, a town in the mountainous area of Yugoslavia. The letters were a bit one sided, because he knew very little Yugoslavian and had to write all but the first and last words in English. Still, this didn't matter because his new friend wanted to practise her English skills. She also had a friend, who Dave desperately tried to find a pen pal for and somehow he persuaded me to start writing to her. I am not certain as to whether I saw it as an opportunity to improve my English writing skills, or whether it was because Dave said she was "a bit of a looker"! Her name was Georgia Papic Durda and I wrote to her each month about nothing in particular. She would write back detailing what a lovely time they all had in Dubrovnik and what a good looking and wonderful boy Dave was. I think Dave was getting on slightly better with his friend and soon became desperate to meet up with her the following summer.

This is when we both started to plan a trip to Yugoslavia. We scheduled the trip to start immediately after we had taken our A level examinations. I rarely ventured very far from home, mainly because we couldn't afford to, and here I was planning a two month trip across Europe. I suppose dreaming about this exciting trip made it difficult to revise and prepare for my all-important examinations in June, but again there was little or no encouragement or guidance from Mom and Dad. Dave and I were enthralled about the whole romantic idea of hitch-hiking across Europe to meet two girls. It was okay for Dave, he knew what to expect, but for me it was an awfully long way to go just for a blind date! In the weeks leading up to our trip we spent more time together than we had previously done in seven years at Harold Malley. We joined the Students Union and the Youth Hostelling Association, bought rucksacks and camping equipment, purchased train tickets for the start and end of our journey and learnt a number of useful phrases. The one that sticks in my mind and the one I will probably never forget is "*Wollen sie mit meiner luftmatratze spielen?*" This is German for "Would you like to play with my airbed?" a chat-up line that has never really taken off.

The family next door lent me a 'top of the range' sleeping bag and Shirley whom I worked with at the Plough restaurant said we could borrow her tent to save ourselves some money. The guy next door, whose name I cannot remember, worked in the stores of Her Majesty's armed forces and was able to lend me a sleeping bag used by our troops out in tropical locations. It was filled with eiderdown and was guaranteed 100 per cent water-proof, giving me the option to zip myself up in it completely. It was so unbelievably warm and dry, just what I needed. Needless to say, whilst I was very grateful for Shirley's tent, it was not quite to the same exacting standard as the sleeping bag. My rucksack was packed with all of the other essentials items including:

Wash kit, toothpaste and toothbrush,
Deodorant, shampoo and Nivea sun-cream,
Galvanised plate and mug,
Knife, fork and spoon,
Two pairs of jeans,
Two Ben Sherman short sleeved shirts,
Seven pairs of pants and a pair of socks,
A pair of swimming trunks,
Passport and documentation,
A hundred and ten pounds in cash and traveller's cheques,
And finally the things I can never do without, two combs.

A few days before we were due to leave, I received the latest letter from Georgia enclosing a photograph; apparently she was getting really excited about my imminent arrival. I had to read the letter several times to work out exactly who was in the picture she had enclosed. Initially I thought it was a photograph of her brother or cousin because the person had short, almost cropped hair and was wearing a pair of 'jack' boots. After a third reading of the letter I realised Dave had been economical with the truth about Georgia. She wasn't "a bit of a looker" as he had led me to believe, but was in fact a well-built tomboy with very few feminine characteristics.  Up until that point I hadn't really been nervous about the trip, but all of a sudden I developed a sick feeling in my stomach. It didn't last long, because I soon accepted that there was no point in panicking; all of the arrangements were in place and the cost of the train tickets was non-refundable. Ever the optimist, I convinced myself she wasn't that unattractive and probably had a fantastic personality. That's what Dave must have seen in her!

Soon the first of July 1972 arrived and I said my goodbyes to Mom, Dad and my brothers, as I was about to set out on an unforgettable adventure; a trip like I had never come close to encountering before. Dave's Dad kindly offered to drop us in London in time to catch our train to Brussels. Both the car and train journey gave us the start we needed. It catapulted us on to mainland Europe, meaning we were well into our trip within a very short space of time. Progress from there would be slower, but it would not be long before we arrived at Vukovar, in deepest Yugoslavia, to be greeted by our awaiting pen pals. For the first night we had booked a bed in the city's Youth Hostel, just to ensure we had somewhere to stay on our first evening. Having planned my trip with military precision, I had taken a small amount of cash for the countries we were travelling through so as not to waste time looking for a bank while we were on our way to Vukovar. Unfortunately Dave hadn't made the same provision and only had English traveller's cheques, which the hostel didn't accept. Being mates I agreed to use my currency and pay for all food and lodgings on the way to Yugoslavia and Dave would then reimburse me later.

The next morning we ate an early breakfast and made our way to the outskirts of the city to begin our hitchhike through Belgium, Germany and Austria, towards the western border of Yugoslavia. It wasn't long before we received our first lift; the drivers seemed to be queuing up to take us to wherever we wanted to go to. Dave and I had both bought "GB" car stickers to fix to the back of our rucksacks and we were holding signs indicating our desired destination. Our meticulous planning was already paying-off; at this rate we would be in Vukovar in less than a week. We made great progress in the first two days passing through Frankfurt, Stuttgart and Munich, finally ending up in Salzburg, some 582 miles later. My Dad had told me about the wonderful German autobahns and how they were recognised as the best roads in Europe. Everyone had said how great they were, but to be honest Dave and I were not that impressed. They were made from concrete blocks and were far noisier and more uncomfortable than the tarmacked M1 we had driven down two days previously. The cars were much better though, usually our lift was in a large Mercedes. They were so different to what I was used to. The cars were large and roomy and appeared to have just two speeds: zero or 160 kilometres per hour. Every driver drove at a hundred miles per hour and about three feet from the car in front. I remember turning around in the back seat of one car and being able to see the whites of the eyes of the driver behind. It was quite scary, particularly when our hosts were driving at the same speeds while turning around to try out their English skills on us!

We arrived at the edge of Salzburg quite late on in the evening. We were dropped off at the West Salzburg exit of the A1 autobahn by our kind driver just as it was getting dusk. Conveniently, at the end of the slip road, there was a large piece of grassland, perfect for pitching Shirley's tent. This was the first time we had tried erecting it, having stayed our second night in a youth hostel in Stuttgart. I have always been good at putting together flat-pack furniture, so one six foot, two person tent was no problem to me. Twenty minutes later Dave and I were snuggled up in our respective sleeping bags, listening to the hum of the passing traffic. By this time it was dark and rain clouds had appeared overhead. Within five minutes of climbing into the tent it was raining – we had made it just in time!

Half an hour later it was still pouring down with rain, the canvas tent had got soaked through and the first drop of rain began to fall from the apex of the roof. It all happened very quickly, but within five minutes we may well have been sleeping in the open-air, because the tent was affording no protection at all. Perhaps our planning had not been as thorough as we had first thought, or perhaps Shirley should have told me the tent wasn't waterproof. It didn't take us many minutes more to decide to pack up and find somewhere drier to stay. I soon began to wonder if we had made the right decision, because I had been completely dry in my sleeping bag. By this time the rain was coming down in stair rods and we were walking along a road, not knowing where the hell we were going. On top of this, the sodden tent was in my rucksack, which now weighed more than the wooden fishing creel my Dad had made for me some years previously. I am sure you can visualise the scene quite clearly: two young lads wearing jeans and short sleeved shirts, struggling along the road in the dark and looking like drowned rats! Luckily for us it wasn't long before a couple of locals took pity on us and came to our rescue. They took us in their car to the nearest information centre, where they organised a local 'pension' for us to stay at. They even dropped us right outside the front door, for which we were so grateful. This was just one example of the kindness shown to us by everyone throughout our whole journey. Well before midnight we were out of our wet clothes and asleep in a double bed with clean white crisp sheets. I was momentarily concerned, because Dave was the first bloke I had ever slept with, but under the circumstances I decided to make an exception!

The next morning we were up early, fully refreshed and ready to be on our way. All traces of the previous night's rain had evaporated away and the sun was now shining. Before we left I tried to wring as much water out of the tent as I could, so that my shoulder wouldn't give way under the weight, while we travelled across Austria. To speed up our journey we had already decided to catch an Alpine train through the mountains. This was by far the easiest and quickest way to escape Austria. The last thing we wanted to do was to have to use the tent in the mountains; the next time we might not have been quite so lucky. Before catching a train towards Yugoslavia, we decided to take the opportunity of doing a little sight-seeing. After all, Salzburg was reputed to be one of Europe's prettiest cities. We both enjoyed our whistle-stop tour of the city, probably Dave more than me, because I was dragging the tent around. Exhausted from the morning's efforts I chose to buy an ice-cream. Of course Dave still didn't have any cash so I offered to buy one for him. He declined the offer and sat watching as I licked my way through the most gorgeous blackberry and apple dairy ice-cream I have ever tasted. The choice at the stand had been phenomenal; I had never come across so many and such unusual flavours in all my life. I had not quite finished when Dave said longingly, "I wish that I had said yes now."

"Was it a particular flavour you fancied?" I replied.

"No," he countered, "it just sounds so nice!"

Ow! I thought, where did that come from? I may have been brought up on a council estate, but Mom and Dad always taught me to eat with my mouth closed and told me never to make a noise whilst eating. It was only a moment's thought though; I soon forgot about what he said and before I knew it we were arriving in Yugoslavia.

We had been told that hitchhiking in Yugoslavia would be difficult, but no one told us we would spend three whole days at the roadside in one tiny village, without a single offer of a lift. Even the "GB" stickers weren't enough to entice drivers to stop for us. What made matters worse was the weather was pretty poor. Luckily it didn't rain but it was very overcast and cool. Having not packed any jumpers, I spent most of the time in my sleeping bag. By the end of the third day we would have gladly gone anywhere in Europe, but not one driver slowed down to even look at us! We slept on the beach for two nights, that is if you can call it a beach. It was more of a rocky outcrop, definitely not a golden sandy beach like the one Dave had spent the previous summer on in Dubrovnik. The great thing about hitchhiking is you get to meet many other interesting and more experienced travellers. We stuck it out for three days, while dozens of seasoned travellers had more sense, gave up and turned back towards Italy. I had a good reason to be more determined than them though. I was on my way to a blind date with a Yugoslavian 'wrestler' in Vukovar!

On the fourth morning, despite my protestations, Dave said he was turning back and making his way to Italy, so that is what we did. I felt quite bad about not continuing to Vukovar, because there was no way of letting Georgia and her friend know about our change of plan. Still to this day I don't know for certain how disappointed they both were. I have a feeling they were not best pleased, because Georgia never wrote to me again. It was either being stood up on our blind date, or that she didn't take to the photograph I put in the post before I left. Perhaps she wasn't impressed and I appeared to be far too feminine looking for her – who knows?

We could not even get a lift out of the country so were once more forced to spend our scarce cash on a train to Trieste, in Italy. One of the more experienced guys we met advised us to buy a ticket to the border and then to purchase a ticket on the train for the remainder of the journey. This way we paid for local travel, which was a fraction of the cost of an international, cross border ticket. He said the whole journey would cost us less than a pound, instead of five. That had got to be worth doing.

The new plan went well and we were soon speeding our way through the countryside,; hopefully towards warmer climes and easier lifts. That was until we crossed the border and were confronted by the ticket collector. He was very officious looking, more like a policeman than a railway worker and he couldn't speak a word of English. We were proud of the way in which we managed to make ourselves understood: two single tickets from the border to Trieste in Italy. However we soon came back down to earth when he said he wanted 2,400 Dinars from us in exchange for the tickets. This was one time when I wished I hadn't been great with numbers, because with 24 Dinars to the pound I immediately knew this was coming out at fifty pounds each. The guard could probably see the blood literally draining from our faces, as we told him we didn't have enough money to pay. I had only taken a hundred and ten pounds in total for the two months. Fifty pounds out of that and I would have been living on bread and water for seven weeks, until I caught the train home from Milan. For ten minutes we sat there arguing with him that fifty pounds each, for a half hour train trip into Italy, was extortionate and we would rather walk the twenty miles than pay that sort of money. He was just about to throw us off at the next station, when a gentleman who had obviously noticed our distress, came over and asked if he could help. When we explained the situation to him, he half smiled and spoke to the ticket collector in Croatian. He then turned to us and explained it was in fact only 24 Dinars. There had recently been a devaluation of the currency and the collector was talking in 'old money'. Apparently many of the older locals were resisting the change and refused to recognise the new rate. After handing over our 12 Dinars each, equivalent to fifty pence, we wiped the sweat from our brows, settled down in our seats and enjoyed the remainder of the journey!

We arrived in Italy in a much better frame of mind. There was a cloudless, lovely azure sky and as we stepped off the train it was noticeably much, much warmer. Little did we know that every day for the next seven weeks the weather would be exactly like this. I felt considerably more comfortable being in Italy. I had started to learn Italian in the final year at Harold Malley so was happier in an environment where I could now speak the language, or at least make myself understood, a little. "*Eravamo arrivati.*"

Exhausted by permanently standing on our feet for three days and the trauma of the morning's train journey, Dave and I made straight for the beach for a well-earned rest. The sand was fabulously golden and clean and the water of the Adriatic was both clear and warm. The cold overcast days spent on the roadside in Yugoslavia seemed a long way away and thoughts of my blind date were long gone. I was so tired, the embarrassment of showing off my pure white body amongst a beach full of bronzed Adonises melted with the thought of lying on the warm sand. On went the swimming trunks and I lay down by the water's edge, soaking up the warm rays of the midday sun. This was heaven – well worth the long trek across Europe. True to form, I was fast asleep within minutes of my head hitting my rucksack, which was being used as an improvised pillow.

I awoke some three hours later as the rising tide lapped against my toes to discover I was "done to a crisp". At first I just felt a little warm, but by the time we were booked into a campsite, the front half of my body was starting to tingle all over. I knew what was required, but standing under a cold shower just took my breath away. There was so much heat in the upper layers of my skin, as soon as I stepped under the shower head I sizzled like a red hot pan being lowered into the washing up water! That night I honestly thought I would either die or end up in hospital. My skin was so tender to the touch, I could not bear to have anything touching my chest or legs and the slightest movement meant I was in agony.

For the next week, I decided it best to keep covered while my body recovered from its ordeal. I intuitively knew when it was safe to expose my body to the sun again. After seven days the skin on my chest and legs peeled off in one complete sheet, to reveal a somewhat still pink body below. From then on I made certain I used the sun-cream Mom packed for me. I also rationed myself religiously to twenty minutes per area at the beginning, gradually increasing it as the days went by. I was adamant I would not be caught out again. The plan worked brilliantly. Within three weeks I was using suntan oil and by the end of the trip I needed very little protection at all. It was a lesson I learnt the hard way. Since that day I have always been very careful, usually ending up under an umbrella with a towel over my legs, while everyone else enjoys the sun.

We had not been in Italy long, when Dave asked me how much money I had left from all of the different currencies I had changed back in England. There wasn't a great deal; only the odd note and mainly coins. I was really taken aback when he accused me of being dishonest and withholding the truth about how much he owed me. He felt we could not have spent as much as we had and to be honest I found it difficult to remember every occasion I had put my hand in my pocket. Having paid out for all accommodation, transport, meals, drinks and items bought while travelling to Yugoslavia, I could not account for every last penny, but I knew exactly what I had left. I was hurt, but in the interest of keeping the peace I tried to forget about the accusation and made sure I stayed friends with Dave and enjoyed the rest of our time in Italy.

During the next month we did experience numerous fantastic and memorable situations and met many wonderful and generous people. We travelled down through the centre of Italy as far as Rome and turned back, along the western coastline, towards Milan, our final stop. Without doubt the highlights of our journeys were visiting Venice, Florence and Rome. Italy has so much history and culture, and the food, wine and people in my opinion are second to none. *"Tutti sono meravigliosi"*. Apart from when we were stuck in Yugoslavia for three days it appeared everyone wanted to stop and offer us a lift and on many occasions much more. Many of the drivers went out of their way to drop us off exactly where we wanted to be. Others bought us drinks and snacks; one German in Stuttgart provided us with a ten Deutsche Mark note, because he had taken too long to get there and the banks were shut when we arrived. Without doubt though, the kindest person we came across was also a German. He stopped to offer us a lift on our way to Livorno, which is on the coast just south of Pisa. At the time, together with our experience with the guy in Stuttgart, it completely changed my attitude towards Germans; they didn't behave how I had expected them to. We were hitching a lift on the edge of a small village when the guy in question pulled up in, yet again, a large Mercedes car. Livorno wasn't far away, we only needed to travel along the coast road for around fifty miles. We jumped at the chance of his kind offer, particularly when he asked if he could buy us a coffee before we set off. Apparently he was on his way back to Germany and therefore had a long day ahead of him. He said his name was Hartwig, which kind of amused our schoolboy humour. At the café Hartwig made short shrift of his espresso and left Dave and I to finish our cappuccini and '*bomboloni*', while he went to the bank to change some Deutsche Mark into Italian Lire. Our choice of refreshment was easy to make, because for the previous three weeks our breakfast had generally consisted of coffee and doughnuts.

Five minute later Hartwig arrived back at the café, we put our rucksacks in the boot of his car and climbed into the plush leather seats for the trip ahead. I suppose the journey took no more than an hour, which flew past while we were discussing the successes of the England and Germany national football teams. We were quite buoyant because of our great recent win over Germany in 1966, but he was more interested in Mexico 1970 and the accusations against Bobby Moore. On arrival at Livorno Hartwig surprised us both by saying he had inadvertently changed too much money and could he buy us lunch. I looked at Dave and Dave looked back at me. He had only been to the bank an hour ago, surely it wasn't an accident that he had too many Lire. We were both thinking the same thing: what did he want in return? Perhaps we should have said no, but up to then everyone had been so kind; surely he was too?

Hartwig seemed to know all of the local restaurants and soon settled upon a lovely little café, with tables outside looking across at the sea. We all had similar meals: veal, potatoes and salad, washed down with a bottle of Peroni and followed by a huge bowl of fresh fruit. Again over lunch we chatted about sport, but probably football mostly; it was all very civilised and certainly the most substantial meal we had eaten in weeks. On most days since arriving in Italy, lunch comprised bread rolls, Bel Paese cheese, ham and tomatoes, or if we were feeling flush, pizza. Incidentally, with a budget of one pound a day, that was not very often. Not being accustomed to such cuisine we left the table feeling rather full but highly contented, perhaps though with a little apprehension. Surely Hartwig would not foot the bill and just drive away; what was our contribution expected to be? It turned out to be absolutely nothing. We collected our rucksacks from the boot of his car, shook hands and thanked him for his generosity, before he waved goodbye and drove off into the distance. *"Molto gentile."*

A few days into the trip we had been so disappointed with Shirley's tent, after we discovered it was far from being waterproof. In the rain it was about as much use to us as 'a chocolate teapot'. However, after the horrendous experience in Salzburg, Shirley's tent then became an asset to us. For the rest of the trip, the weather during most evenings was kind to us, so it didn't matter that the tent leaked like a sieve when it rained. However, there were two occasions when during inclement weather the tent became a 'chick magnet'!

The first time was when we booked in at the local camping site in Mestre, just outside Venice. Apart from sleeping on the beach, camping was by far the cheapest accommodation, which meant we had more of our pound per day to spend on food. The first task when we arrived was to find a suitable pitch: somewhere flat and reasonably close to all of the facilities. Late at night we didn't want to be fumbling about in the dark, trying to find our way to the toilets. We found a very convenient spot and began to put the tent up, but were soon dismayed by the dark clouds overhead and the threat of rain. When the raindrops started to fall, we both looked at each other and hesitated about whether or not we should continue. Our indecision had not gone unnoticed by the occupant of a tent nearby. She was about twenty years of age and what I would describe as an 'Italian beauty'; blonde hair, dark tan and stunningly attractive. "*Bellisima.*" Not only was she good-looking, but her English was impeccable. She asked us if we were having difficulty in putting up the tent. When we told her it was not waterproof and recalled the Salzburg nightmare to her, she made us an offer we couldn't refuse. "Would you like to join my sister and me, in our tent?" she asked. "My parents have gone off to Milan for a few days and left us on our own." I hope I didn't seem too keen, but without hesitating I replied positively with a "*Si, grazie*".

We sheltered in their tent from the rain and got chatting about where we were from and our European trip. I say a tent, but compared to ours it was like Buckingham Palace. It had multiple rooms, you could stand upright in it and it had proper furniture; table, chairs and beds. Her English was so fluent because she was studying it at university. Unfortunately because I was so taken by her good looks I cannot remember her name, so will refer to her only as 'Bella'. It wasn't long before Bella's sister arrived back at the tent and Dave and I were introduced to her. It was hard to believe they were related. She was considerably older and looked nothing like her younger sibling. Never mind, I was the one that spoke Italian, so hopefully I would have first choice.

We got on really well and I was becoming more confident with my Italian. I had only studied it to O level, but it all came flooding back to me. For anyone who has ever learnt any Italian you will know one of the first questions you are taught is: "*Sei sposata?*" which translates to "Are you married?" Without really thinking I tried out this phrase and of course she wasn't. Bella replied with a smile and complimented me on my accent, but I think she was just being kind. The girls invited us to join them for dinner, saying they could cook enough pasta for us all. I said, "*Si per favour,*" and made an offer to lay the table, which they readily accepted. Just when Dave and I had got excited and built our hopes up, Bella asked me to lay up for six. Were her parents coming back tonight? We hoped not! Their parents were not returning from Milan for another week, but what 'Bella' had forgotten to tell us was their two older brothers were also staying with them. They were quite a bit older, even older than her sister, and they were very athletic looking – not the sort you would want to mess with. After initially feeling a little deflated, it didn't really spoil our evening, because not unsurprisingly the lads were interested in football. With a few glasses of wine, good food, great company and banter about football the evening passed quickly and before we knew it, it was time for bed. We may well have been disappointed about sleeping on our own that night, but at least we were well fed, comfortable and dry.

That is more than can be said on one evening in Viareggio when we had an almighty thunder storm, about an hour after we settled down for the night; it was Salzburg all over again! The rain was undoubtedly heavier and there were frequent flashes of lightning that lit up the inside of the tent so well, that we could see the water dripping off the roof. Outside of the tent it was like Clapham Junction; there were dozens of campers shouting and running in every direction, trying to dodge the rain and make their way to cover. We were just thinking about escaping to the nearby toilet block when some idiot ran past and tripped over a couple of our guy ropes; ripping the tent pegs completely out of the ground. They hit them so violently that the tent poles came out of the ground as well and the whole thing collapsed in a soggy heap on top of us. If we hadn't decided to make a run for it by then we weren't going to be hanging around for much longer! We picked up our sleeping bags and headed for the toilet block! Not the best or most comfortable place we had found to sleep in the last five weeks. I soon settled down on the hard concrete floor and found no trouble in closing my eyes. My sleeping bag, borrowed from my next door neighbour kept me beautifully warm and dry. Not so for Dave though. He had brought along a bright, flowery bag made from nylon or polyester. Dave was already damp from being in the tent and it definitely wasn't keeping him warm or dry. After approximately ten minutes he started to shiver, so I had a decision to make. There were three options. I could let him join me in my sleeping bag, let him die of hypothermia, or I could go back to the pile of wet canvas that was our tent and find him some extra clothes. In the blink of an eye, I was out of the toilet block searching through our belongings.

The rain was still hammering it down and the light was not particularly brilliant. I wasn't having a great deal of success in locating Dave's jumper, when the lady from the tent behind us asked me if there was a problem. She could clearly see our tent was no longer usable in its current state, so why did she ask? I quickly explained some idiot had been kicking out the tent pegs and we were sheltering in the toilet block for the night. Without hesitating she said, "You must come and stay the night in my tent. There is only myself and my daughter and we have plenty of room." Once more we had been rescued from disaster by a kind generous female. Dave was unbelievably grateful to me for sorting it and even more so when he discovered the couple were French. This time he had the advantage and could practice his language skills. Soon we had forgotten our demise and after a few glasses of wine, great food and good company we had comfortable camp beds to retire in. I lay there pinching myself for a while, because as I mentioned earlier I don't really like the French, but here were a couple of French ladies offering compassion to two complete strangers – how kind!

Kindness was all I ever encountered in the two months of my trip. No one tried "to put one over on us", or showed the slightest bit of a negative reaction towards us. Everyone engaged us in their conversations, allowed us to join their games of football and offered us shelter and refreshments. From the drivers who stopped to give us lifts to the group of Austrian students who paid for our bar bill. Perhaps this was unusual, we were very lucky or just nice lads; I don't know. I have since heard many tales of how travellers have been chased, mugged and robbed during their journeys across Europe. Whatever the truth, it made for a memorable experience, one I will never forget.

I suppose I told a little white lie when I said "Kindness was all I ever encountered", because as the weeks went past Dave and I began to get on each other's nerves more and more. It is hardly surprising when you consider how much time we had previously spent together. Being friends at school is one thing, but living in each other's company 24 hours a day, for six weeks is very different. There had been Dave's earlier questioning of my honesty and integrity and towards the end, each day there were little disagreements and snide remarks. There were still two weeks to go before we had to catch the train home from Milan and we were camping on a site in what looked like a disused quarry. It resembled a huge bowl and as such, absorbed every ray of sunshine throughout the day, which meant the temperature in the tent was unbelievable. Immediately the sun came up, the temperatures rose and by the end of the day we couldn't even contemplate entering Shirley's tent. This meant the evenings were pretty unbearable and the occupants of our tent immeasurably irritable.

On about our third morning Dave went off to the shop to purchase breakfast and asked if I wanted him to buy me anything. I said "no". I was too hot and bothered, felt thirsty, but not very hungry; I just wanted to escape the heat as soon as possible. He arrived back ten minutes later with a couple of dry crusty rolls and began to tuck in, which made me feel even thirstier. I probably wasn't feeling at my best, when suddenly things got much worse. It hadn't happened all trip, but now for some reason the little man appeared on my left shoulder shouting, "Go on, say it." You can tell how low I was feeling, because the other guy never even bothered to make a show, to put up any resistance. So without considering the consequences I leaned towards Dave and whispered, "I wish that I had asked you to get me something now".

"Are you feeling hungry then?" he replied.

"No," I countered, "yours sounds so nice!"

Ow! Dave went red in the face and screamed, "That is it, I'm leaving!" Five minutes later he was walking up the road, on his way, never to be seen by me again for almost thirty years. He tried to persuade me to give him the tent poles, so neither of us would have a tent for the rest of the trip. I told him firmly that he didn't have to leave, but if he did, it would be without any of Shirley's tent. Two weeks later, I half expected to meet him in Milan, but didn't. At the time I had the feeling he was home sick and could no longer stand the rough living. I later discovered he had stayed in a pension for two nights and caught an early train home.

I enjoyed being on my own for the next couple of weeks. I have always enjoyed my own company and have never minded the solitude, like my Dad really. I continued to meet numerous wonderful people and to have many memorable experiences; none more so that the night I awoke to find a scorpion crawling up the inside of my tent. Not wishing to harm it, I caught it alive and went down to the toilet block, where there was enough light to make a positive identification. It soon attracted quite a crowd around the urinals until the owner of the site came in to see what the commotion was all about. He took one look at it, threw it to the floor and squashed it with his size nines, saying with some authority, *"Che non e un scorpione!"* He may well have said it wasn't, but I knew a scorpion when I saw one and there was no way I was sleeping in my tent that night. Luckily for me kindness abounded again and an English family gave me a camp bed under the awning of their caravan for the night.

The last thing I did before catching the train home from Milan was to spend the day looking for a fishing tackle shop. It wasn't easy, but I eventually located one and bought myself a roach pole with my last five pounds. I carefully transported the rod back to England, guarding it with my life. I would be the envy of the Red Lion Angling Club. Roach poles were only ever used by Europeans; you could not even buy them in the shops back home. I could not wait to see Les' face when I showed him.

Kindness from drivers continued right up to the very end of my trip. Arriving at Victoria station in London I still needed to get up the M1 and back to the Midlands. Expecting this to be the most difficult part of the trip, it only took five minutes before I was on my way. The final lift was from a young mom and her 12 month old son, who was on her way home to Wolverhampton. I cannot imagine this happening today. It would be difficult to obtain any sort of lift, let alone from a female. The lady even went out of her way to drop me at the end of the A38 Aston Expressway, from where I was able to catch a bus for the final leg of my journey. I cannot remember her name, or that of her son, whom I entertained for two hours, but I felt so grateful to that kind lady. I was desperate to arrive at Arbury Hall Road and to a few home comforts.

When I finally made it back to Shirley, that day in early September, Mom and Dad were extremely pleased to see me. They got to find out about Dave's early return from cousin Jackie. She worked at Dave's dad's music shop. Therefore, during the previous week, not knowing where I was, they had been concerned for my safety. I certainly had changed in two months. I had dark skin and weighed a stone and a half lighter! Mom wasn't quite sure if it was a tan or just grimed in dirt. After putting me on the scales, she sent me straight up stairs for a long hot soak in the bath, while she cooked me the largest fry up I have ever eaten. I had returned from a memorable journey, tired but with many life changing experiences and countless tales to tell. Most of them would have to wait until the morning though. My bed was calling me: it was great to be home.

# Chapter 12

## ON THE SHELF AT 19 (THE KEY TO SUCCESS)

There were lots of stories to tell Mom and Dad and much to catch up on about what had been going on at home. One of those things was my A level results, which had arrived by post a few weeks earlier. I suppose you could say it wasn't the best news I had ever received, with just one grade D in Chemistry. My other result was for what was supposed to be my strongest subject, Mathematics. I wasn't even given any classification at all; I failed it completely! It still amazes me today that I managed to do so poorly in my best subject. Had there been a mistake in the marking? I will never know because Mom and Dad weren't the sort of pushy parents to question the result, or challenge the Examining Board.

This meant with little chance of a half decent job, I needed to find work quickly. Mom and Dad could not afford to keep me, so it was imperative I started to bring a wage home. I landed on my feet really when I visited the local Tudor Grange Swimming Pool to show off my tan before it disappeared. A lad I knew, called Dave, told me the manager was looking for an extra lifeguard and asked if I would be interested. Within fifteen minutes, Mr. Pocklington watched me drag a person the full length of the pool, carry out mouth to mouth resuscitation and surface dive to pick up a brick from the bottom of the deep end (12 feet six inches). He didn't bother to ask any questions about me personally; that was it, the job was mine! It was a good job too. It didn't take too much effort, it paid well and it attracted plenty of girls. There was however a certain amount of cleaning necessary each day before the pool opened. If you have ever worked at a public swimming baths I am certain you would never go swimming there again! One of the daily tasks involved clearing the scum off the surface of the water that built up overnight. The water inlets meant the scum accumulated at the deep end where the diving boards were. The scum usually covered an area of more than 500 square feet and lay several inches thick. It was mostly white, topped with a deep yellow; a result of body oils, cosmetic residues, waste and chemical by-products forming insoluble materials. Most of the foam could be scraped off the surface into the waste channels around the edge of the pool, but the residual was broken up only to reform the following night. The final job meant diving to the bottom of the pool to clear debris and other undesirable objects off the outlet grills. You just never knew what you may end up with in or on your hands!

Most swimmers were completely unaware of what was needed to keep everything looking pristine each day. There were certainly many regulars at the pool, none more so than 'One Blue'. This was the nickname given to a gentleman who swam every Sunday morning and could be found queuing up at the door, at half past seven, a full half an hour before opening time. The reason for him trying to be first in the queue each week was down to the procedures at the pool. Clothes were put into wire baskets and handed in to the attendants on duty to be stored in racks in a secure location. In exchange for your clothes, you received a coloured wrist band with a number on it. This allowed bathers to get back their own clothes after their swim. Racks were filled up in a specific order, so that at peak times swimmers with a certain colour of band could be called out, to make way for people waiting. The first band of the day to be handed out was number One Blue, hence the reason for the nickname. He did everything in his power to ensure his clothes went in 'One Blue'. He never took a band, he would just say, "One Blue, please". Others did their best to obtain the elusive 'One Blue' on a Sunday morning, but never managed it. 'One Blue' was already changed when he joined the queue – trunks on and bare footed. He was obsessive about diving into the pool first each week and woe betide anyone who denied him the pleasure!

The quietest time was weekday mornings when local schools had their swimming lessons. By far the quietest sessions were when the girls' schools were in; generally more girls sat on the side of the pool than swam. They always seemed to have justified reasons for not entering the water. This was in complete contrast to the boy's schools, when nobody sat out of lessons. When I became a lifeguard, I was almost 19 and couldn't really say I had been out with any girls. I often wondered whether there was something seriously wrong with me, which would mean me being alone for the rest of my life. Yes there were crushes throughout my school days and the occasional girlfriend, which usually lasted for just a week or two, but generally I was shy with members of the opposite sex. It may have had something to do with attending an all-boys grammar school, but I had also been scarred by Mrs. Ricardo. She was a neighbour who lived two doors away from us, at number 88. Mrs. 'R' was of South African origin and hence loved the sun. She had dark, wrinkled skin and the most ginormous bust you have ever seen, probably about 44GG. Mrs. 'R' smoked heavily and had a deep scary voice, which she used to tease Gra and I. Whenever she saw us, she would creep up behind us, corner us and say, "Give us a kiss." I don't know about Gra, but I was petrified of her and would do anything to avoid her or escape her grasp. It may have been fifty years ago, but even today I can still visualise her bust, scary face, and hear her voice.

There were many young girls at school whom I fancied, some I have already mentioned, like Lynne from recorder group. My very first sweetheart was Sonia, better known as Poppy. She lived on the Stratford Road near Monkspath and our moms knew each other from the Young Wives Club. Our most romantic encounter occurred during the Church Fete, when we shared a swing boat and I presented Poppy with a plastic ring I'd won on the hook–a-duck stall. The romance went a little pear shaped after I went to her fifth birthday party and apparently 'showed myself up'. Poppy's Mom recalled something I said at the party. When asked if I wanted anything else to eat I replied with an anxious voice, "Yes if I get the chance." Also at the party was Roberta, a lovely blonde girl with a twin sister in another class and a very unusual double barrelled name. I think every boy in the class liked Roberta, who loved playing kiss chase. Being rather an unusual name I recently Googled it to see if I could find out what ever happened to her. To my surprise I discovered a girl with the same name who appeared in the men only magazine Mayfair, Volume 11 Number 8, in 1976. Is it a coincidence that she was born in 1953 as well? Surely there cannot have been two girls with such an unusual surname, born the same year.

There was also Amanda, the tallest girl in the class who was not the prettiest, but who had a distinctive twitch that attracted me to her. For those of you who can remember Samantha from the 1960s and 70s TV series 'Bewitched', her twitch was reminiscent of Amanda's. Amanda was permanently contorting her face to stretch her nose and wiggle it from side to side. The infatuation didn't last very long because during the second year at school she left and moved to another part of the country. Perhaps I should have realised then that I was destined to be on the shelf until I was much, much older.

When I attended Harold Malley there were girls who I fancied, but it was only ever from afar; I was just too shy to approach them. There was Maureen, Bernadette, Lynn and Liz, to name but a few. The only girl I really dated while at school was a friend of Cousin Jackie. She must have made a big impression, because I cannot for the life of me remember her name. I think it may have been Carol – I am not sure. I first met her at a party. That may sound pretty normal and exciting, but this was no ordinary party. Carl, the lad who caddied at Shirley Golf Course with me all of those years ago, was sixteen, a year younger than me. Mrs Swan arranged a birthday party for him at her house in Widney Lane. I was invited and not having much of a social life, jumped at the chance. Perhaps with hindsight I should have thought about it a bit longer.

When I arrived, Mrs Swan told me Cousin Jackie would be coming along and was bringing an 'old flame' of mine. It kind of surprised me, because I couldn't recall any old flames. I could honestly say my candle had never been lit! Carl was already at his own party and I was the first to arrive. We made polite conversation for ten minutes until Cousin Jackie arrived with 'Carol', whom I had never seen before. Mrs. Swan announced that now we were all here, we could start the party. It definitely was not the sort of party I had expected. Instead of dozens of party goers, with good music, flowing booze and a gourmet buffet, there were four of us, eating crisps, drinking orange squash and listening to one 'Long Player' record on a gramophone. It was a good job I took along my 'Tighten Up' volume one, or else there would have been no music to listen to. Carol made a bee line for the chair next to mine and sort of attached herself to me, in more ways than one. Receiving Carol's full attention, the party soon turned from what should have been a nightmare into the best party I had ever been to: she was all over me like a rash. I did feel a little guilty. It was Carl's birthday and he was sitting there like a gooseberry, while I was having a great time.

Before I knew it, Carol and I were going out together; my first real girlfriend. Our first date was arranged for the following weekend. Carol said there was something on at the cinema that she really wanted to see. She explained that it was an X rated film and therefore we needed to go dressed up, in order to appear to be the correct age. This was easy, I had been buying drinks in the George and Dragon for the last three years, so with my suit on I would easily pass for eighteen. However, I was more concerned about Carol who was three years younger than I was.

I need not have worried, because when we arrived at the Odeon cinema, in Shirley, the attendants never questioned our ages. Carol chose the back row where we made ourselves comfortable. Up until then the only film I had ever seen at the cinema was 'The Battle of the Bulge' (a World War II film) with Dad. So it was a bit of a shock when I discovered the film she wanted to see was the Derek Ford film, 'Wife Swappers'. There is no need to explain what the film was about, suffice to say there was not a great deal of dialogue in it. This didn't appear to bother Carol, who quickly became very excitable at what can only be described as very graphic scenes. I think it was approximately halfway through the film when I decided the relationship with Carol was starting to move too quickly for me and perhaps we should end it. A week later Carol and I were no more and once again I was single and available.

Once I was working as a lifeguard, there was a choice and I could have taken my pick of the girls. With my uniform of white shorts and t-shirt complementing my recently acquired tan, it was difficult not to notice me on the poolside. The role of a lifeguard was to be aware of everything going on in the pool, constantly on the lookout for bathers in distress. This involved sitting for hours on end in a very tall, strategically placed chair, or walking up and down the side of the pool, swinging a whistle around your finger; first one way and then the other. The whistle was to let swimmers know they were breaking the rules or to attract attention if you were about to dive in to save someone. Most of the girls who went swimming were regulars, so you got to know them by name. They would either stand at the base of the chair and chat to you or shout out comments as you walked past. The strangest comment I received during my time at the baths was, "Have you got sand on your legs?" I am unsure whether it was the tan they were referring to or my hairy legs.

Somehow one of them got to know my birthday and bought me a wallet, making another girl jealous. Her name was Chris, who at the time was probably the only person shyer than I was, if that was possible! She had younger twin sisters who came and chatted me up on behalf of their elder sibling. Although Chris only said a few words, she was nice looking and in a way was more my kind of girl than Carol had been, so I agreed on a date. We arranged to meet in Shirley at 19:30 on Friday evening, so we could catch a bus into Birmingham. The plan was to visit one of the night clubs and do some serious dancing. It appeared we both liked similar styles of music.

I had already been frequenting clubs in town on a regular basis, places like Rebecca's and Barbarella's. I used to go with a few lads from the estate, usually on a Friday night. I can hear you saying to yourself, good looking lad, above average dancer, why hadn't he met someone already? I think it had something to do with the fact Ossie and Graham who organised the trips into town were heavy drinkers. So by the time I was onto my tenth pint of lager, I probably wasn't so good looking and not much of a mover either. There was many a time I would ask a girl to dance, only for her to need a visit to the washroom. I must have had one of those forgettable faces, because nine times out of ten they never recognised me and managed to find their way back again!

When I recall those nights on the town, I find it difficult to understand how we are all still here. Graham was the chauffeur, driving us all to and from the clubs. He probably had more to drink that I did and still managed to get behind the wheel. With eyes like 'piss holes in snow' he must have found it difficult to see, let alone drive eight miles home. In the late sixties, it was not an offence to drink and drive. The police could not stop anyone and could only take action if you were involved in an accident. Thank goodness things are different today!

Getting back to my date with Chris, I turned up on time at the bus stop on the Stratford Road by St. James' Church in Shirley, dressed in my smartest clothes and best dancing shoes. Chris arrived five minutes later escorted by one of the twins. I thought as they were walking towards me how considerate the twin was to make sure her elder sister met me safely. However, as they approached the twin announced her sister didn't feel like going into town and wanted to know if I wished to go back to their house for the evening. Being ever the gentleman I agreed and followed them both a hundred yards around the corner to spend the evening with all three of them. What Chris lacked in confidence, the twins more than made up for. They got to know me quite well and I found out loads about Chris, through them. We went out for about two weeks, although that is not strictly true. We never went out anywhere, we always stayed in and whenever I saw Chris, I saw at least one of the twins. Having never seen Chris alone in two weeks and without so much as a peck on the cheek, I finally decided to put a stop to it. She was the complete opposite to 'Carol': a shrinking violet as opposed to a budding nymphomaniac. I felt like Goldilocks from the fairy-tale, my girlfriends were either too... fast or too... slow. Would I ever find someone who was... just right, or was I destined to be on the shelf at nineteen?

Shortly after I ended my 'ménage a quatre' relationship with Chris and her sisters, I started going out with a few of the other lads from the baths, Jeff, Al and Dave. Jeff and Al had transport, which allowed us to cast our nets even wider; we could visit clubs and pubs off the 154 bus route! One of the clubs we frequented was the Boot at Honiley. It played great music and the drinks were much cheaper than the prices we paid in Birmingham. We would all arrive together, but then split into pairs for the night when looking for girls to ask to dance. My partner was Dave – a big advantage for me. He was not the best looking of our group and certainly not the most confident guy with the girls either. On one particular Saturday Dave and I met a couple of girls from Warwick, fairly early in the evening. Myself and my partner got on really well together. She was petite, lovely looking, but more importantly had a great personality: it wasn't long before we were chatting like old friends. Chatting soon turned to close dancing, warm embraces and the occasional long kiss. She asked me my name and told me hers was Maggie. "Maggie what?" I asked.

"Promise you won't laugh," she replied coyly.

 "Of course I won't," I replied sincerely.

"OK then, it's Maggie Spaggins."

I remember trying successfully to keep a straight face and saying something like "That's unusual, I never would have guessed," then moved in close again to distract from her embarrassment.

Ever aware of what was going on around him, Dave noticed us enjoying ourselves, so tried it on with her friend. This resulted in him receiving a sharp slap around the face and having to spend the rest of the night on his own. I am not sure whether time dragged for Dave, but for me the evening sped by and it was soon time for us to say our goodbyes. Maggie and I reluctantly parted, promising to meet up again the following week – perhaps this was it?

I spent the whole week thinking about the time we spent together and how Maggie Day sounded much better than Maggie Spaggins. I hoped she thought so too; I could hear wedding bells already. The ringing in my ears didn't last for long because Jeff and Al decided against going to the Boot the following week. The club was so far off the beaten track, there was no way of me getting there on my own and Maggie did not have a telephone. I can recall being so disappointed. What would she think of me when I never turned up? I imagine it would have been something along the lines of, "Typical bloke, they are all the same – unreliable." But that is just not me!

I soon put the disappointment behind me when Jeff and Al announced we were going to 'The Barn' in Hockley Heath. It had recently opened as a night club and everyone wanted a piece of the new scene. It played a great selection of music and had a revolving dance floor. At the time there was nothing else like it in

Birmingham. The advantage as we saw it was that you could stand, beer in hand, around the edge of the dance floor and watch out for the best girls as they danced by; a bit like at a cattle market. Hopefully the girl you wanted to dance with was passing close by as the next record began to play. It didn't always work out like this; often the girl you fancied was on the opposite side of the room.

Towards the end of the evening I remember asking a young girl to dance. She was attractive, very slim, had long, darkish hair and was wearing a full length burgundy halter neck dress. I had been attracted to her by the good looks and a great sense of rhythm to the dance tracks being played. She accepted my offer of a dance, which turned out to be a lot more than one. She said her name was Heather, she was fifteen and a half and just about to sit her mock O level examinations. Little did I know, my life was about to change forever. I clearly remember telling her off, saying she should really be at home revising. I was a fine one to speak with my exam track record, but I had learnt from bitter experience!

During the next hour we danced and chatted endlessly. I suppose I should have been put off by an early comment she made, but I was too smitten to care. Apparently she had noticed me standing on the side and had been secretly hoping I would ask her to dance. I immediately wondered whether it had it been my looks or my dance moves? No, it just happened to be the shoes I was wearing. They were my white leather and brown suede brogues I bought from Dolcis. Apparently a guy Heather fancied, but who wasn't interested in her, had an identical pair.

Heather was in a small group of friends, all around the same age and whose Dads took it in turn to take and collect them from dances. So a few minutes before twelve, just like Cinderella, she told me her carriage awaited and ran off to catch her lift home. I ran after her and managed to quickly ask if I could see her again. She gave me lovely kiss and replied with a beautiful smile that she would be coming to The Barn the following week. My heart almost stopped as I thought back to the Boot at Honiley and my 'what might have been' with Maggie, only seven days before.

My anxiety soon dissolved into anticipation, when Jeff and Al announced they had enjoyed themselves so much they would be going back the following week. I don't know how I got through the next seven days. Every spare moment of each day I thought about Heather; I could not get her out of my mind and kept wishing my life away. Saturday 27 January 1973 eventually arrived and I dressed myself appropriately for the evening ahead. The first things to go on were my shoes. They were what Heather first noticed about me; I had to wear them. Luckily my checked Oxford Bags had extremely wide legs, which meant it wasn't too much of an ordeal putting them on over my shoes. With a cream shirt and dark jacket to finish, I was ready to make a suitable impression.

I met up with Jeff and Al in Solihull for a well-earned drink. A day working at the swimming baths meant you needed more than a pint to rinse the smell of chlorine from the back of your throat. We were all in a jovial mood and left the Masons Arms just after nine o'clock, as The Barn was only a short drive away – around fifteen minutes. We parked the car and approached the reception, where a crowd of people were gathered. I think it was Jeff who said "It looks busy tonight lads".  Then disaster struck. My heart sank as I heard one of the bouncers say, "Sorry lads we're full up. There will be no one else coming in tonight." There were more than a few choice words said in the heat of the moment. Why did we have to buy that last round of drinks? It was happening all over again: the 'Spaggins' curse!

I remember my heart beating quickly and the adrenalin pumping around my veins, when I heard a voice shout, "The gents' toilet window is open!" The gents' toilets were located on the side of the building, towards the back where it was reasonably dark. The window was not large, probably about two feet wide by four feet high, but was fairly low to the ground. I don't remember my feet touching the ground as I darted towards the window. I reached it in time to see the first pair of feet disappearing through: I was the second one in. The first lad to make it stood guard on the door, while others piled through the illegal entrance. In total there must have been twenty of us clamber through the window in as many seconds. Then one by one we made our way out, inconspicuously so as not to arouse suspicion. All four of our group made it. Hopefully we were in for a great night.

After grabbing a quick drink from the bar I scanned the dance floor to look for Heather, but to no avail; she was nowhere to be seen. Perhaps she had taken my advice and stayed home to revise for those all-important exams. I chatted to the lads for most of the night and I know I definitely wasn't good company. I constantly searched the crowds for a glimpse of Heather's face and didn't really want to dance with anyone else. My night was ruined. Perhaps I was too upset and agitated to be able to recognise Heather – what would she think of me? She would think I was rude and perhaps had had a change of heart and didn't fancy her. I cannot remember what state I was in, but I was completely unaware that she had spotted my shoes again and was trying to get my attention. Apparently on several occasions she brushed past me, purposefully almost knocking the drink out of my hand. It went on for about an hour and still I never noticed her. The time for her carriage was getting closer and closer.

After a couple of drinks I made one of my usual visits to the washroom and stood there looking at the window, which by this time was now closed. What a waste of time. I had risked doing myself a mischief by scrambling through the window, and for what? I left the toilets somewhat dejected, hoping the time would pass quickly. I was not having a good time. On leaving the gents a girl I knew approached and spoke to me. It was Nicola, a friend of Jeff's. She had a large grin on her face when she excitedly told me, "There is someone looking for you." I sort of grunted an acknowledgement and continued towards the entrance of the dance floor. The noise was always loud and the disco lights usually very bright, but as I turned the corner and stepped into the room it was different this time. The music appeared to be muffled and the room seemed dark, so dark I could not see the faces of anyone. I looked over to where I had left Jeff and Al and could not see them. They were all a blur. Then I noticed a single lonely figure walking towards me, as clear as anything, standing out from everything else. It was Heather and she was surrounded by the brightest light I have ever seen. A light comprised of every colour of the rainbow in an arc surrounding her completely. Heather appeared to have an aura around her, appearing to me like I imagine the Angel Gabriel appeared to the shepherd thousands of years ago. It may sound cheesy and you may think I have 'gilded the lily' a bit, but I can honestly say it is exactly how I remember it.

We were both pleased to see each other and relieved we were finally together. I believe I danced for the first time that evening – everything seemed so right. We never left each other's sides for the rest of the evening, dancing to many a great tune. None more so than 'Me and Mrs. Jones', sung by Billy Paul. Heather and I agreed it was our favourite tune of the moment and from then on it became our song. Whenever we hear it, it is a constant reminder of a very special time in both of our lives. Determined not to miss out on future times together, Heather gave me her telephone number before she left in her carriage. There were no mobile phones in the early seventies and why would I carry a pen and paper with me, so I had to memorise her number and promise to call one night in the week. Heather was concerned I might forget it, but I assured her there was no way I would forget. Her number and the memories of that evening were etched on my brain forever.

I did worry myself that I may not remember the telephone number, but on the Tuesday evening I made the all-important call. I thought all weekend about what I might say and whether Heather would still be so keen. I need not have worried, my fingers tapped out the number as though I had known it all my life and Heather answered before it had time to ring a second time. We arranged to meet on the Friday evening, at 8:00, in the High Street, Solihull. This was all a new experience for me and for the first time ever I was excited with anticipation about seeing a girl. There were butterflies in my stomach and I could not think about anything else, even, most unusually, food. The night arrived and I waited for half an hour at the bus stop in the High Street wondering whether or not Heather had been having second thoughts. I was almost on the point of walking to the pub for a miserable pint on my own when a very apologetic Heather arrived in quite a state. The half past seven bus decided not to turn up and she was half expecting me to have given up waiting. Still we would have a great evening together, wouldn't we?

The Mason's Arms was the 'in' pub at the time, so that's where we went for a drink. Heather not being quite sixteen drank a soft drink and I had my usual pint. Once again we enjoyed each other's company and soon chatted away as though we had known each other for ever. Talking to her came so easily, not something I was used to. Heather was extremely surprised when she discovered I was a lifeguard at Tudor Grange. It suddenly dawned on her that she had seen me before, walking up and down the side of the pool, twizzling my whistle. Heather was amongst the girls sitting on the side, not taking part in the lesson. She told me she had noticed my legs and quite fancied me, but she had not recognised me with my clothes on!

It seemed as though we had only been together for five minutes when she announced she had to be home for ten and should really be catching the next bus home. We had been in The Mason's approximately half an hour and I hadn't even managed to finish one drink, but I was determined to make an impression and agreed to see her safely home. Unfortunately for me, home happened to be in completely the opposite direction to where I lived. It was a ten minute bus ride and a good ten minute walk on top. I walked her to the top of her path, kissed goodnight and was saying my farewell, when she asked if I would go inside and meet her mom and dad.

To my surprise her mom and dad were expecting me; they had only allowed Heather to meet me on condition she took me home for them to vet. Possibly if I had not agreed to go in, I may not have seen Heather again, who knows? I think they were surprised by my looks. Heather told them I had blonde hair and dark skin, but nothing could be further from the truth. Although in fairness the Italian sun had bleached my hair and my tan was still quite evident. Heather's mom and dad were both very pleasant to me, her Mom in particular fussing around me to make me comfortable and feel at home. She even brushed down my jacket, which by this time had one completely white arm. Heather had been wearing a white fur jacket – not a real one, but one with simulated fur where the fur comes out and sticks to anything and everything. They were very grateful to me for walking their daughter home and her Dad offered to give me a lift back into Solihull, which I readily accepted. I think they felt

Heather was safe with me and therefore could meet me again, which she did.

Over the next few months we arranged to see each other once or twice a week. Not too often, after all Heather had her studying to think about. During that time I met the majority of her family and most of them appeared to take to me. Heather's Mom said to her, "He's a nice lad, but not the one for you," and Heather's Gran was more concerned with my appearance: "He's a nice lad, but I wish he would get his hair cut." Her Dad was never one for many words, he was just impressed by my time keeping. If I said I would be there for seven o'clock, I was there for seven. No earlier and no later. He often commented that he thought I came early and waited at the top of the road until the time I promised to arrive. The only member of her family who seemed to resent me, was her brother (although I have now won him over with my charm and wit). Maybe he felt protective towards his younger sister and felt she was too young to become romantically involved. After ten weeks most of Heather's close family were becoming attached to me, but Heather herself was starting to have second thoughts. I didn't know at the time, but she told me some months later that she felt I was being too nice to her. I was kind, considerate, and thoughtful and paid her too many compliments, which she felt could not be sincere. Heather was not used to being treated like this, but why would I treat someone I cared for any differently? That's what my Dad would have done.

If Heather's brother was not keen on us being together at the start, what happened in the April was about to harden his resolve even more. Our relationship was becoming serious and we both felt being together was right and that it would naturally last forever, so why didn't we get engaged? If we did I was determined to do things correctly, so I asked her Dad for his daughter's hand in marriage. Bearing in mind Heather was still only a fifteen year old schoolgirl, her dad took it quite well. I dropped Heather off one Saturday evening and popped in to see her Mom and Dad, as I usually did. I had been nervous all day, wondering how I might broach the subject and had rehearsed the words over and over again in my mind. Heather's Mom was upstairs and her Dad was just about to leave the living room when I said tentatively, "Will it be all right if Heather and I get engaged on her sixteenth birthday in July?" I have never seen the colour run from anyone's face quite as quickly as her Dad's did that evening. He went ashen white as he appeared to slowly slide down the wall, close to the door. After picking himself up off the floor, he replied, "I'll go and talk to your mother." We waited nervously for around ten minutes for her Dad to reappear with her Mom. "We have had a discussion on the matter," they said, "and feel it is too early for you to become engaged. If you still feel the same in twelve months' time, you can buy Heather a ring for her seventeenth birthday." We both accepted their reply, but were not best pleased. We both knew how we felt and that we would not change our minds; besides we were both old enough to make decisions like this, or so we thought. It was not until exactly twenty four years later when our daughter Kerry was fifteen, we realised just how young and immature we must have been at the time.

The next fifteen months soon passed by and Heather's Mom and Dad arranged an engagement party for us with everyone invited. Most people, but not quite everyone, were happy for us and gave us their blessings. Malvern Hall Girls' School was one of those not celebrating the engagement, especially with Heather being voted as Head Girl. They definitely had never had a Head Girl wearing an engagement ring before and they were "not going to start now; it would not be a good example to the rest of the girls." A similar situation occurred when Heather went to Birmingham University, Teacher Training College in Dudley. At her interview they made her aware they had noticed she was engaged to be married and took great delight in telling her, "Girls who are engaged when they come to the college do not stay engaged for long." Heather must have been the exception to the rule because on 1 July 1978, a week after she completed her degree, we were married at Solihull Methodist Church. This became the day when I definitely realised I was not a person to hide my emotions. It was the day I had been waiting for so long; the day when I wept buckets because I was so happy and the day 'I was finally off the shelf'.

Marrying Heather is without doubt the best thing that has ever happened to me. From the day we first met she has been so supportive, providing me with the motivation and a reason for making the most of myself. I have so much to thank her for, when she encouraged me to reach for my goals and supported me in my further education. Without her, who knows where I may have been today – I might well have still been a lifeguard! I doubt I would have earned myself two degrees and gone on to hold successful jobs with a large FTSE100 company. I believe Heather has been the key to unlocking the potential inside of me by giving me the encouragement and support, which I don't feel I ever fully got from Mom and Dad. Please don't take this comment the wrong way, because I have an awful lot to thank Mom and Dad for. They sacrificed many things to ensure their children never went short and had the very best start in life given our family circumstances. They instilled in me values and principles of life, which I will never change; values which probably can only best be learnt from being brought up in a 'poor' environment. However, whatever nature or nurture influenced the first nineteen years of my life, I sincerely believe the next forty years spent with Heather has brought out the best in me. I can compare my life with that of a plant or flower. The start in life, which Mom and Dad were responsible for, allowed me to set down firm roots that are essential for a plant's vigorous growth. Without strong roots plants become weak and unstable. Roots provide stability and hold plants firmly in the ground, providing nutrients to ensure healthy growth. However, without the further nurturing and 'tender loving care' provided by Heather, this plant probably would not have blossomed in the way it has. But good blossoms are only possible with strong roots and a healthy plant. What I am trying to say is I have Mom, Dad and Heather to thank: Mom and Dad for a wonderful start in life and Heather for finally completing the 'Making of a Ginger Nut'. I certainly would not have been enthused or motivated to put pen to paper and write this book without Heather. After all, she was the one who first got me thinking about whether it is nature or nurture that moulds our lives.

*Gran and Grampy's Wedding Day in 1924*

*Gran and Grampy.*

*Grampy in the garden;*
*flat cap and with a cigarette in his mouth.*

*'Home Farm', 1130 Stratford Road.*

*Gran, and Mom with Grampy*
*cutting dahlias in the garden at 'Home Farm'*

*I spent many a long and happy hour by the pond at 'Home Farm'*

Mr. A. Carter

Our portrait this week is of Mr. Arthur Carter, hon. sec. of the National Viola and Pansy Society. Mr. Carter, who has been actively associated with the Society since its revival, about thirteen years ago, was its Show Superintendent before taking over the duties of Secretary, and has carried out the secretarial work faithfully and well for the past five years. The cultivation of Violas is a great hobby of Mr. Carter's; he has secured several prizes, including the Society's Silver Medal, and has been awarded a First-Class Certificate for his own seedling, "Mrs. A. Carter."

## Who's Who in the Gardening World

No. 202.—Mr. A. Carter, hon. sec. of the National Viola and Pansy Society

*The newspaper cutting about my Great Granddad, Mr. Arthur Carter.*

*Best in Show' fuschia*

*Receiving my cup at the Hartshill Garden and Allotment show - Grampy would have been so proud*

*A prize winning garden; - two years running*

*The 'Granny' boots I wore, were not like those worn by the other lads on the estate!*

*and my canvas hockey trainers were not quite as robust as the real thing!*

*…. but the shoes that attracted Heather to me, when she was just 15, are still going strong!*

*Out of short trousers at last*

*The haircut that earned me a detention!*

*Class photograph – circa 1967 (6<sup>th</sup> from the left on the front row)*

*Uncle Les, doing what he loved;*
*how I remember him best.*

*Those slippery eels, caught on our infamous trip*
*to Bosherston lake in South Wales.*

*Making the most of my roach pole;*
*bought during my adventures in Italy 1972.*

*Mom and Les at mine and Heather's*
*Silver Wedding.*
*(the last time I saw my Uncle)*

*No wonder they got a shock in the gent's
Toilets at the motorway services!*

*Marathon training in 1992.*

*Heather, as she was when we first met in 1973.*

*Dad in a familiar pose;
with the pianola in the background.*

# Chapter 13

## NATURE OR NURTURE (THE CONCLUSION)

"An open-minded, logical thinking, introvert, who cares for and considers others, while being able to cope with the stresses and problems thrown at me by life." These are the words I used at the beginning of the book to summarise my personal traits. I have to impress on you that this is only my personal opinion: the way in which I see myself. Of course these views may well be biased. However, I believe that deep down, most individuals (me included) will generally have a good idea of what sort of person they are. Many of an individual's views about themselves will be based upon what psychologists refer to as 'reflective appraisal'. Reflective appraisal occurs when a person observes how others respond to them in certain situations. For example a comment such as, "You don't ever appear to worry about anything," together with the individual's knowledge about how they feel, may well lead them to believe they are calm under pressure or are well equipped to cope with the stresses and problems thrown at them by life. This is not always true, particularly if a person is given a false impression by somebody, or if the individual chooses not to believe someone else's remarks or comments. Do I behave how I perceive myself to be, or am I living with a deluded belief of what I am really like?

In the mid-1990s, while on holiday in Bournemouth, I recall paying a few pounds to have my hand writing analysed. Only a few months ago, while conducting research for my book, I uncovered the results produced for me. Graphology is the pseudoscientific study and analysis of handwriting, especially in relation to human psychology. Its use has been controversial and at the heart of much debate for more than a century. Although supporters point to the anecdotal evidence of thousands of positive testimonials as a reason to use it for personality evaluation, most empirical studies fail to show the validity claimed by its supporters. Perhaps you would like to read the results for yourself, to see if you feel it comes close to how I perceive myself.

*You show immediately from your handwriting that you have a sympathetic nature. You are the sort of person who will always be on hand for others and your kind considerate personality will be respected by those around you.*

*You are forgiving and will give people the benefit of a second chance, even if you have been hurt by their harsh and unkind behaviour. You believe in being fair, often this will be abused as you can be too easy on others.*

*You are fun-loving and easy going. You should be popular with friends and acquaintances and people will take to you very quickly.*

*You are trustworthy and will easily be offered positions of authority because of this.*

*You are not a person who requires fame or recognition. You are confident and happy as you are.*

*You are a person who does not expect your partner to be successful and you do not demand material goods, but you will need a stimulating and loving relationship to keep you well balanced and happy.*

*You are romantic and loving and you will expect your partner to be the same otherwise you may be discontented.*

*You are organised and methodical.*

*Your negative characteristics show that you can become possessive with a partner and sometimes you are forced to be jealous. You are also touchy and volatile.*

I remember thinking at the time how 'spooky' the remarks on my personality seemed; how similar they were to what I thought about myself. Therefore I am going to use this as a template for my final chapter.

Modesty prevents me from giving specific examples of perceived acts of kindness. Dad was always supportive and caring, even to complete strangers. He would always help someone who was struggling or clearly in need of assistance. Like him I will go out of my way to help others whether it is to carry shopping, change the wheel on a car, apprehend thieves, administer first-aid or go to their assistance in a crisis. I have never been put in a position where I have had to put my own safety at risk to help others. However, I would like to think despite any danger to my own health, that I would always go to someone's aid. If I saw a child, woman or even man being attacked, I hope I would intervene to try to prevent unnecessary harm coming to them. I may get hurt myself but I hope others would do the same if my grandson, daughter, wife or son were in a similar situation. I am not saying I would be reckless, I would always assess the situation and act appropriately to minimise the personal risk, but I don't think I could live with myself if I stood by and did nothing. After all I know for certain my Dad would have acted, so it must be the right thing to do. I am almost certain this is an example of nurture!

I won't elaborate further about acts of kindness, but I will relay to you an example of how these actions have impacted on my life and not always in a positive way. In 1990 I was working as a Data Information Officer, when a more senior post became available for me to apply for. I got an interview, during which the Senior Manager commented, "Oh yes, I did hear you were a bit of a Marje Proops!" Rebecca Marjorie Proops was best known as an agony aunt, writing the column *'Dear Marje'* for the Daily Mirror newspaper and the Manager was referring to incidents where I had gone out of my way to help a team member. For example a female member of my team who was experiencing severe relationship problems. I was an independent, non-judgmental person to whom she could unburden herself and discuss her options available. I felt flattered and privileged that she thought she could trust me to keep her confidence about something so personal and sensitive. I got the distinct impression the Senior Manager's view about my personality was seen as a weakness and went against me when making the appointment. Unfortunately for me I was not given the opportunity to explain why someone might have said this about me and what my motives had been. During my time as a supervisor/ manager my philosophy had always been that a manager's role is to "remove the barriers that prevent your team from doing a good job". I sincerely believe, if your team is happy, both in their personal and working environments, they will work hard and perform well. The Senior Manager in question had perceived my kindness as a weakness and not a strength in building a stronger and more reliable workforce.

I recently came across an appropriate quote, which says

*"Don't ever mistake my silence for ignorance, my calmness for acceptance or my kindness for weakness. "* ANON

How very true these words are, but sadly how often does the opposite occur in life today? None more so that the first phrase, "Don't ever take my silence as ignorance." I have sat in many a meeting where people have spoken just for the sake of speaking, irrespective of whether or not they had a valuable contribution to make. This type of person generally progressed in the company and those people like me who only spoke when they had something valid to say didn't. In deciding whether these traits I have are down to nature or nurture, I have concluded most of the influence is nurture, the way in which Mom and Dad brought me up. In particular the values and principles they instilled in me as a boy and the way in which they provided role models.

I suppose the second element of the unattributed quote, "Don't ever mistake my calmness for acceptance" is linked to the second graphology point, *"You are forgiving and will give people the benefit of a second chance, even if you have been hurt by their harsh and unkind behaviour. You believe in being fair, often this will be abused, as you can be too easy on others."* I do believe this is also true of me. For as long as I can remember, I have always tended towards supporting the underdog, people who are being picked on or 'badmouthed' by others. Often I feel the stance I take is perceived as me being deliberately obstinate, as if I am taking this person's part, just to spite everyone else. This could not be further from the truth, because I am a firm believer that people generally deserve a second or even third chance, irrespective of what they have done. Of course there are exceptions to this, but for everyday mistakes and misdemeanours that others make, it does warrant another chance. It might not be as a result of a wrongdoing that others 'gang-up' on someone else; often it can be a prejudice resulting from 'hearsay'. The best way to overcome your prejudice is to associate, or get to know the person better. Don't follow the pack, just because of what others say. Get to know the true facts and if necessary empathise with the individual. People only act in a certain way for a reason and often that reason can be the result of nurture – their life experiences.

I suppose some people may feel I am forgiving just for a quiet life. There could be an element of truth in that, but I like to think it is a forgiving nature and a belief that people are generally good at heart! I don't remember whether or not Dad was a forgiving sort of person. There weren't any occasions I recall where he had cause to be forgiving, so I have no examples to go on. I suppose there might have been his relationship with the rest of his family, but was this Dad's fault or was it the responsibility of others? Certainly Dad and Mom could have done more to build bridges; assuming there were bridges to be built. If there weren't they could have made more of an effort to have a closer relationship. I feel Mom was certainly more inclined not to be forgiving; she had a long memory and could be quite obstinate when she wanted to be. Not to say Mom was completely unforgiving, but perhaps not as tolerant as me. Is this trait in me nature or nurture? If it is the former, whom did I inherit it from? Not Mom or Dad. So was it some other relative further along the family tree or was it nurture? I think it was the latter! With hindsight Mom and Dad must have been forgiving at times, or else how would I have made it this far in life?

I may be caring about others, but it will never be at the expense of my family; family always comes first. Just like Dad I am very protective about my family and would do anything to ensure its wellbeing and safety. I am also very defensive about others criticising members of my family. It is fine for me to criticise them and what is said may well be true, but I will always defend my loved ones vigorously. Again this is one of Dad's traits and I believe I learnt it from him, I didn't inherit it.

The next graphology point, *"You are trustworthy and will easily be offered positions of authority, because of this."* I feel is also true. I know I am generally honest. There have been times in my life when through peer pressure I stole penny chews from Mr. Lewis' shop, in Marshall Lake Road. And yes, I have also told little lies, but I was never allowed to get away with either misdemeanour. Mom and Dad always found out and taught me the correct way to behave. In fact today I believe I am too honest. Who else do you know who has given a ten pound note back to a bank, because its ATM machine had dispensed too many to them; I did? Not everyone would own up to a restaurant that they had not been charged for items they had eaten or drunk. There have been numerous occasions when I have sent the bill back, because a bottle of wine had been omitted, or a round of drinks had not been charged for. Why wouldn't you? I religiously check every restaurant bill I receive and I always let the establishment know if they are trying to overcharge me, so why not tell them if the opposite has occurred? Besides I worked in restaurants for many years and know staff can often have the money deducted from their wages, if tills are short at the end of the night!

One of the graphology points I don't necessarily agree with is the, *"You are not a person who requires fame or recognition. You are confident and happy as you are."* It is true I am confident and happy and I don't particularly want to be famous, but everyone needs some degree of recognition.  That is recognition for what they do and who they are. Perhaps I desire recognition more than the next person. Let me explain. I was once on a training session, regarding the implementation of a new performance related pay scheme. (Incidentally this is something which I totally disagree with, unless it is judged on the performance of a team and not an individual.) Anyway during the workshop the Senior Manager went around the table asking attendees what it was that motivated them in a job. Without exception everyone said "money", that is until he reached me. I replied, "Yes money makes the job worthwhile, but it isn't my main motive. I just want to be loved by everyone." I don't think he had ever had a reply quite like it. I went on to explain further that recognition for doing a great job is important to me. I am motivated by people recognising my contribution and believing that I am a reliable, honest and caring individual. I basically want people to like me and I get upset if they don't. I am not sure what the driver is. Am I reliable, honest and caring to make people like me, or do I want people to like me because I am reliable, honest and caring? Perhaps I am too close to the answer to make a true judgment.

The graphology results said *"You are organised and methodical,"* which is generally true, but not entirely. Throughout my working life I have been organised and methodical. With my educational background in statistics, data collection and analysis, I have had to be. My whole career has been built around spread sheets, experimental designs and project plans. Even today I get great excitement and satisfaction from building a spread sheet or producing a plan to ensure things turn out the way I want them to. What's more there are plenty of examples where I have used my organisational skills in my personal life. For example when Kerry got married, I used 'Management and Planning Tools' to ensure nothing was forgotten and everything was executed in the correct order. Each task and its dependencies were rigorously recorded and monitored. I even used a 'traffic light' system to monitor progress against what was needed to be done! On the actual day, a schedule was produced and pinned up in the hall, with precise timings to ensure everyone had a shower and got fed before the big event – how sad is that? Not enough people know about and use these techniques to ensure important elements of their lives run efficiently and effectively. Where would I have been without an 'inter-relationship' diagram to plan the contents of my book? Where does this trait come from? Certainly not Mom or Dad. I believe it is the 'organised and methodical' trait that has driven me towards this career, rather than the other way around. I was born with it, rather than learnt it from life experiences, therefore it must be nature and not nurture.

I did say it wasn't entirely true because to a certain extent I am definitely not a 'completer finisher'. When doing a job I usually tend to leave a small part of it unfinished. For example when I decorate a room, I usually leave part of it unpainted. This comes from my Dad. Mom was forever asking him to finish a job, but he never did. This has to be nature – nobody teaches you to leave a task incomplete, do they?

I cannot leave the negative comments without a mention, that would be remiss of me. *"Your negative characteristics show that you can become possessive with a partner and sometimes you are forced to be jealous. You are also touchy and volatile."* I think it is true that I could be possessive and become jealous of Heather, but she has never done anything to warrant my jealousy. We have an open and trusting relationship, which thankfully means we rarely, if ever, have any doubts about each other; not from my side of the relationship anyway! Dad was certainly jealous of Mom at times. He didn't feel comfortable with her working as a waitress, because of the tales of affairs and unfaithfulness that are common place in the catering industry. I could tell many a tale of 'goings on' at the Plough when I worked there! He need not have worried though. There was only ever one man in Mom's life and that was Dad. She didn't look at another man, even in the thirty years after his death.

'Touchy and volatile'? Not usually me, but if I am honest I can be occasionally. Unfortunately it is usually Heather that takes the brunt of it. She is the one who generally gets snapped at, or receives a 'withering' look (her words, not mine), when I am irritable and short tempered. Luckily for me, Heather puts up with it and luckily for her it doesn't happen very often. I know I shouldn't, but hopefully Heather knows I don't mean to. She is the last person I would ever want to hurt.

Reflecting on the preceding chapters, there are a number of my personality traits I can definitely attribute to nature and I believe all of them are inherited from Dad. They include a good sense of balance, quick reflex actions, painting and decorating, the desire to win, politics, the ability to improvise, the love of sport, particularly running and without doubt being able to sleep anytime, anywhere.

The last trait can only be influenced by nature; it's the way I am made. I have many memories of Dad asleep in his armchair, head to the left with it resting on the arm. Night after night he could be found in this familiar pose with the television on, but clearly not watching it. Nothing seemed to disturb him, that is except for someone creeping in and changing channels on the TV. As soon as it changed he would open one eye and say, "I was watching that!" There were many frustrating nights when we had to find alternative entertainment because Dad was watching a Spaghetti Western with his eyes closed! I do have empathy for him though, because I know just how it feels when you have no control over your eyes. If I sit in a comfy chair after eight o'clock in the evening, nine times out of ten I will fall asleep. Even if there is something I really want to do or watch on television, there is nothing I can do to stop my eyes closing! I can be talking to Heather and literally within a matter of seconds I have 'dropped off'. Heather often moans about my sleep habits, but we are made differently. She is wide awake in the evening, but struggles to get up in the morning. I am the complete opposite. Like Dad was, I am usually 'up with the lark', requiring very little time to awaken and be alert, ready for the day ahead.

Decorating and improvising are definitely nature. I feel they have to be, because although Dad was brilliant at both, he didn't teach me how to be good at them. I did watch from a distance, but I never got to see the detail. Decorating was self-taught from a minimal reference to books and magazines, while improvisation has just been picked up over the years. By improvisation I mean being able to 'fix' a spin dryer, or toy without the correct part or component. Or using old inappropriately sized nuts and bolts to hold some furniture together. Perhaps the best example was when I 'fixed' the headlight on my car. It was my second car, an old, teal blue, Morris 1100. British Leyland cars did not have a great reputation in the early seventies, but it was all I could afford. It was full of rust, filled with fibreglass and had very dodgy suspension. Oh yes, and it had a boot full of water every time it rained. The suspension comprised of four MacPherson struts, one on each wheel, which were filled with hydraulic fluid. Due to the poor build quality, the fluid was forever leaking out and required topping-up on a regular basis. Being unable to afford this regular expensive maintenance, unless it was a few days before the annual MOT, most of the time the ride was very hard. The knock-on effect of this was the driver's side front headlamp was forever failing. Driving over bumps with the lights on, when you didn't have decent suspension, regularly resulted in a broken filament. Good old British Leyland had ensured they would profit from their poor reliability by fitting expensive sealed units that I could not afford to buy every month. The solution? Buying a second-hand headlamp, fitted with bulbs, which were much cheaper to replace. The only problem was there was no way of keeping the unit in place, so I ingeniously solved the issue with a very large and strong elastic band. It got me through MOTs, lasted me until I sold the car and saved a substantial amount of money. The only down side was slight water ingress, which sometimes affected the brightness of the lamp. However, a quick drying of the unit and a cleaning up of the contacts solved everything!

I suppose you could say I was a 'Jack of all trades, but master of none'! This particularly applies to sport, where I was an average player at most sports, but not exceptional or brilliant at any of them. I played football, cricket, hockey, darts, lacrosse, golf, swimming, diving, dominoes and running (long distances) but didn't really excel at any of them. Perhaps that was due to not having the proper instruction, or being unable to buy the right equipment or join a club to enhance my skills. Who knows given the right opportunity and encouragement I might have been great at one of them and gone on to play professionally? Or perhaps it was my resolve and determination that was not strong enough? They say if you want something badly enough you can always achieve your goal.

The one thing in my life I have 'wanted' and worked at is the love of Mathematics and numbers. Many years after my disappointing A level result, I was lucky enough to have had the opportunity and support available to make this happen. My employers paid for my part-time education to obtain a BSc and MPhil and Heather encouraged and supported me for more than twelve years while I completed the courses, for which I will be eternally grateful. If this support and encouragement had not been readily available, would I have been so determined to see it through? This determination does it come from a gene, or not? If it does then maybe nature never intended me to be great at anything. My Dad certainly instilled in me the desire to win, but is that enough to make someone successful? Do I want to win at all costs? I suspect not. Dad always taught me to play fairly and to care and respect others. Maybe that's where it all went wrong, not using others to further my own aspirations. Perhaps it was never meant to be!

The only two characteristics I can think of which may have originated solely from nurture are worrying about my looks and dress sense and being careful and aware of Health and Safety issues. It is almost certain both of these are a result of Mom and Dad persistently nagging me as I grew up. Almost like Pavlov's dogs I have learnt from repeated, but in my case bitter experience. Pavlovian conditioning is a form of learning in which the conditioned stimulus (for me scruffiness and accidents) comes to signal the occurrence of a second stimulus (Mom's nagging and pain). I am sure I have an obsession with combing my hair, because every morning Mom spent ages getting my hair 'right' and every afternoon, after school she would spend just as long telling me what a mess it looked. Similarly, Mom and Dad were forever 'drumming in to me' the need to be careful, as I experienced one accident after another.

Everything else feels as though nature was the biggest influence, although not without nurture also having an impact. My past suggests many of my personal characteristics are inherited; my genes tend to point me in a certain direction. How far you develop a personal trait, or whether or not you do at all, depends on that skill or quality being nurtured. I believe some people have hidden talents that have never been nurtured and hence have not come to the fore. They have the ability to be good at something, but have had no opportunity or encouragement to fulfil their potential.

Similarly nurture or life's experiences can have a different effect on different people. Life is almost like a game of 'parlour bagatelle'. When the ball bearing hits a pin sometimes it will go left and other times it will go to the right. Only the slightest difference in the shot can make a huge difference to where the ball eventually ends up. Life appears to be like this as well. For example there are many young boys who grow up in a home where their mother is abused by the Dad or partner. Some boys grow up believing this is 'the Norm' and treat their partners in a similar way. However, there are others who reach adolescence and reject this behaviour. Seemingly they have had the same life experience, but they end up going in completely different directions. Is it nature that influences their reaction to what they have witnessed, or is it some minor difference in what they experienced?

In chaos theory, the 'butterfly effect' is the sensitive dependence on initial conditions in which a small change at one place in a system can result in large difference later in time. The name of the effect, coined by Edward Lorenz, is derived from the theoretical example of a hurricane's formation being dependent on whether or not a distant butterfly had flapped its wings several weeks earlier. I believe everyone's life can be tremendously affected by small and insignificant changes to their life experiences. The extent to which an individual is affected by these small variations may depend upon their genes and hence nature. Is the person focused, or are they easily influenced?

Irrespective of this I sincerely believe life is one large casino, dependent upon chance and random variation. If you think about it, we are all very lucky to be alive today; certainly I consider myself to be very lucky. Those of us alive today are just a very small proportion of the population that COULD be on this planet. Consider the 16 million brave soldiers and civilians who died in World War 1 alone. If either of my granddads had been one of those unlucky souls, I wouldn't be writing this book. What if the mortar that injured Dad had exploded a fraction of a second earlier and he had died on the battlefield? What if it had exploded a fraction of a second later and he had not been injured at all – he probably would not have met Mom. In either scenario I would not have been born. Some people believe in destiny or fate, that is our lives have a predetermined course of events. I don't subscribe to this theory because to ensure everyone's life turned out as planned, everyone and everything would have to have their actions timed to the finest detail.

People die on our roads every day of the year. In 2012 there were 1,754 fatalities. Each traffic accident would not have occurred exactly as it happened if just one of thousands of people had delayed their car journey by a short time. Setting off a couple of seconds later would have changed the order and flow of traffic. Maybe only by a small amount initially, but ten or fifteen minutes later, things could be completely different. How can everything be controlled to such a fine degree? It can't: life has to be one big game of chance! It isn't necessarily completely random and we can control certain elements of our life and in a way 'make our own luck'. However there will always be external influences, outside of our control, that could come along and change our life forever. My philosophy is to enjoy life while you can and make the most of what you have, because you never know what tomorrow may bring!

You can see why I feel so lucky, by the great hand I have been dealt. My whole life may be influenced by random events, mostly out of my control, but I doubt whether I would change anything about it. From Mom and Dad, Gran and Grampy, Uncle Les, Heather and Kerry and Matt, I have been very blessed. For the education I have had, the jobs I have held and the wonderful people I have had the privilege to work with, again I am very fortunate. I may not be in the Sunday Times rich list yet, but a person's wealth cannot be judged by money alone. Family, health and happiness also need to be taken into consideration. If you do that, then I am one very rich 'ginger' nut!

Lightning Source UK Ltd.
Milton Keynes UK
UKOW06f0921141215

264684UK00019B/1216/P